GREAT TWENTIETH CENTURY
JEWISH PHILOSOPHERS

BERNARD MARTIN is Abba Hillel Silver
Professor of Jewish Studies and Chairman
of the Department of Religion at Case Western Reserve University in Cleveland. His
books include *The Existentialist Theology
of Paul Tillich* and *Prayer in Judaism.*

Great Twentieth Century Jewish Philosophers

SHESTOV

ROSENZWEIG

BUBER

With Selections from Their Writings

EDITED AND WITH INTRODUCTIONS BY

Bernard Martin

THE MACMILLAN COMPANY
COLLIER-MACMILLAN LTD., LONDON

The Macmillan Company

Library of Congress Catalog Card Number: 79-85787

FIRST PRINTING

ACKNOWLEDGMENTS

I. *Shestov*

"Athens and Jerusalem" (pp. 51–72). From *Athens and
Jerusalem* by Lev Shestov. Copyright © 1966 by Ohio Uni-
versity Press. Reprinted by permission of Ohio University
Press, Athens, Ohio 45701.

"Morality and Pessimism" (pp. 72–76). From *In Job's
Balances* by Lev Shestov. Reprinted by permission of Ohio
University Press, Athens, Ohio, 45701, from its forthcoming
book *In Job's Balances* by Lev Shestov.

"What Are Questions Made Of?" (pp. 76–82). From *In
Job's Balances* by Lev Shestov. Reprinted by permission of
Ohio University Press, Athens, Ohio, 45701, from its forth-
coming book *In Job's Balances* by Lev Shestov.

"*Cur Deus Homo?*" (pp. 82–88). From *In Job's Balances*
by Lev Shestov. Reprinted by permission of Ohio University
Press, Athens, Ohio, 45701, from its forthcoming book *In
Job's Balances* by Lev Shestov.

"*De Novissimis*" (pp. 88–94). From *Potestas Clavium* by
Lev Shestov. Copyright © 1968 by Ohio University Press.
Reprinted by permission of Ohio University Press, Athens,
Ohio 45701.

"Pensées from *Athens and Jerusalem* and *Potestas Clavium*"
(pp. 94–117). From *Athens and Jerusalem* by Lev Shestov.
Copyright © 1966 by Ohio University Press. And from

II *Rosenzweig*

III *Buber*

"The Faith of Judaism" (pp. 321–334). From *Israel and the World* by Martin Buber. Copyright 1948 by Schocken Books, Inc. Reprinted by permission of Schocken Books, Inc., New York.

Grateful acknowledgment is made to the Central Conference of American Rabbis for permission to use material previously published in its Journal and Yearbook.

Contents

Preface

THE THREE MEN with whose work this book is concerned would undoubtedly appear in any thoughtful listing of the foremost Jewish religious philosophers of the twentieth century. While each has unique and distinctive qualities, certain affinities, both in the content and style of their thought, are discernible. It is clear, first of all, that all three may be regarded as belonging to that rather ill-defined but powerful movement known as existentialism which has played such an important role in the religious thought of recent decades and which, though its popularity has somewhat ebbed of late, is still very far from having exhausted its vital forces.

Lev Shestov, Franz Rosenzweig and Martin Buber all share, though in different degree, in the protest, so characteristic of existentialist thinkers, against the fundamental assumption of rationalism that the nature of reality can be grasped entirely by intellectual means, especially by that instrument which Paul Tillich aptly called "controlling reason." Each in his own way denies that this instrument can by itself give man the ultimate truth that he seeks about himself and his world.

All three also make important use of the distinction, typical of existentialism, between subjective and objective, or public and private, truth. While Shestov protests most vehemently against the rule of Spinoza prohibiting the introduction of any human interest or emotion into the search for knowledge—*non ridere, non lugere, neque detestari, sed intelligere*—and insists most strongly that the ultimately significant truths are not those objective statements which are accepted "always, everywhere and by all men" but rather those truths which the individual has obtained for himself through painful struggle and which may be true only for him, Rosenzweig also emphasizes personal truths that are verified only through the individual's commitment, decision and risk. And Buber, of course, speaks of the knowledge, particularly the knowl-

edge of God, that is accessible only in the *I-Thou* attitude
in which the whole person is involved and that is forever
closed to the *I-It* attitude of detachment and objectification.

Each of our philosophers also participates in the existentialist revolt against the tendency to reduce man to the
status of an object, a quasi-physical system of functions
and responses to stimuli. Shestov rebels against the inclination of philosophical naturalism and mechanism to
view man as only another, and rather insignificant, link in
the causal chain of phenomena and as subject to all-
powerful Necessity. Rosenzweig attacks Idealism for its
subordination of the particular individual, with his name
and surname, his life and death, to the all-embracing,
abstract Whole. Buber reacts to the dehumanization of man
and the destruction of authentic personal relations wrought
by the technological, objectifying orientation of contemporary civilization with a passionate plea for a return to
the life of dialogue in which persons as such are confirmed
in their wholeness and uniqueness.

All three thinkers, finally, share the existentialist concern for dealing with man in his concrete existence with
all its contradictions and ambiguities. Certainly their
thought cannot do altogether without abstract conceptions
and ideas, but they never lose sight of the particular
individual whose conflicts and struggles cannot, in their
endless complexity and contrariety, be reduced to precise
definition or find adequate expression in any comprehen-
sive, logically consistent system of thought.

Shestov, Rosenzweig and Buber have in common not
only their existentialist orientation, but the thought of all
three is also profoundly rooted in the Bible. These two
facts are, of course, not unrelated, for some of the basic
existentialist modes of thought find perhaps their most
powerful expression and exemplification in the Bible.

Though sharing a common reverence for the Bible, our
three philosophers emphasize different aspects of it. For
Shestov the Biblical proclamation of an omnipotent Creator
God for whom nothing is impossible is central; in this he
sees the liberating truth of faith which can overcome
the constraining truths of scientific knowledge. Buber
regards the Bible as exemplifying the life of dialogue; it
is itself the record and witness of dialogical encounters

between God and Israel, and it summons men to responsibility and presentness in their meetings with one another and with God. Rosenzweig sees in the Biblical affirmations of Creation, Revelation and Redemption the profoundest indication of the way God, man and the world are related in time. All three thinkers have contributed importantly to the revitalization of Biblical faith that has begun to manifest itself in contemporary Jewish life and thought.

In the expository chapters of this book I have given a statement not only of what seem to me the main themes of each philosopher's thought but also a brief account of his life, for, in the case of an existentialist thinker particularly, life and thought are inextricably interwoven.

The selections from the writings of Shestov, Rosenzweig and Buber included in the volume are by no means exhaustive of the vast range of each man's interests and concerns, but they will give the reader direct acquaintance with at least a few of the major ideas that have made these three philosophers of decisive importance in the history of modern religious thought.

BERNARD MARTIN

Case Western Reserve University
Cleveland, Ohio
February 1969

Lev Shestov
1866-1938

THOUGH HE HAS ENJOYED a very substantial reputation in
Continental philosophical circles for more than half a
century,[1] Lev Shestov is still relatively unknown in America
and England, even among professional philosophers and
theologians. Several reasons suggest themselves for this.
First of all, until quite recently little of his work had
appeared in English translation. It is true that English
versions of three of his early books—*Penultimate Words
and Other Essays*,[2] *All Things Are Possible*,[3] and *In Job's
Balances: On the Sources of the Eternal Truths*[4]—*were*
published, but these seem to have made little impression
when they appeared, and they have long since gone out
of print. Secondly, Shestov founded no school and had
no real disciples, with the one exception of the brilliant
Rumanian-born Jewish poet and essayist Benjamin
Fondane, who died in the gas chambers of Birkenau.
True to the existentialist tradition, Shestov denied that he
had any clearly defined philosophy that could simply be
handed on to students and appropriated by them. Thirdly,
Shestov's thought is difficult and unpopular. To the reader
who looks to philosophy for guidance in the conduct of
life he has little to offer; to one who seeks moral edifica-
tion he has even less to say; for the lover of system he
provides nothing; and the analytically inclined will find
little that is of interest to them in his work. Fourthly,
Shestov is stubbornly and unrelentingly anti-modern. The
gods of the nineteenth and twentieth centuries—science,
technology, the idea of historical progress, autonomous
ethics—are for him nothing but vain and destructive idols.

Despite the fact that it is so little known, the body of
Shestov's work represents one of the most fascinating
philosophical contributions of the last century. In a much
more genuine sense than Spinoza, this Russian Jewish
thinker was, in his maturity, a God-intoxicated man. For
him, God was the beginning, the center and the end of
all true philosophy. With a mastery not only of the entire

Western philosophic tradition but of European literature in general, he used his vast knowledge, as well as the ardent passion of his being and his extraordinary literary talents, to forge a powerful indictment of rationalist and pseudo-scientific metaphysics in order to regain for man what he considered the most precious of human gifts: the right to God and to the primordial freedom that God has given man.

Lev Shestov was born Lev Isaakovich Schwarzmann in 1866 in Kiev.[5] His father was a wealthy merchant and a prominent member of the Jewish community. Though considered by the more traditionalist Jews of Kiev as somewhat heretical, Isaak Moisseevich Schwarzmann had a genuine love for Hebrew literature, which he was able to read fluently, and a sincere loyalty to Judaism. He engaged a tutor to come to his large house in the Podol quarter of Kiev to give instruction in Hebrew and Jewish literature to Lev and his other children.

Jews who managed to obtain a higher education could expect special privileges from the Czarist regime in Russia in the last decades of the nineteenth century. Desiring to obtain these for their son, his parents sent Lev Isaakovich to a gymnasium in Kiev. Both the secondary schools and the universities of Russia were hotbeds of political ferment at the time. As a consequence of his involvement in a political affair in the gymnasium at Kiev, the young Shestov was expelled from the institution and was sent to Moscow, where he finished his secondary studies. He then entered the University of Moscow, first studying mathematics and later law. As a result of another political involvement, Shestov had to leave the University of Moscow and return to Kiev, where he pursued his studies at the local university, graduating in 1889 with the title of Candidate of Laws. Shestov's interests during his university days were centered on social and economic problems. The doctoral dissertation that he wrote for the University of Kiev dealt with the situation of the working class of Russia. The work was accepted by the faculty of the university but suppressed by the Committee of Censors in Moscow who felt that it was far too radical and politically dangerous. Because of the suppression of his dissertation, Shestov did not receive the degree of Doctor of Law. He was inscribed on the official list of lawyers at

St. Petersburg but never practiced law and in time lost virtually all of his interest in legal matters.

In his twenties, after finishing his studies at the university, Shestov began to work in his father's textile firm. Business activity was not at all congenial to his restless and inquiring spirit. Nevertheless, he developed enough ability in merchandising and accounting to prevent the bankruptcy that at one point threatened the family firm as a result of his father's overextension of credit to customers. Working in business during the day, Shestov spent his evenings writing for the avant-garde press of Kiev. In this period he published several articles, including one on the work of Vladimir Soloviev and one entitled "Georg Brandes and Hamlet."[6] The latter served as the basis for his first book, *Shakespeare and His Critic Brandes*, published in St. Petersburg in 1898.

In 1895 Shestov finally managed to escape the stifling atmosphere of his family's business, which he had put in solid financial order, and went to Italy to travel and study. In Rome, a year later, he married a young medical student, Anna Eleazarovna Berezowsky. Two daughters were born to Shestov and his wife, Tatiana in 1897 and Natalie in 1900. In 1898 Shestov and his wife settled in Switzerland, where Anna finished her medical studies at the University of Berne. Shestov's own interests during these years were centered largely on poetry and music. Possessing a splendid voice, he contemplated for a time a career as a singer. However, finding himself drawn ever more strongly to literature, he soon abandoned this idea and devoted himself to writing.

From his youth Shestov had been deeply interested in the novels and short stories of Tolstoy and Dostoevsky. Now, toward the end of the 1890's, he became acquainted with the work of Nietzsche, whom he recognized as kindred, in certain respects, to the great Russian writers. The result was his second book, *The Good in the Teaching of Tolstoy and Nietzsche: Philosophy and Preaching*, published in 1900. This was followed in 1903 by *Dostoevsky and Nietzsche: The Philosophy of Tragedy*. In 1905 he published *The Apotheosis of Groundlessness*, a collection of brilliant statements, in the style of Pascal's *pensées*, on philosophy, religion and literature. In 1908 *Beginnings and Endings*, containing among other things a major essay on Anton Chekhov, was published. Three years later, *Great Vigils* appeared.

In the years before the First World War, Shestov made his home alternately in Russia and in Switzerland or Germany. During the war years, spent entirely in Russia, he continued to write. Several of his articles written in this period were later included in his volume entitled *Potestas Clavium*, in which the religious direction in which his thought had begun to move as early as the time of the writing of his book on Tolstoy and Nietzsche became clearly apparent. In this period he also maintained contact with a group of philosophers and writers in Moscow and St. Petersburg, including Chelpanov, Gershenson, Lurie and Ivanov, as well as his lifelong friends Nikolai Berdyaev and Sergei Bulgakov.

Despite the disfavor in which he stood with the Bolshevik authorities after the revolution, Shestov was permitted to teach and in the winter of 1918–1919 gave a course of lectures on Greek philosophy at the People's University of Kiev. However, a growing disenchantment with the Soviet regime finally led him to the decision to exile himself from Russia. In 1920 he and his family joined the large colony of Russian *émigrés* residing in Paris. Several years later he was appointed professor of Russian philosophy in the Institut des Études Slaves and also served intermittently as a lecturer in the extension division of the Sorbonne. After Shestov settled in France, most of the books that he had written earlier in Russian were translated into French and German, and some also into other European languages.

In the decade of the twenties Shestov's reputation as a brilliant and creative thinker was firmly established in European literary and philosophical circles. His genius was acclaimed by such figures as Jules de Gaultier and Lucien Lévy-Bruhl in France and D. H. Lawrence and John Middleton Murry in England. In his apartment in Paris he continued his research and writing, which had for some years now been concentrated on the Bible and on an intensive study (he called it "a pilgrimage through souls") of such great religious thinkers of the Western tradition as Plotinus, St. Augustine, Spinoza, Luther and Pascal. Under the auspices of the Nietzsche-Gesellschaft of Berlin, of which he was elected an honorary president, he lectured in Berlin, Halle and Freiburg. Invitations came from other countries as well, and he addressed philosophical meetings in Prague, Cracow and Amsterdam. In Amsterdam Shestov met Edmund Husserl, with whom he maintained a close friendship for some years despite the radical difference in their philosophical orientation.

In 1923 *Potestas Clavium* was published in Russian in Berlin. This volume contained, along with a number of striking essays on religion and philosophy, a long article on Husserl's theory of knowledge entitled "Memento Mori." In 1929 Shestov's book *In Job's Balances*, which included important essays on Tolstoy, Dostoevsky, Spinoza, Pascal and Plotinus, appeared in Russian in Paris. Seven years later he published his book on Kierkegaard, to whose writings he had first been introduced by Husserl in 1929 and whom he studied with great interest. In Kierkegaard he recognized a deeply congenial spirit, since his own thought had moved in the same direction as that of the great Danish thinker long before he discovered the latter's work. The book, which has been translated into English, French, German, Spanish and Danish, is entitled *Kierkegaard and the Existential Philosophy: Vox Clamantis in Deserto*.

Shestov's last work and his *magnum opus, Athens and Jerusalem*, on which he worked over a period of more than twenty years, was completed in 1937. Ever since the cataclysm of the First World War he had been brooding over what he called, in a letter to Bulgakov, "the nightmare of godlessness and unbelief which has taken hold of humanity." He had become convinced that only through "the utmost spiritual effort," as he termed it, could men free themselves from this nightmare. And he had decided to devote himself to a relentless struggle against the "self-evident truths" of speculative philosophy and positivistic science which, as he believed, had come to possess the mind of European man and made him impervious to the rationally ungrounded but redemptive truths proclaimed in the Bible. That struggle is most fully reflected in *Athens and Jerusalem*.

The essays and aphorisms of *Athens and Jerusalem* represent, in many respects, the culmination of Shestov's entire lifetime of intellectual inquiry and spiritual striving, and they bring together the diverse strands appearing in his earlier writings. In this monumental book Shestov set himself the task of critically examining the pretension of human reason to the capacity for attaining ultimate truth. Surveying the thought of the great philosophers and scientists from ancient Greece to his own day, he concluded that, instead of giving man true knowledge and freedom, they have only brought him to a cul-de-sac where he has lost both the primordial freedom granted him by God and all possibility of envisioning utlimate truth. Against speculative philosophy and science (Athens) must be set the revelation of the Bible (Jerusalem) with its paradoxical but, according to Shestov, profoundly true and liberating proclamation that, through faith in the God who transcends all rational categories and human expectations, man may not only again find that "nothing is impossible" for him but also catch a glimpse of that true reality which the light of human reason only obscures.

Shestov's last days were shadowed by the approach of the Second World War, but he continued his work until the very end. After finishing the manuscript of *Athens and Jerusalem* in the spring of 1937, he personally supervised the preparation of French and German translations of the Russian text. The German version was barely published in Graz and distributed to libraries throughout Europe before Hitler annexed Austria to the German Reich. On November 20, 1938, after several months of illness, Shestov died peacefully at the Boileau Clinic in Paris. At his bedside was an open Bible and the Deussen translation of the Vedas open at the chapter "Brahma als Freude" where he had underlined the following passage: *Nicht trübe Askese kennzeichnet den Brahmanwisser, sondern das freudig hoffnungsvolle Bewusstsein der Einheit mit Gott.*

II

"All things are possible"—this is the basic idea which the young Shestov, writing at the turn of the century, was eager to proclaim.[7] It is an idea that came to be echoed in all his later books, up to his final and greatest work, *Athens and Jerusalem.*

According to Shestov, though the relationships between the phenomena of the natural world which science is concerned to discover and describe exude an air of regularity, permanence and necessity, they are, in an ultimate sense, completely arbitrary and ungrounded; the truth is that anything may come from anything. We see all around us phenomena that manifest law and order, but there is nothing to prevent us from believing that the universe may be so constituted as to permit at any moment the most fantastic metamorphoses.

. . . we are forced to admit that anything whatsoever may result from anything whatsoever . . . from our own minds and our own experience we can deduce nothing that would serve us as a ground for setting even the smallest limit to nature's own arbitrary behavior. If whatever happens now had chanced to happen quite differently, it would not, therefore, have seemed any the less *natural* to us.[8]

The dominant tradition of Western scientific and philosophical thought has held that there is an eternal and immovable barrier between the possible and the impossible and that the contours and limits of this barrier may be known not only through empirical investigation but even a priori. This, Shestov brands as a myth, a pious fable. Perhaps there has been or still is a barrier, but who knows if it may not suddenly be removed? In an essay entitled "On Method" he makes the point strikingly:

A certain naturalist made the following experiment: A glass jar was divided into two halves by a perfectly transparent glass partition. On the one side of the partition he placed a pike, on the other a number of small fishes such as form the prey of the pike. The pike did not notice the partition, and hurled itself on its prey, with, of course, the result only of a bruised nose. The same happened many times, and always the same result. At last, seeing all its efforts ended so painfully, the pike abandoned the hunt, so that in a few days, when the partition had been removed, it continued to swim about among the small fry without daring to attack them . . . Does not the same happen with us? Perhaps the limits between "this world" and "the other world" are also essentially of an experimental origin, neither rooted in the nature of things, as was thought before Kant, or in the nature of our reason, as was thought after

Kant. Perhaps indeed a partition does exist, and makes
vain all attempts to cross over. But perhaps there comes
a moment when the partition is removed. In our minds,
however, the conviction is firmly rooted that it is impossible to pass certain limits, and painful to try: a
conviction founded on experience. But in this case we
should recall the old skepticism of Hume, which Idealist
philosophy has regarded as mere subtle mind-play,
valueless after Kant's critique. The most lasting and
varied experience cannot lead to any binding and universal conclusion. Nay, all our a priori, which are so
useful for a certain time, become sooner or later extremely harmful. A philosopher should not be afraid of
skepticism, but should go on bruising his jaw . . . How
can you tell when the partition will be removed? Perhaps at the very moment when man ceased his painful
pursuit, settled all his questions and rested on his laurels,
inert, he could with one strong push have swept through
the pernicious fence which separated him from the unknowable.[9]

In his early years Shestov saw considerable merit in
science, particularly in its empirical methods, which he
felt must replace the deductive and inferential methods of
scholastic logic and philosophy if genuine knowledge is to
be obtained. "It is surely time to give up conclusions,
and get truth a posteriori, as did Shakespeare, Goethe,
Dostoevsky; that is, every time you want to know anything,
go and look and find out."[10] But as the years went on
Shestov came to believe ever more strongly that science,
while undoubtedly useful to man for practical purposes,
cannot pretend to ultimate truth. By the time he had
finished *In Job's Balances* (1929), Shestov had become
even more firmly persuaded than when he wrote *All
Things Are Possible* (1905) that science can yield no real
truth because, by its very nature, it will not and cannot
seek truth. The fundamental principles upon which the
scientific enterprise is based—the idea of causality and
the principle of the regularity of phenomena—are, he now
categorically declares, totally ungrounded and, indeed,
erroneous. These principles, as well as the whole idea of a
self-sufficient natural order, are fictions, created out of
deference to the limitations of the human mind and de-

signed merely to serve man's utilitarian interests.[11]

The idea of a self-sufficient order of nature—independent, indifferent to all things and manifesting invariable and eternal causal relationships among its parts—cannot be defended, he argues, in the face of the appearance of life, particularly of the living phenomenon that is man. The very search for causal relationships is dependent on the emergence of a living being with needs, interests and desires.

> . . . before life appears with its "need" there are and can be no questions. Even the question of causality, outside living needs, is an empty and senseless question; it is even no question at all, but the purest illusion. Water turns into steam or ice—we ask why? The question has only a sense if *we* decide in advance that steam is not water and ice also not water; that the one was there first and then the other appeared and we want to explain to ourselves how the one turns into the other, how something "new" appears on the earth. But if we were not, ourselves, beings for which "all is not one," beings which wish, endeavor, and "value" according to their wishes and their endeavor, then steam and ice would be nothing "new," "different" in relation to water; in the same way the beauty of heaven, of the morning star, or of a sequence of notes would be nothing to us.[12]

The basic reason, however, why science cannot attain truth is that it stubbornly and wilfully refuses to see "miracles," understood as phenomena that are unexpected or rationally inexplicable. Man, especially scientific man, has an overwhelming horror of anything that is unanticipated or fails to fall into his customary categories of explanation, and he defends himself by simply refusing to recognize the reality of such things.[13] How, Shestov demands, can science claim to be based upon free inquiry when it arbitrarily refuses to "see" anything that is "incomprehensible" and that cannot be caught in the net of "universal and necessary judgments"? If science will not rest content until everything "miraculous" vanishes from its field of vision, this can only be because it is under the spell of what Pascal once called an *enchantement et assoupissement surnaturel*.[14]

Where science further goes astray, Shestov declares in *All Things Are Possible*, is in its determination to classify and pigeonhole all phenomena. To understand a thing, according to the scientist, is to include it in a list of other things previously known. But the attempt to understand persons, life and the world in general in this way prevents us from knowing them at all. There is a difference between understanding and knowing.

> . . . since all our mental aspiration reduces itself to understanding the universe, we refuse to know a great deal which will not adapt itself to the plane surface of the contemporary world-conceptions. For instance the Leibnitz question, put by Kant into the basis of the critique of reason: "How can we know a thing outside us, if it does not enter into us?" It is non-understandable; that is, it does not agree with our notion of understanding. Hence it follows that it must be squeezed out of the field of view—which is exactly what Kant attempted to do. To us it seems, on the contrary, that in the interests of *knowing*, we should sacrifice, and gladly, understanding, since understanding in any case is a secondary affair.—*Zu fragmentarisch ist Welt und Leben!*[15]

Science, Shestov admits, has given us much that is useful and significant, but we must not make an idol of it or accept its pretensions to set before us ultimate truth. The scientist wishes to make everything remarkable unremarkable, but the fact is that truth "lies there where science sees the 'nothing,' in that single, uncontrollable, incomprehensible thing which is always at war with explanation, the 'fortuitous.' "[16]

Many scientists seem to believe that they can penetrate to the secret "intentions" and "purposes" of nature, but they are mistaken. Furthermore, they search in the wrong place. The "purpose" of nature, according to Shestov, is "pain and pleasure, joy and sorrow, hopes, fears, passions, expectation, devotion, anger, hatred, etc., everything which fills human souls and of which human speech can tell, even in approximations. . . ."[17] The most unpromising way to discover these is by studying, through scientific and experimental methods, the life of the amoeba and mollusc or the fossilized remains of extinct animals. Instead of learning something from such study, we are likely to lose our capacity for discovering anything at all about the final secrets and wonders of the universe. What we must rather do is "project our thought and feeling into the most intensive and complex seeking and struggling of the boldest and greatest representatives of humanity, of the saints, philosophers, artists, thinkers, prophets, and 'conclude' and judge with them on the beginning and the end, on the first and the last things."[18]

Science and common sense cannot be disregarded with impunity. Thales, Shestov reminds us,[19] provoked the mocking laughter of a Thracian girl when, as a result of fixing his gaze on the heavens and failing to look before his feet, he fell into a muddy well. But we must remember that a still greater punishment awaits those who abandon themselves completely to common sense and science. They are swept away by death, with no trace of them remaining and without ever having attained anything of ultimate truth.

Did the Thracian girl who laughed at Thales escape the abyss? Where is she? What has become of her merry laughter? History does not tell us. History, a strange science which tells of the actions of men long since passed away, never remembers what awaited the "victor," nor what abysses were prepared for him.[20]

III

Philosophy or, more properly, much of what has passed for philosophy in the Western world during the last two and one half millennia, is criticized by Shestov no less than is science, and, to a considerable extent, on the same grounds.

The fall of Western philosophy, he suggests,[21] practically coincided with its birth. Thales and Anaximander, who were among its founders, were also those who set it on the road to ruin. The former declared that All is One, and the latter saw in multiplicity an audacious impiety, something that ought not to be. Ever since their time most philosophers have systematically fled from and denied multiplicity, while seeking and esteeming uniformity as the highest good. "The comprehensible and the uniform became synonymous with the real and with that which ought to be. The individual, the independent, the different were looked on as unreal and audacious."[22] But if man wishes to attain truth, Shestov insists,[23] he must not yearn for a return to the womb of the One or to the blissful, undisturbed peace of super-individual being. Somehow he has managed to escape from the One and become an individual. This escape is not a sin or a crime; it is rather an achievement—indeed, the supreme achievement. Man as a single, independent being is confronted with eternal restlessness, tensions, tortures and doubts, but he must also realize that, precisely because of his individuality, unlimited possibilities are open to him.

Reason, which most philosophers take as the prime source of their thinking, is terrified both by the difficulties and the possibilities which flow from man's affirmation of his individuality. But such affirmation is the only way to truth. Among the ancient Greek philosophers it was Protagoras, Shestov maintains, who pre-eminently understood this. Contradicting all the canons of common sense, logic and reason, Protagoras boldly declared that man is and must be the measure of all things. The great Sophist, according to Shestov, was probably not thinking, when he said this, of empirical truth but of "metaphysical truth, as the immortal gods bear it in themselves."[24] What Protagoras meant is that man himself can and must *create* metaphysical truth.

I will illustrate this with an example. A queen and her ladies-in-waiting enter a box in a theatre. The queen sits down without looking round. Since she sat down, therefore there was a chair under her. The ladies-in-waiting looked round first, and after they had convinced themselves that chairs had been pushed forward, they sat down. A queen does not have to look round first and convince herself. She has a "logic" all her own: there is a chair there *because* she sits down. Common mortals, on the other hand, only sit down when there is a chair. This was perhaps Protagoras's thought. Although daily experience testifies to the contrary, he saw, or perhaps believed, that it is granted to man to create truth, and that royal blood flows in man's veins. One need look round at each step and ask "truth" for permission only in so far as man belongs to the empiric world, in which rules, laws, regulations, real and imaginary, do in fact reign; where all things, even truths, have a weight and fall unless supported. But man strives for freedom.[25]

Man belongs not only to the empirical world where his life is ruled by law and constraint, but also to a transcendent realm where he may enjoy limitless freedom. This, Shestov repeatedly declares, is a basic truth about himself that man must recognize, though ordinarily he flees in terror from it. Terror was precisely the reaction not only of Aristotle but also of Socrates and Plato to the doctrine of Protagoras. Despite their uprightness and honesty and their wholehearted desire to serve the truth, they were afraid, Shestov tells us, "that if they let Protagoras prevail, they would become μισόλονοι, despisers of reason, that they would commit spiritual suicide."[26] But the fears of these philosophers were unfounded. They misunderstood Protagoras, for the acceptance of his doctrine does not commit one to despise or reject reason but only to the recognition that *man is above reason.*

The besetting sin of reason or, rather, of the philosophers who worship at its shrine, according to Shestov, is their pretension that the power of reason is unlimited. This claim must be clearly and resolutely rejected. Reason has its proper place, namely, in the realm of empirical phenomena, but it cannot and must not be allowed to determine the directions of man's metaphysical quest.

Rationalist philosophers by and large have maintained that, while it may be true that empirical facts are arbitrary and contingent, the basic axioms of traditional logic at least are necessary, universal and eternal. This Shestov emphatically denies. That A equals A is not a necessary, but an empirical, truth. It is true only for our phenomenal world. Other worlds are conceivable in which it is false.[27] Shestov does not wish completely to discard Aristotelian logic as an instrument for acquiring knowledge. What he does refuse to admit is that it is the only or primary road to truth. "Against this one must fight, even if he has against him all the authorities of thought—beginning with Aristotle."[28]

The major difficulty with logic is that it destroys the

power of imagination, which is the only faculty competent to deal significantly with the ultimate questions of human existence. From this Shestov concludes that "philosophy must have nothing in common with logic; philosophy is an art which aims at breaking the logical continuity of argument and bringing man out on the shoreless sea of imagination, the fantastic tides where everything is equally possible and impossible."[29] The essential function of the philosopher is to think, but there is an incalculable difference, according to Shestov, between thinking and employing logic. The drawing of logical inferences is a natural function which gives man considerable pleasure. Not so thinking.

> . . . to think—really to think—surely this means a relinquishing of logic. It means living a new life. It means a permanent sacrifice of the dearest habits, tastes, attachments, without even the assurance that the sacrifice will bring any compensation. Artists and philosophers like to imagine the thinker with a stern face, a profound look which penetrates into the unseen, and a noble bearing—an eagle preparing for flight. Not at all. A thinking man is one who has lost his balance, in the vulgar, not in the tragic sense. Hands raking the air, feet flying, face scared and bewildered, he is a caricature of helplessness and pitiable perplexity.[30]

The final task of the philosopher, Shestov maintains,[31] is not to construct a system, or to explain our scientific knowledge, or to reconcile the obvious contradictions of life. All these transitory needs of men are to be served by the positive sciences. Philosophy has an altogether different purpose. The best and only complete definition of philosophy, according to Shestov, is to be found in Plotinus who, when asked "what is philosophy?" replied το τιμιώτατον, "what matters most."[32] So the last of the great Hellenistic thinkers connected philosophy with religion and art, at the same time setting it in irreconcilable opposition to science, which is ultimately indifferent to everything.

The chief sin of most of the philosophers is precisely that they have sought to make philosophy a science. If Plotinus' definition is accepted and if, further, Plato—who held that philosophy is nothing but a preparation for death and dying—is also right, then philosophy can have nothing to do with science, which seeks to serve the practical purposes of life. "The task of philosophy," says Shestov, "is to tear itself loose from life during life, if only in part."[33] Life is essentially a sleep, a sleep from which philosophy must seek to awaken man. A few great men— notably artists like Aeschylus, Sophocles, Dante, Shakespeare, Dostoevsky and Tolstoy—have recognized this and have tried to tell others of their own awakening. But their attempts have met with very limited success because, in communicating what they had discovered, they had perforce to use words, and the "word," according to Shestov, "has an enigmatic power of only letting through that which is suitable to life."[34] By giving names to things, by classifying them in species and genera, man virtually destroyed his capacity to understand anything except "essences" and general characteristics. Words serve the practical purposes of life, but they hide from man the secret of the individual and the particular.

Shestov indicts modern philosophy, particularly since Spinoza, for having been, and having wished only to be, the handmaid of science. All that is most precious in life— beauty, goodness, ambition, tears, laughter and curses—it has dismissed as useless rubbish, forgetting "that out of this material and this alone, genuine, truly philosophic questions have to be moulded."[35] In its desire to serve science, or rather to be itself a science, it has insisted upon regarding all of the "sudden, wonderful and mysterious transformations" which occur in the world as merely "natural developments."[36] The philosophers, like the scientists, want to count, measure and weigh automatically, under the assumption that this will allow them to live in what they call peace but what Shestov calls a vegetative slumber.

One of the major differences between the positive sciences and philosophy, Shestov points out, is that scientific knowledge develops cumulatively, whereas in philosophy there is no such thing as cumulative progress. The present-day scientist does not concern himself, except incidentally, with the history of his science, with the theories of the ancient physicists or botanists. He is basically interested only in the present state of knowledge in his field, in the sum of facts and theories that are now

Lev Shestov

regarded as valid. But in philosophy we cannot dismiss the ancients. "We need Plato, Aristotle, Plotinus no less than Kant or Hegel. Indeed, even more; one can get along without modern philosophers such as Wundt or Spencer, but not without Plato or Plotinus."[37] The ancient philosophers are eternal and irreplaceable teachers. In art and religion the same situation prevails. The modern poets, Shestov maintains, show no advance over Homer, Sophocles, Aeschylus or even Horace or Virgil. As for the Bible, it remains "the book of books, the eternal book" and, he adds, "it would be no loss to exchange the theological literature of a whole generation of later epochs against a single Epistle of St. Paul or a chapter from Isaiah."[38] Unlike the knowledge of the positivist scientist, the "knowledge" of the genuine philosopher, artist or prophet is not automatically transmittable. It does not enter into man's everyday life as an article of use and can only be appropriated, and then no more than partially, by a great effort of sympathetic imagination.

In the face of the positivist scientists and philosophers, with their confident belief in the endless progress and accumulation of knowledge, Shestov hurls the charge that, as far as the really important and ultimate problems are concerned, we have not advanced one step beyond the wisdom of the ancients.

> If we compare our knowledge with that of the ancients, we appear very wise. But we are no nearer to solving the riddle of eternal justice than Cain was. Progress, civilization, all the conquests of the human mind have brought us nothing new here. Like our ancestors, we stand still with fright and perplexity before ugliness, disease, misery, senility, death . . . We, the children of a moribund civilization, we, old men from our birth, in this respect are as young as the first man.[39]

If we would attain genuine philosophic insight and wisdom Shestov insists, what we must do is precisely this: to become as children again. The knowledge of children is usually dismissed as foolish and insignificant, but, says Shestov,

> My view is that this is a very great and sad error. The contrary should be the case. We should learn from

children and await revelation from them. Our whole
philosophic interest, our whole pure thirst for knowledge
should be directed towards restoring in our memory
what we received in the happy time when all impressions of being were new to us and we took up into
ourselves reality without submitting ourselves to the
postulates dictated by practical needs. If we want
"absolute" knowledge, if we want to see "directly" as
a living and reasonable being sees which is bound by
no presuppositions, which still fears nothing and is not
even afraid of becoming "terrible," then our first commandment must be: Be as children.[40]

Most of the philosophers of antiquity, with the exception
of Aristotle and his followers, did—at least at times—
manage to achieve the posture of children in their philosophic quest. They were not bound by presuppositions,
they were not afraid, and they were not harried by the
need to fulfill practical purposes. Beginning with Socrates
these philosophers, believing what Plato later put into
words, that philosophy is nothing else than a preparation
for death and dying, undertook a bold "flight from life."
Not only Socrates and Plato and their direct disciples, but
also the Cynics and Stoics, and Plotinus as well, were,
according to Shestov, "endeavoring to escape from the
hypnotic power of reality, of the *dream* reality with all its
ideas and truths."[41] They did not, as did most people in
their time and as do many still today, regard death as a
kind of sleep, the most perfect and final sleep. They were
convinced that it was life that is a sleep. And in this
conviction, Shestov maintains, they were profoundly right.

Not only is sleep still life: our life itself, strange as it
may seem at first sight, is three-quarters or more sleep,
i.e., the continuation of the original non-being out of
which we were torn by some incomprehensible and
mysterious power, unasked, and perhaps even against
our will. . . . It is precisely for that reason that the
mechanist theories seem to us the only true ones, and
any attempt to fight against immemorial necessity seems
fore-doomed to failure: it troubles our waking sleep
and arouses only a sense of injury and irritation, such
as a sleeper always shows towards a man who awakens

him. Whenever anything unexpected, inexplicable, either from without or within shakes us out of our accustomed cherished equilibrium, our whole being is filled with unrest.[42]

But the ancients, unlike modern positivist philosophers, were not afraid of awakening; indeed, it was precisely this that they sought with all the power of their being. When Euripides said "Who knows if life is not death and death life?" he pronounced words that will remain forever puzzling and problematic. No precise meaning can be attached to them, and obviously the statement itself is incapable of verification. The significance of these words, according to Shestov, lies perhaps "in the very fact that they deliver us from certainty; that they make us hope that what is called evident can be conquered."[43]

It is flashes of thought, sudden inspiration—which are derived from Eros—that are the proper foundation of philosophy, rather than "thought-out thoughts . . . brought into relationship with the past and serving as basis for future thoughts."[44] This was the case with much of the thought of Plato, in whom dialectic is dominated by the mythical.[45] Plato is unconcerned whether others hear the harmony that his ears have caught or whether the ideas that inspiration has whispered to him correspond with reality. "The 'love-lorn philosopher' troubles little whether or not other men share his delight in the beauty he has discovered. He is in love. His love is final aim and self-justification. Indeed, is anything more necessary?"[46]

Scientists rarely, if ever, claim that they do not understand one another. They may differ and disagree. One may claim a theory to be valid and well established while another regards the same theory as unproven or insufficiently warranted by the evidence. But it is difficult to imagine a qualified scientist saying that he simply does not understand a scientific theory put forward by a colleague. Not so with philosophers. Aristotle could not understand Plato's theory of Ideas. He rejected it, feeling in it something absolutely hostile and repugnant and seeing in it an unnecessary duplication of the empirical world. But, as Shestov points out, "what was unnecessary to Aristotle seemed to Plato the *supreme necessity*, the *supremely important and essential*, το τιμώτατον, for whose

sake both he and all his true disciples went to philosophy."[47] If in the natural and visible world violence
prevails and Anytus and Meletus, the enemies of Socrates,
triumph, then there must be for Plato another, supernatural world in which no evil can befall a good man such
as Socrates. Aristotle, however, was not at all concerned
about the fate of Socrates. His "metaphysical destiny,"
Shestov would have it, was different from Plato's. While
the latter was destined for the ideal world, Aristotle was
destined for the empirical.

The insights that any philosopher achieves, it is suggested, are a matter of individual temperament and fate.
To try to reconcile the vision of one thinker with that of
another is pointless. There is no necessity even for re-
conciling the contradictions within one philosopher's
thought. Plotinus, Shestov notes, was guilty of a glaring
contradiction. At the same time that he tried so desperately
to transcend the boundaries of the empirical world and to
escape through his "ecstasy" from the enchantment of
the "self-evident truths" which bind man to the earth,
he loved this world with all his soul and strongly opposed
the Gnostics who preached hatred of it. But in this very
contradiction lies Plotinus' greatness. It is foolish to seek
to reconcile his statements with each other, and even more
so to try to supplement his thought with that of other
great metaphysicians, who had an essentially different
vision. "Plotinus cannot be supplemented at all. He can
only be heard and, so far as possible, felt."[48]

Even in the ancient world there were more than a
few philosophers besides Aristotle who dreamed of a
strictly scientific metaphysics or, at least, a metaphysics
that would be in no way inconsistent with science. In
modern philosophy the search for such a metaphysics
has been the dominant concern. Since Descartes, and
particularly since Spinoza, practically every officially
recognized philosopher has sought to develop his metaphysical constructions with the help of scientific methods
and principles. Spinoza boasted that he had constructed
an *ethica, ordine geometrica demonstrata*. Like Kant after
him, Spinoza wished to banish everything "arbitrary"
from his metaphysics.

He aimed at the strictly scientific, and if he clothed his thoughts in the form of mathematical conclusions, he did so precisely because he, like Kant . . . was chiefly concerned with putting an end, once and for all, to the capricious multifariousness of opinions and creating a permanent uniformity of judgments, bound up with the idea of necessity.[49]

Spinoza believed that mathematics was the supreme science and that it was derived completely from reason. But he, like many other great philosophers, including Kant, never troubled to give a precise and adequate definition either of science or reason. They took it for granted that everyone knows what these are. But, Shestov writes,

. . . if we try to gather from the works of the philosophers an idea of what reason and science are, everything comes just to this: reason and science give us judgments of universal validity. And where, by this path or that, we attain to universally valid judgments, all doubts and arguments have an end and must have an end; there everyone has always thought alike and will always think alike, and there, consequently, lies eternal truth.[50]

Spinoza seems to have believed that human reason, insofar as it admitted or at least did not resolutely exclude the passions and interests of men, was imperfect and could not be trusted to yield eternal truth. His ideal was God's reason, which he held to differ completely from man's reason and to have as little in common with the latter as the dog star has with the dog, the barking animal. For God's reason what men call beautiful, perfect, good, etc., has no meaning whatsoever. If men wish to raise themselves to the level of God's understanding—and this is what Spinoza believed himself to have done—the great commandment is: *non ridere, non lugere, neque detestari, sed intelligere.*[51] Men must give up laughter, tears, anger, and all questions relating to the things they value most, and seek instead purely to understand. That Spinoza himself did not by any means consistently follow his professed principle, that—on the contrary—he sought

the beautiful and never asked any questions that he did
not need the answers to nor found any answers that did
not concern him, failed to prevent him, Shestov points
out,[52] from constantly emphasizing that this principle
provides the only road to truth.

Spinoza formulated what has been a conviction of most
philosophers ever since the beginning of speculative
thought, namely, that men are "in the power of an eternally
existent, incorporeal and indifferent might, to which it is
given to decide not only what is the sum of the angles of
a triangle, but also what fate awaits man, the peoples,
and even the universe itself."[53] This is a conviction that
has been burned into men through the centuries and has
become for them a patent, self-evident and invincible
truth. But, Shestov never tires of repeating, it is a conviction that is absolutely false. Moreover, it is evil and
destructive, since it has taken away from man the primordial freedom given to him by God.

Kant, Shestov maintains, merely continued the work of
Spinoza. Despite his claim that he had been awakened
out of his "dogmatic slumber" by Hume's criticism of the
idea of necessity, Kant never took Hume seriously. Nor,
for that matter, did Hume himself really grasp what he
had seen and act upon it. No sooner had the Scottish
philosopher discovered the groundlessness of the idea of
necessity than he forgot the wonders that he had glimpsed
and began to speak of "custom." Kant, according to
Shestov, "exiled the wonders, in order not to be forced to
see them, into the field of the *'thing in itself,'* and be-
queathed to mankind the 'synthetic a priori judgments,'
transcendental philosophy, and his three miserable 'postulates.' "[54] Neither he nor Hume ever really awakened
from the dream world in which the idea of necessity has
enveloped men. Had they been truly awakened, says
Shestov, "any further slumber, any further faith in understanding, in *intelligence*, would become impossible and
useless, and . . . they, like Tertullian, withdrawing themselves from the power of the devil's whisperings and
awakened to final reality, would break all their fetters of
pudet, ineptum, impossibile."[55]

Kant, betraying Hume as Hume had betrayed himself,
developed the conceptions of autonomous reason and
autonomous ethics and asked men to bow down in rever-

ence before them. After him came Fichte and Hegel, who, like Kant, carried on Spinoza's program. Despite his loudly proclaimed opposition to Spinoza and his attempt to overcome Spinoza's "static" with his "dynamic," Hegel only strengthened man's belief in the autonomy of reason. For him philosophy "was the 'self-development' of the spirit, i.e., the automatic unfolding of the absolute, which in the 'ideality' of its nature and in its lifelessness surpassed the mathematical conceptions themselves."[56] The rational, Hegel proclaimed, is the real. But he was wrong, and his philosophy of history, Shestov emphatically declares, "is a crude and noxious falsification of life."[57]

Kant believed that he had written the final and exhaustive critique of reason, but he was mistaken. According to Shestov, it was not Kant who gave us the true critique of reason, but rather Dostoevsky, and that primarily in his *Notes from the Underground*.[58] In an extraordinary essay entitled "The Conquest of the Self-Evident: Dostoevsky's Philosophy," Shestov declares that what Kant gave us was not a critique of, but an apology for, pure reason. The protagonist of *Notes from the Underground*, however, unlike Kant, does not permit the positive sciences to judge metaphysics. On the contrary, for him it is metaphysics which judges the positive sciences. The underground man refuses to accept the wall constructed by the natural sciences. He rejects also the soothing balm offered by those religionists who say that God does not ask the impossible. This, for him, is an utter falsehood. God *does* ask the impossible. God asks nothing but the impossible. With unparalleled passion and power, Dostoevsky denounced the legitimacy of the rights of reason, of common consciousness, of "omnitude" (the ideas accepted by all). For him, assuming that the protagonist of the *Notes* represents his thinking, it is the living individual and his freedom that are ultimate—not natural laws or universal truths. The latter "are perhaps only magic, auto-suggestion or influences from outside which hypnotize us as a goose is hypnotized if we trace round her a circle of chalk."[59] Do not admit them, refuse to pay any further respect to them, and perhaps they will lose all of their power. That two times two equals four may be acceptable mathematics, but for Dostoevsky it is not ultimate truth. " 'Twice two is four,' gentlemen, is not life, it is the beginning of death."[60]

The only answer to the death-dealing power of reason, Shestov agrees with Dostoevsky, is not argument, for all arguments are rational and are therefore subject to the judgment of reason; it is mockery, invective, a categorical No.

Both science and philosophy—the one with its empirical approach and the other with its rationalist, deductive methods—have sought to give men definite, assured and permanent truths, along with the sense of tranquility and certainty that these are supposed to produce. What they have brought about, however, is the complete enslavement of men, though often it is not recognized as such by the enslaved. Moreover, the search for permanent and universal truths, for *veritates aeternae*, is fruitless; the fact is that there are no such truths. A serious reflection on history and even a slight use of imagination will readily convince one, according to Shestov, of the relativity and fallibility of everything that men have held to be eternally true.

> To escape from the grasp of contemporary ruling ideas, one should study history. The lives of other men in other lands in other ages teach us to realize that our "eternal laws" and infallible ideas are just abortions. Take a step further, imagine mankind living elsewhere than on this earth, and all our terrestrial eternalities lose their charm.[61]

The passion for constant and immutable truth is, as we have seen, an ancient one. It is this passion, Shestov maintains, that explains the preoccupation of Socrates and Plato, in one of their moods, with eternal "forms" and "ideas." They, as well as many other philosophers, found it difficult to grasp this "agitated, capricious life," and so they concluded that it is not real life but a figment. Truth is then sought not in objects but in the ideas or forms of objects. Thus a weakness in human understanding is unjustifiably exalted into a philosophical virtue.[62] But it is time that philosophy surrender its search for *veritates aeternae*. "The business of philosophy is to teach man to live in uncertainty—man who is supremely afraid of uncertainty, and who is forever hiding himself behind this or the other dogma. More briefly, the business of philosophy is not to reassure people, but to upset them."[63]

It is perhaps primarily because he has sought pleasure and comfort that man has been so grievously misled and enslaved. The positive sciences and the eternal truths of rationalist metaphysics have made available to man all the riches of the kingdoms of this world for his use and enjoyment. But enjoyment or pleasure is the greatest danger, threatening the living creature with final destruction, destruction both of the soul and the body. Shestov recalls with approval the words of the Cynic Antisthenes, "I would rather lose my understanding than feel pleasure," and the saying of St. Theresa, *Pati, Domine, aut mori*— "Suffer, Lord, or die."[64]

> For the vast majority of mankind, pleasure is sleep, or in other words, death of the soul, its return to nonexistence. Pain, suffering, is the beginning of awakening. A pleasurable, even, unperturbed existence kills in man all his humanity, leads him back to a vegetative existence, to the womb of that nothingness out of which he was brought in so inexplicable a fashion by some mysterious power.[65]

Death alone, with all its monstrousness and horror, Shestov concludes, can shake us loose from our enchantment and free us from the power of "necessary" and "universal" truth. That death is natural or pleasant is a lie. On the contrary, death is agonizing and frightful. Men instinctively fear death, and they are right in doing so. To try to make death less horrifying and problematic is foolish and misguided. The fear of death should be precisely the starting point of our philosophical thinking, for

> . . . only before great terror does the soul resolve to apply to itself that compulsion without which it could never raise itself up above the commonplace; the ugliness and agony of death make us forget everything, even our "self-evident truth," and force us to seek the new reality in those fields which seemed to us before to be peopled with shadows and ghosts.[66]

How shall men find the way to the truth? Only by becoming like the author of the Twenty-Second Psalm who said, "I am poured out like water and all my bones are out of joint. My heart is like wax; it is melted in the midst of my bowels." It is not enough, says Shestov, "for man to declare himself ready to live in filth and cold, to endure injury and sickness, to be burned in the brazen bull of the tyrant Phalaris."[67] In addition what is needed is that of which the Psalmist speaks: "to melt inwardly, to shatter the skeleton of one's own soul and to break that which is held to be the basis of our being, all that ready certainty and clear-cut definition of conception in which we are accustomed to see the *veritates aeternae*."[68] For a man to be able to glimpse ultimate truth, everything in him must become broken and fluid. He must feel that complete desolation and lostness experienced by the author of the same Psalm when he cried, "My God, my God, why hast Thou forsaken me?" Only when one feels that there is no God, that man is utterly alone and abandoned to himself, is there hope that he will escape from the dream-world of empirical reality and begin to create for himself both causes and aims. Only when he has first gone through the experience of despair, believing that God is not and that man must himself become God and create all things out of nothing, can he hope to catch a glimpse of the true God and of ultimate reality.

Philosophy is not calm and disinterested reflection, what Edmund Husserl, whom Shestov sees as the latest and one of the greatest examplars of the age-old attempt to create a thoroughly scientific philosophy, called *Besinnung*.[69] It must be, instead, a passionate and agonizing struggle. To the charge that such a struggle is a beating of the head against a stone wall, Shestov has no answer except the answer that to beat one's head against the wall is possibly the noblest and best thing a man may do. The world as logic and science conceive it—governed by universal and immutable laws, constrained by the iron hand of necessity—is, as far as Shestov is concerned, a humanly uninhabitable world. He seconds the paradoxical cry of Dostoevsky's protagonist in *Notes from the Underground*:

> Merciful heavens! but what do I care for the laws of nature and arithmetic . . .? as though such a stone wall really were a consolation . . . simply because it is as true as twice two makes four. Oh, absurdity of absurdities! How much better it is to understand it all, to

recognize it all, all the impossibilities and the stone wall; not to be reconciled to one of those impossibilities and stone walls, if it disgusts you to be reconciled to it.[70]

This, and Shestov's echo of it in *All Things Are Possible*, in *In Job's Balances*, and in *Athens and Jerusalem* is the cry of despair, of hopelessness. But despair and hopelessness are not altogether negative and destructive. For in his very abandonment, man may catch a glimpse of the road to salvation. As Shestov put it, "Hopelessness is the most solemn and supreme moment in life. Till that point we have been assisted—now we are left to ourselves. Previously we had to do with men and human laws— now with eternity, and with the complete absence of laws."[71]

IV

If philosophy is understood, as it was by Plotinus, to be a search for το τιμιώτατον, "what matters most," then obviously there is no necessary conflict between philosophy and religion. Indeed, their goal is essentially similar. But if philosophy is regarded, as it has been by most of the "scientific" metaphysicians of the West, as the search for eternal truths and universal principles, then religion—at any rate, the religion of the Bible—must be in irreconcilable conflict with it. This is Shestov's fundamental thesis in *Athens and Jerusalem*.

For the man of the Bible, God is not only at the center but at the beginning and end of all things. God created both the world and man and endowed man with freedom. Having created man, God blessed him and gave him dominion over everything in the universe. By the philosopher who aspires to be scientific, however, man is regarded as only one link in the endless chain of phenomena and as living in a universe governed by necessary laws. For the Psalmist, who represents Biblical thought, no empirical fact is ultimate; every fact is in the power of God who, in answer to man's cry, can suppress it or make it not to be. A fact is something which rose one day, which had a beginning, and therefore may, if not must, have an end. The philosopher, however, seeks to transform even a single, non-recurring fact or event into an eternal and unchangeable truth. For the man of the Bible, knowledge is not, as it is for the philosopher, the supreme goal of human life. Unlike the philosopher, who holds that knowledge justifies existence, the man of the Bible feels that it is from existence that knowledge must obtain its justification.

There can be no reconciliation, according to Shestov, between that philosophy which would be scientific and biblical revelation. Athens, he follows Tertullian in proclaiming, can never agree with Jerusalem. And yet, for two thousand years, the foremost thinkers of the Western world have firmly believed that a reconciliation is possible and have bent their strongest and most determined efforts toward effecting it.[72]

The work of the Alexandrian Jew Philo represents the first major attempt to reconcile the revelation that came out of the Orient with Western science and philosophy. But, Shestov declares, what Philo called reconciliation was in fact treason.

> A few Fathers of the Church—Tertullian, for example— were aware of this. But not all of them saw, as Tertullian saw, wherein lay the essence of the Hellenic spirit and the danger of its influence . . . He alone resolved, and that only once, in the famous saying which I have often quoted and which, in my opinion—as I have also said—each of us should say daily before sleeping and repeat on waking—resolved to recognize the formula of incantation which alone can give us freedom from the magic spell of centuries: *non pudet, quia pudendum est; prorsus credibile—quia ineptum est; certum—quia impossibile*—I am not ashamed—because it is shameful; it is absolutely credible—because it is absurd; it is certain—because it is impossible.[73]

Philo's attempt was a betrayal of the Bible because, in "explaining away" from the Bible the *pudendum, ineptum,* and *impossibile* which, according to reason, must be banished from our thought, it removed all that is most meaningful and valuable in the Scriptural outlook. Philo subordinated the Bible to Hellenistic wisdom and required Jerusalem to seek her justification and her blessing in Athens. The Alexandrian philosopher's work was extremely influential. As Shestov reminds us,

Philo's thought has even made its way into Holy Writ and has given the Fourth Gospel a tinge of its own. "In the beginning was the Word"—that meant: first Athens was, and only later Jerusalem. And consequently everything which proceeded out of Jerusalem must be weighed in the balances of Athens.[74]

The task which Philo set himself was continued by many of the doctors of the Church in the Middle Ages. Their thinking, according to Shestov, was as deeply influenced by Greek modes of speculation as was Philo's. While they revered the Bible and constantly exercised themselves with the question of its authority, they seem, in discussing its relation to the dominant Aristotelian philosophy, to have utterly neglected its content. Even as incisive a thinker as Duns Scotus never thought of looking in the Bible for the critique of reason or for the critique of the knowledge that reason brings to man. And, Shestov tells us, "when in the Middle Ages the voice of Peter Damian rang out, proclaiming that God could bring it about that that which had been had not been, it seemed like the voice of one crying in the wilderness. No one, neither of our time nor even of the Middle Ages, dared to admit that the Biblical "very good" corresponded to reality, that the world created by God had no defect."[75]

The ontological proof for the existence of God, which was so attractive to many medieval philosophers and which still retains a measure of popularity today, means nothing else, says Shestov, than the surrender of Jerusalem to the judgment of Athens. "The idea of the supremely perfect being had arisen in Athens, and the Bible God, if He wished to attain the predicate of existence, had to seek it on His knees in Athens, where all predicates which cannot dispense with universal recognition were forged and distributed."[76]

It is, however, against Spinoza's treatment of the problem of relating Biblical religion to philosophy that Shestov vents his sharpest anger. In the *Tractatus Theologico-Politicus* Spinoza made it very evident that, in his judgment, the Bible contains no truths but only moral lessons. Its affirmations about reality are to be understood as symbols and poetic images. Feeling, however, that the word "God" is important and valuable insofar as around it cluster so many pious associations and moral sentiments, Spinoza did not hesitate to identify nature, or substance, which is the ultimate in his philosophy, with the traditional word "God." But it is perfectly clear that Spinoza's God has nothing to do with the God of the Bible. Spinoza denies not only man's freedom but God's as well. In his system the freedom of God consists simply in submitting to an order which is nothing more than the expression of the divine being. "*Deus ex solis suae naturae legibus et a nemine coactus agit*—God acts only in accordance with the laws of His own nature, and none compels Him."[77] In speaking about God, then, "honest" Spinoza did not shrink, according to Shestov, from proclaiming a lie, and it is a lie that has been accepted by most philosophers since his time.

> Spinoza's formula, "Deus = natura = substantia," like all the conclusions drawn from it in his *Ethics* and his earlier works, simply means that there is no God. This discovery of Spinoza's became the starting point for modern philosophical thought. However much one may talk of God, yet we know with certainty that we are not speaking of that God who once lived in Biblical days, who created Heaven and earth and man after His image, who both loves and also desires, is excited and repentant, strives with man and even sometimes gets the worst of it in that strife. Reason, the same reason which rules over triangles and perpendiculars and which, therefore, thinks that it owns the sovereign right to distinguish truth from lies; reason which seeks, not for the best, but the true philosophy—this reason declares with the self-sufficiency peculiar to itself, in a tone which admits no contradiction, that such a God can be no supremely perfect being, not even a perfect being at all, and can consequently be no God.[78]

Kant and Hegel—though they proclaim themselves to be, and are regarded by others, as Christian thinkers—merely continued the work of Spinoza. Kant concluded that the existence of God is philosophically unprovable, as is also the immortality of the soul and the reality of human freedom. All three are to be accepted as "postulates of faith." What Kant meant in effect, Shestov urges, is that

God, immortality and freedom are illusory and non-
existent. But even if we take him at face value and
accept his statement that God, immortality and free will
are legitimate postulates of faith, we must nevertheless
question his sincerity, or at least his lack of a sense of
proportion. Kant was deeply disturbed by the apparent
inability of philosophy to prove the existence of external
objects, and he regarded this as a great scandal. But is
not the real scandal of philosophy, Shestov asks, that it
cannot prove the existence of God?[79] Kant employed
the language of biblical religion but denied its substance.
In this respect, Hegel, who has often been portrayed as the
great Christian restorer to metaphysics of the rights which
Kant had taken away from it, is, according to Shestov,
even more anti-biblical; in Hegelianism the religion of the
Bible is completely subverted and denied.[80]

   The biblical revelation can neither be defended by argument nor harmonized with rationalist or "scientific" metaphysics. Biblical man, Shestov maintains, as we shall
presently see in considering his views of the Bible and
its God, based his life on faith, which is not a weaker
form of knowledge but a completely different dimension
of thought; and the substance of this faith, denied both
by science and philosophy, is that "nothing is impossible."
When Adam ate the fruit of the tree of the knowledge of
good and evil, according to Shestov's interpretation of the
legend of the fall, faith was displaced by autonomous
reason and autonomous morality. Ever since, the sin of
Adam has been repeated by his descendants. The consequence has been a suffocation, a choking, of the springs
of life.

   Man as he now exists is enthralled by reason and enslaved by knowledge. He languishes under what Pascal
called "a supernatural enchantment." How can the magic
spell be broken? Shestov answers: only by returning to the
truths proclaimed in the Bible. And the first step is for
man to realize his own fallen condition as Scripture
portrays it.

   For Shestov the story of Adam's sin in the third chapter
of Genesis, which he regards as simultaneously legend and
divine revelation, contains the essential key to understanding the reality of the human situation. No naturalistic or
simple historical explanation can tell us

how a little, uneducated, nomad people could come upon the idea that the supreme sin which deformed human nature and brought with it the expulsion from paradise, with all the consequences of that expulsion: our heavy, tortured life, labor in the sweat of our brow, sickness, death, etc.—that the supreme sin of our forefathers was trust in "reason," and that man in plucking the apple from the tree of knowledge did not save himself, as one would suppose, but damned himself for ever.[81]

This immemorial legend of the fall has been repeated many times—by Isaiah, by St. Paul, by Luther, by Nietzsche in his *Beyond Good and Evil* and by scores of others—but men still find it hard to grasp and strenuously resist accepting its message. According to Shestov, some theologians, in interpreting the story, seem to have deliberately distorted its essential point. St. Augustine, for example, understood it as meaning that man became mortal because he disobeyed the commandment of God, and not, as the text clearly states, specifically because he ate of the fruit of the tree of the knowledge of good and evil. Others have been even more obtuse and interpreted the original sin to be the *concupiscentia* which Adam, seduced by Eve, was unable to conquer.[82]

Of all those who have pondered the Bible, it was Dostoevsky, Shestov suggests, who best understood its mood and spirit. It is only, however, after a whole series of *exercitia spiritualia* that a reader can perceive the truth of the Biblical affirmations that are echoed in the works of the Russian novelist.

Only thus can one perceive that time has not one, but two or even more dimensions, that laws have not existed for all time, but are "given" and only in order that the offence might abound, that it is faith and not works which can save souls, that the death of Socrates can shake the formidable "twice two is four," that God demands always and only the impossible; that the ugly duckling can change into the beautiful white swan, that everything has a beginning here but nothing ends, that caprice has a right to guarantees, that the fantastic is more, real than the natural, that life is death and death is life, and other truths of the same sort which look out at us with strange and terrible eyes from every page of Dostoevsky's writing.[83]

It is in his short story entitled "The Dream of A Ridiculous Man" that Dostoevsky retells and comments on the biblical legend of the fall. The protagonist of the story, to whom everything has become indifferent, has decided upon suicide, but before doing away with himself, he goes to sleep and in his dreams sees what the opening chapters of Genesis relate. He dreams that he is among men who have not yet tasted the fruit of the tree of the knowledge of good and evil, who possess no science, who know neither shame nor anxiety, and who have neither the power nor the wish to judge. They are beautiful, more beautiful than anything on earth, these children of the sun. The ridiculous man realizes that the inhabitants of this paradise know without having scientific knowledge, that theirs is a knowledge which is incomprehensible to him. But the earthly man, despite his admiration for these children of paradise, corrupts them all. How? By endowing them with scientific knowledge and with moral principles. Immediately they come to feel shame and their entire world is utterly changed. It is now hedged about with laws. Instead of free creatures, they have become automata.

By eating the fruit of the tree of knowledge, man, the Bible and Dostoevsky thus tell us, has fallen into a world of necessity, of limitation, where his life is ringed about by impossibilities and impassable boundaries. How can he transcend this world? Only, Shestov replies, by that means which St. Paul pointed to when, commenting on the legend of the fall, he declared "all that does not come of faith is sin." But faith as Shestov understands it is not what St. Paul seems to have understood by the word *pistis* or what most of the exponents of the Judeo-Christian tradition have understood by it. For Shestov faith is not simple trust in God or a surrender and obedience to His will. Certainly it is not, as it has sometimes been defined, an intellectual or emotional assent to unproved propositions which are set forth in a book alleged to be the product of divine revelation. Faith, for Shestov, is rather "a spiritual exertion of quite peculiar nature, which we describe as 'audacity.' Only when we have forgotten the 'laws' which bind us fast to the limited existence, can we raise ourselves up above human truths and human good. To raise himself, man must lose the ground under his feet."[84] Or again, as he puts it in *Athens and Jerusalem,*

> . . . to find God one must tear oneself away from the seductions of reason with all its physical and moral constraints, and go to another source of truth. In Scripture this source bears the enigmatic name "faith," which is that dimension of thought where truth abandons itself fearlessly and joyously to the entire disposition of the Creator: *"Thy* will be done!" The will of Him who, on His side, fearlessly and with sovereign power returns to the believer his lost power: . . . "what things soever ye desire . . . ye shall have them."[85]

Faith, then, is audacity, the denial of necessary laws, the refusal to regard anything as impossible. It is the demand for that absolute, primordial freedom which man supposedly had before the fall, when he still found the distinction between truth and falsehood, as well as between good and evil, unnecessary and did not even know that these existed. Faith, for Shestov, is becoming like God, for whom there are neither moral sanctions nor reasons.

> He (God) does not need, as mortals do, a reason, a support, a firm ground. Groundlessness is the basic, most enviable, and to us most incomprehensible privilege of the Divine. Consequently, our whole moral struggle, even as our rational inquiry—if we once admit that God is the last end of our endeavors—will bring us sooner or later (rather later, much later, than sooner) to emancipation not only from moral evaluations but also from reason's eternal truths. Truth and the Good are fruits of the forbidden tree; for limited creatures, for outcasts from paradise. I know that this ideal of freedom in relation to truth and the good cannot be realized on earth—in all probability does not need to be realized. But it is granted to man to have prescience of ultimate freedom. Before the face of Eternal God, all our foundations break together and all ground crumbles under us, even as objects—this we know—lose their weight in endless space, and—this we shall probably learn one day—will lose their impermeability in endless time.[86]

But Shestov's God—the God of whom the Bible speaks and before whom all human foundations crack and crumble —is clearly not the God of Spinoza or of Kant. Spinoza's God is the eternal substance or order of nature. Kant cannot accept a living God who is active in the affairs of men and nations. Such a God would, for him, destroy all reason and philosophy, which rest upon the Spinozist idea that what is is necessarily just as it is throughout all eternity.[87] Kant, says Shestov, "rescued piety and morality, but betrayed God by replacing Him by an idea, which he created after the image of the highest criterion of mathematical truths."[88] Against all rationalist theologies, Shestov himself wishes to speak, as did Pascal, of "the God of Abraham, the God of Isaac, the God of Jacob, and not the God of the philosophers. The God of the philosophers, whether He be a material or ideal principle, carries with Him the triumph of constraint, of brutal force."[89]

The God of the Bible is not to be found as the conclusion of a syllogism. His existence cannot be proved by rational argument or inferred from historical evidence. "One cannot demonstrate God. One cannot seek Him in history. God is 'caprice' incarnate, who rejects all guarantees. He is outside history, like all that people hold to be το τιμιώτατον."[90] How shall one arrive at this *Deus absconditus*, this hidden God? "The chief thing," says Shestov, "is to think that, even if all men without exception were convinced that God does not exist, this would not mean anything, and that if one could prove as clearly as two times two makes four that God does not exist, this also would not mean anything."[91] To the complaint that it is not possible to ask one to take a position which negates a universal conviction of men and flies in the face of logic, Shestov replies, "Obviously! But God always demands of us the impossible . . . It is only when man wishes the impossible that he remembers God. To obtain that which is possible he turns to his fellow men."[92]

Perhaps modern man can reach the God of the Bible only by first passing through the experience of his own nothingness and feeling, as Nietzsche and others have, that God also is not. This feeling, Shestov suggests, is a profoundly ambiguous one, capable of leading men in diametrically opposite directions.

"The fool said in his heart: There is no God." Sometimes this is a sign of the end and of death. Sometimes of the beginning and of life. As soon as man feels that God is not, he suddenly comprehends the frightful horror and the wild folly of human temporal existence, and when he has comprehended this he awakes, perhaps not to the ultimate knowledge, but to the penultimate. Was it not so with Nietzsche, Spinoza, Pascal, Luther, Augustine, even with St. Paul?[93]

Our task if we would find God—and this, Shestov urges, is also the way to true philosophy and genuine knowledge —consists "in the Psalmist's image, in shattering the skeleton which lends substance to our old ego, melting the 'heart in our bowels.' "[94] Experiencing the abyss that opens before him when all his *veritates aeternae* and certainties are taken away, the desperate soul feels that "God is not, man must himself become God, create all things out of nothing; all things; matter together with forms, and even the eternal laws."[95] When a man has felt this complete abandonment to himself and to boundless despair, he may—as such irreconcilable enemies as St. Ignatius Loyola, the founder of the Jesuits, and Luther, the renegade monk, both testify—direct his eyes toward ultimate reality and see the true God who will restore to him the limitless freedom with which he was created and again make all things possible for him.

V

In typical existentialist fashion Shestov rebels against the attempt to describe man in abstract and generic conceptions. These, he urges, do violence to the endless variety and multifariousness of human individuals. Men differ from each other in innumerable ways, including what he calls their "metaphysical destiny."[96] Aristotle, for example, was destined for the empirical world, Plato for the ideal. Hence it is improper to speak of "man" generally. In obviously ironic and overstated terms, Shestov declares, "there is a Plato, Aristotle, Socrates, and Alexander's groom, but each of these differs from the other far more strongly than he does from a rhinoceros, a peacock, a cypress, or a cabbage, perhaps even from a tree trunk or a rock."[97]

Not only is the general conception "man" inappropriate, but we must also beware of applying any general attributes to man in a univocal sense. This becomes apparent, for example, when we consider the all-important question of man's freedom. "It is impossible," writes Shestov,

> to speak of free will (as of anything affecting the first and last truths) in the language of pure conceptions purged of contradictions, if one wishes form and content of the word to correspond even approximately. Either one must simplify reality, i.e. distort it past recognition, or permit oneself inevitable, almost paradoxical contradictions, or else, like Plato, have resort to myths. Or— and this is obviously the right way out—one must not be above either contradiction or myth. One must agree once for all that all our conceptions, however we construe them, are bi-dimensional, while truth is tri-dimensional or more. Therefore in speaking of free will it is impossible to start from an exceptional case, like Buridan's example. Still less can one rely on the general principle of no effect without cause. Between the "freedom of will" of Buridan's ass, or even of no ass, but a man confronted with a similar dilemma, on the one hand, and Augustine saving his soul or Plato meditating on Socrates' death and the fate of the just, on the other, there is so great a difference that to reduce all these cases to a single problem would mean having eyes and not seeing, having ears and not hearing.[98]

In the empirical world, Shestov maintains, man obviously does possess a measure of freedom. "He can go right or left, choose which he will of several like objects, even act in more important cases (I should not care to say which) without considering anything but his fortuitous whim."[99] But in the face of the ultimate choices and dilemmas man's freedom of action disappears. "To choose between good and evil, to decide his metaphysical destiny, is not granted to man."[100] Here Shestov is no ordinary determinist, who seeks "natural" explanations for everything and refuses to see anything mysterious or enigmatic in the powers that control man's fate. Such a refusal, Shestov believes, would be a deliberate closing of the

eyes to reality. "But wilful blindness towards the unknown
and fear of it do not alter the facts: something imperious
and irresistible fetters our freedom and guides us towards
ends unknown and incomprehensible to us."[101]

The loss of freedom, however, is a symptom of man's
fallen condition. But this condition—Shestov, as we have
seen,[102] believes—may be transcended. Through faith man
may regain his primordial freedom, and this is God's
strongest wish for him. To affirm his freedom and individuality through the audacity which is faith is also,
according to Shestov, man's primary task. Once he has
escaped from the womb of the One, he must not seek
to return to its safety and comfort but rather reaffirm
the audacity that he once exercised. That God wanted to
teach man this lesson, Shestov ingeniously suggests, may
well be the best explanation of the classical Christian
doctrine of the Incarnation.

> *Cur Deus homo?* Why, to what purpose, did He become
> man, expose Himself to injurious mistreatment, igno-
> minious and painful death on the cross? Was it not in
> order to show man, through His example, that no de-
> cision is too hard, that it is worth while bearing anything
> only in order not to remain in the womb of the One?
> That any torture whatever to the living being is better
> than the "bliss" of the rest-satiate "ideal" being?[103]

Man lives in time, and this is a fact about him that is of
special importance. Time, Shestov points out,[104] has generally been regarded as the enemy of man, bringing death
and destruction to him and his works. This is a great
error. It is matter, whose basic predicate is eternity and
immutability, that is the true enemy of man; and eternity,
which is the absence of time, is the very symbol and
incarnation of death. Time itself is the chief ally of life
and alone gives man the hope of escaping the power of
dead matter, which, without time, would remain forever
inert and unchanging. Eluding the jealous watchfulness of
eternity, time came into the world simultaneously with the
human soul, and together time and the soul declared war
on inertia. The beginning of all birth is rightly to be seen
in time, but it is wrong to couple time, as did the ancients,
with destruction.

Time only creates the possibility of changes and great transformations. Destruction, however, does not come from time. And if time is as mighty as it appears to the empirical consciousness, then humanity's supreme hopes must be bound up with its might. In the beginning was immovable eternity and its brother death. When time came, having escaped the fetters of inertia and immutability, with it came life. And since that day life and death fight against one another in the world.[105]

The outcome of the struggle is not yet determined, but thus far, at any rate, death has not succeeded in banishing life from the world. Indeed it appears, according to Shestov, that death and eternity, like matter, have renounced their sovereign rights before time and life. "It seems as though eternity, and death, and matter were turning gradually from substance into accidents, from kings who autocratically lay down the law to being into yielding, conciliatory leaders."[106]

Nevertheless, it is plain that death ends every human life. Shestov is as keenly aware as Heidegger and other existentialist philosophers of human finitude, of man's being as a "being-toward-death"; and both the Russian and the German philosopher acknowledge their indebtedness to Tolstoy who, especially in his great short story "The Death of Ivan Ilyich" and his *Diary of a Madman*, produced the first major existential accounts of the meaning of death.[107]

Men ordinarily seek to escape from the overwhelming anxiety that is created by a genuinely felt sense of their inexorable movement toward dissolution by denying the reality of death or suppressing the thought of it: ". . . death lies in the future, which will not be—so everyone feels."[108] In this, philosophers and ordinary men are alike. But they must be reminded of their mortality; otherwise they will never awaken from the dreamworld in which they spend their days or transcend their accepted values and standards.

Let no one hypocritically pretend, as Plato did in the *Timaeus*, that death is natural, painless and agreeable. It is none of these. What does it mean to say that death is natural? "If the word 'natural' has any meaning at all, we must allow that everything in the world is alike

natural: health and sickness, death in old age and death
in youth. Nothing unnatural, i.e. nothing against nature,
can be. If it exists, it is natural."[109] The perceptive and
honest seeker after truth, however, "sees in death the
eternal problematical, a thing not compatible with the
usual *ordo et connexio rerum* or even *idearum*."[110] Nor,
Shestov insists, is death pleasant and painless, even if it
comes at a great age. "Death is monstrous, agonizing and
frightful."[111] Plato himself, when he wrote the *Phaedo*
under the fresh impression of Socrates' death, was far
removed from the position he took in the *Timaeus*.

> . . . when the Master dies under our eyes, we shall
> hardly entertain considerations of the naturalness of
> death, or of any naturalness. In such a case one thinks
> only of the unnatural, the supernatural. Can we then
> feel convinced that the natural is more legitimate and
> mightier than the supernatural? It is, indeed—at first
> sight—more comprehensible, more thinkable, more ex-
> pected. But what is the value of first sight, thinkable-
> ness, comprehensibility? Socrates has been poisoned, he
> is no more![112]

The supreme importance of an existential experience of
the fact of human mortality—as Plato (in some of his
moods), Tolstoy and a few other extraordinary men have
discovered—is that it reveals new possibilities previously
undreamed of. That *Deus impossibile non jubet* is a self-
evident truth, attested alike by common sense, science and
Roman Catholic theology. "But death takes no heed of this.
It has its own truths, its own self-evidence, its possibilities
and its impossibilities, which do not agree with our
ordinary ideas . . ."[113]

Death, as Ivan Ilyich in Tolstoy's story discovered,
forces us out of the world common to all. According to
Shestov, the terror of mortality turns man away from the
"self-evident truths" of science, common sense and rationalist theology and creates instead the possibility of
exercising the audacity which is faith. Then man ap-
prehends a new, transforming reality.

> Faith, only the faith that looks to the Creator and that
> He inspires, radiates from itself the supreme and deci-
> sive truths concerning what is and what is not. Reality

is transfigured. The heavens glorify the Lord. The prophets and apostles cry in ecstasy, "O death, where is thy sting? Hell, where is thy victory?"[114]

Shestov and Heidegger agree that the existential becoming aware of the human condition as a "being-toward-death" halts man's instinctive flight toward the comfort, anonymity and falsehood of *das Man* or the world of ordinary social experience. But for Heidegger this awareness creates only the possibility of *Entschlossenheit*, a "resolute" or "authentic" individual existence, the anxiety of which is in no way overcome or mitigated, as it is for Shestov in the light of the latter's religious faith.

Beyond believing in the possibility of transforming present life through faith, does Shestov hold out for man the hope of a life after death? He replies, with his characteristic note of paradox, in a paragraph entitled "Two Kinds of Logic":

"A whole eternity thou wast not, and didst not mourn thereover, didst not say thou couldst not comprehend how the world could exist without thee. But with respect to the eternity in the future in which thou wilt not be, thou dost maintain that this is unacceptable. It is clear that thou art inconsistent." Thus reason speaks to man. "It is, indeed, clear to thee, for thee *I* am inconsistent. But there is also another kind of logic. When I am once arisen out of nothingness, then it is done; I shall not return again into nothingness, and the second 'eternity' is mine." This is the answer of the irreconcilable and wilful debater. Against such a one reason can do naught with its own means.[115]

VI

Though it appears that he neither called himself an existentialist or thought of himself as such, Shestov, as we have already indicated,[116] may properly be regarded as belonging to the existentialist tradition and following, in large measure, its distinctive approach to philosophy. It is true that he did not discover and read the works of the great nineteenth century founder of modern existentialism,

Kierkegaard, until fairly late in life, and the thought of its foremost twentieth century representative, Heidegger,[117] seems to have passed by him almost unnoticed. Nevertheless, practically all the dominant motifs of existentialism— as represented in the works of Kierkegaard, Dostoevsky, Nietzsche, Heidegger and even Sartre—figure prominently as elements of his thought, which, in its totality, is thoroughly existentialist in mood and spirit.

Like Kierkegaard, Shestov engages in a great polemic against the abstract, rationalistic and pseudo-scientific thought of Hegel, which, for him, represents the culmination of the modern European mode of philosophizing inaugurated by Descartes and Spinoza and continued by Leibnitz, Kant, Fichte and their disciples. All these thinkers —like their great prototype, Aristotle—erred, he believes, in their immoderate pretension that reason and scientific method can unlock all the secrets of the universe and give man ultimate truth. What they have done rather is bound man still more firmly to the power of that 'Ανάγκη or Necessity which they have put in the place of God and which they so slavishly revere.

Again, like Kierkegaard and most of the other existentialists, Shestov seeks to renounce objective (or, as he calls it, constraining) truth and to turn to subjectivity or inwardness as the source of final truth. Abstract, impersonal truth, though logically consistent and empirically verifiable, is for him ultimately insignificant and superficial, while passionately held, inward truth, even when it is self-contradictory and absurd, is deeply meaningful to the individual who holds it. No more than Kierkegaard does Shestov shrink from contradiction or from the paradoxes that are the results of the renunciation of logical norms.[118] Of course, subjective truth is essentially incommunicable—its distinguishing mark is that it cannot be recognized and shared by "all"[119]—but this in no way lessens its value and importance. Shestov parallels Kierkegaard in his religiously motivated insistence on subjectivity and passion in the search for truth, but he is not obsessed with the Kierkegaardian despair over the nothingness of man and his infinite distance from God. For the Russian Jewish philosopher there is always hope, as we have seen,[120] that the gulf between God and man is bridgeable.

Kierkegaard spoke constantly of the necessity for passion in searching for truth. Shestov echoes his thought in insisting that the metaphysical quest must not be, as Spinoza and those who followed him urged, a purely intellectual affair, conducted with complete detachment and indifference. Man's will and valuations may, and should, enter into it.[121] Heidegger, too, it may be noted, has held that truth is not a property of propositions and that the search for it cannot be the simple rationalistic procedure that most of the "scientific" metaphysicians of the West have recommended. Heidegger's understanding of truth or ἀλήθεία as *Unverborgenheit*[122] (revelation or uncovering) might, it seems, have struck a responsive chord in Shestov, but he would not have agreed that the seeker for truth must renounce all evaluative activity and attempt to attain a passive "openness to Being." Man, with his own will and his own desires, must be an active participant in the creation of truth.

For Kierkegaard, as well as for Heidegger, Sartre and most of the other existentialists, man's freedom is the supremely important fact about him. In this respect, too, Shestov is typically existentialist. The problem of human freedom is one of his major concerns. Kierkegaard emphasized the terror of freedom, the dizziness and anxiety produced by man's awareness of the chasm opened before him by his capacity and his need to decide.[123] Heidegger holds that man's freedom to act and the call of his conscience render him guilty.[124] According to Sartre, man is "condemned to be free."[125] In general, the existentialists have maintained that anxiety or dread is an invariable concomitant of freedom. Man's freedom is manifested in moral choice. But once ethical norms have been dethroned from their traditional status of universal and eternal principles whose validity is guaranteed by the nature of reason itself or by the will of the God who is supposed to be their author, freedom becomes terrible and frightening. Without rational justification, without the support provided by a sense of cosmic meaning and purpose, man, according to the existentialists, must choose himself and create his own values in the face of a world that is utterly indifferent both to him and to his projects. The nothingness of which man becomes aware when he is compelled to choose is, as Marjorie Grene has pointed out in her interpretation of Sartre, "though not death, just as genuinely a kind of annihilation or negation."[126] It therefore necessarily arouses profound dread.

Shestov, as we have seen,[127] regards the freedom of man in his "fallen" condition as strictly limited, but within its boundaries (which he declines to specify) man's capacity to choose is real and undeniable. He knows, too, of the terror which the awareness of freedom arouses in most men, and he reminds us repeatedly how the generality of mankind have fled from freedom, glorified and blessed Necessity, and declined to grant any significant power over it even to God.[128] Nevertheless, he himself regards freedom as the highest of human goods and urges men not only to hold fast to that measure of it which they possess but to seek, through "faith," an ever larger scope for its exercise. He also, like Nietzsche and his existentialist followers, refuses to recognize any divinely ordained or rationally justified ethical norms; Kantian "autonomous morality" and "respect for law" are as repugnant to him as "autonomous reason" and the glorification of Necessity. But the absence of "universal and eternal" moral principles to guide man in his acts of choice does not terrify him. Employing the language of Greek mythology and of the Bible, he declares that those who constantly think and reflect, who never venture forward without looking around in all directions, will be changed into stones at the sight of the Medusa's head which they encounter when they look backward while those who, like Abraham, go forward daringly, without considering where they are going and without demanding in advance guarantees or reasons or directions, will attain the Promised Land.[129] Why this difference between Shestov's estimate of freedom and that of most of the other existentialists? The answer obviously lies in their fundamentally different religious presuppositions. Heidegger and Sartre are, of course, atheists. Kierkegaard, to be sure, believed passionately and totally in God, but his God is "wholly other" and infinitely distant from man. Shestov, however, is confident that God is concerned for man, that He wishes man to regain the divine freedom with which He endowed him at the time of creation, and that though the affirmation of his freedom and individuality involves man in endless tension and restlessness, God will not permit him to suffer ultimate tragedy and destruction through the employment of this, His greatest gift to him.

While he differs radically from the other existentialists in his optimistic view of the results of the exercise of man's freedom, Shestov is at one with them in his clear recognition of the fundamental negativities of the human situation, namely, man's finitude and mortality. He emphatically declines, as we have observed,[130] to gloss over the agony of death or to make it appear a simple, natural phenomenon. But death does not, for Shestov, represent mere unrelieved horror. Out of a genuine, existential experience of the fact of his own finitude and mortality, man may find himself capable of breaking the fetters which bind him to the self-evident, to the world of ordinary consciousness in which logic and common sense reign supreme. The awareness of his mortality may lead man, Shestov would agree with Heidegger, to acceptance of personal responsibility for his life, to a "resolute" and "authentic" existence rather than a cowardly flight into the anonymity of the mass. But for Shestov, this awareness may go much further and endow man with the daring necessary to break into that divine kingdom which, according to Scripture, can be stormed only by violence, and in which, contrary to the world conceived by rationalist philosophy and science, "nothing is impossible."

In concert with most of the other existentialist philosophers of our time, Shestov protests strongly against the widespread mechanization of life and the depersonalization of human relationships produced by modern science and technology. Men have come to feel that they are only small and insignificant cogs in a vast machine. What they now require more than anything else is a fresh reminder of the biblical truth that the entire universe was created for their sakes.[131]

Despite the emphasis of most of the contemporary non-theistic existentialist thinkers on the horrors, ambiguities and anxieties of human life, there is a basic optimism in their doctrine that "man makes himself." This must mean, among other things, that man's fate is always open, that until death there is always another chance. Shestov shares this optimism, which, for him, is intensified by the conviction that not only can man be the master of his own fate but that in his endeavor to achieve this mastery he is not dependent entirely on his own resources. In his struggle for freedom and the affirmation of his individuality, he always has God, the living God of the Bible, on his side.

NOTES

1. V. V. Zenkovsky, the historian of Russian philosophy, considers him one of the greatest thinkers of twentieth century Russia. See his *History of Russian Philosophy*, New York, Columbia University Press, 1953. Vol. II, pp. 780–791.
2. Published by John W. Luce and Co., Boston, 1916, with a foreword by John Middleton Murry.
3. Translated by S. S. Koteliansky with a foreword by D. H. Lawrence and published by Robert M. McBride and Co., New York, 1920. This is a translation of a work originally published in Russia in 1905 under the title *The Apotheosis of Groundlessness*.
4. Translated by Camilla Coventry and C. A. McCartney and published by J. M. Dent & Sons, Ltd., London, 1932.
5. For this account of Shestov's early years, I have relied on H. Lowtzky's article "Lev Shestov As I Remember Him," published in Russian in the review *Grani*, No. 45, 1960, and No. 46, 1961, in Frankfurt-am-Main, and on personal conversation and correspondence with Shestov's daughters, Madame Natalie Baranov and Madame Tatiana Rageot of Paris.
6. Published in the journal *Kievskoe Slovo*, February 22, 1895.
7. Such is the constant and recurring theme of his *Apotheosis of Groundlessness*, published in 1905 (English translation, *All Things Are Possible*). All page references below are to the English version, published by Robert M. McBride and Co., New York, 1920.
8. *All Things Are Possible*, pp. 23–24.
9. *Ibid.*, pp. 142–144.
10. *Ibid.*, p. 218.
11. *In Job's Balances*, translated by Camilla Coventry and C. A. McCartney, London, J. M. Dent & Sons, Ltd., 1932, pp. 193–194.
12. *Ibid.*, p. 190.
13. *Ibid.*, p. 157.
14. *Ibid.*, p. XXIX.
15. *All Things Are Possible*, pp. 129–130.
16. *In Job's Balances*, p. 193.
17. *Ibid.*, p. 155.
18. *Loc. cit.*
19. *Ibid.*, p. XXVIII.
20. *Ibid.*, p. XXIX.
21. *Ibid.*, p. 158.
22. *Ibid.*, p. 159.
23. *Ibid.*, p. 173.

24. *Ibid.*, p. 170.
25. *Loc. cit.*
26. *Ibid.*, p. 166.
27. *All Things Are Possible*, pp. 128–129. Cf. "The Limits of the Power of the Principles of Identity and of Contradiction" in *Athens and Jerusalem*, translated by Bernard Martin, Athens, Ohio University Press, 1966, pp. 409–410.
28. *All Things Are Possible*, p. 116.
29. *Ibid.*, p. 38.
30. *Ibid.*, p. 139.
31. *In Job's Balances*, p. 207.
32. *Ibid.*, pp. 31–32.
33. *Ibid.*, p. 207.
34. *Loc. cit.*
35. *Ibid.*, p. 160.
36. *Loc. cit.*
37. *Ibid.*, p. 234.
38. *Ibid.*, p. 235.
39. *All Things Are Possible*, pp. 68–69.
40. *In Job's Balances*, pp. 188–189.
41. *Ibid.*, p. 151. This, according to Shestov, is what Plato was attempting to do through his concept of "spiritual" as distinguished from "corporeal" vision. Cf. "Parmenides in Chains," *Athens and Jerusalem*, pp. 101 ff.
42. *In Job's Balances*, pp. 149–150. Cf. "Logic and Thunder," *Athens and Jerusalem*, pp. 432–433.
43. *In Job's Balances*, p. 6.
44. *Ibid.*, p. 226.
45. *Loc. cit.*
46. *Loc. cit.*
47. *Ibid.*, p. 220.
48. *Ibid.*, p. 234.
49. *Ibid.*, p. XVI.
50. *Ibid.*, p. XVII.
51. "Foreword," *Athens and Jerusalem*, pp. 56 ff.
53. *Ibid.*, p. XXVI. This is the 'Ανάγκη whose enslaving power is Shestov's major theme in the section "Parmenides in Chains" in *Athens and Jerusalem*, pp. 75 ff.
54. *In Job's Balances*, p. XXVII. Cf. "Parmenides in Chains," *Athens and Jerusalem*, p. 83.
55. *In Job's Balances*, p. XXVII.
56. *Ibid.*, p. XXVIII.
57. *Ibid.*, p. 244.
58. *Ibid.*, p. 21. Cf. "Foreword," *Athens and Jerusalem*, p. 64, footnote.
59. *In Job's Balances*, p. 34.
60. *Loc. cit.*
61. *All Things Are Possible*, p. 22.
62. *Ibid.*, pp. 42–43.
63. *Ibid.*, p. 24.
64. *In Job's Balances*, p. 154.
65. *Loc. cit.*

66. *Ibid.*, p. 241.
67. *Ibid.*, p. 229.
68. *Loc. cit.*
69. See Shestov's essay on Husserl, "Memento Mori" in *Potestas Clavium*, translated by Bernard Martin, Athens, Ohio University Press, 1968.
70. According to Shestov, this was also the answer of Chekhov to the hopelessness and misery of the characters he created in his last plays and stories. See the remarkable essay on Chekhov, "Creation from the Void," in his *Penultimate Words and Other Essays*, Boston, John W. Luce and Co., 1916.
71. *All Things Are Possible*, p. 82.
72. "Foreword," *Athens and Jerusalem*, pp. 47 f.
73. *In Job's Balances*, p. XXIII.
74. *Loc. cit.*
75. "Foreword," *Athens and Jerusalem*, p. 63. Cf. *Ibid.*, "Commentaries," pp. 418 ff.
76. *In Job's Balances*, p. XXIV.
77. *Ibid.*, p. XIX.
78. *Ibid.*, p. XX. For another, more extended polemic against Spinoza, see "In the Bull of Phalaris," *Athens and Jerusalem*, pp. 177 ff.
79. "Foreword," *Athens and Jerusalem*, p. 53.
80. "Parmenides in Chains," *Athens and Jerusalem*, pp. 127 ff.
81. *In Job's Balances*, p. 236.
82. *Ibid.*, p. 238.
83. *Ibid.*, p. 64.
84. *Ibid.*, p. 239.
85. *Op. cit.*, "Foreword," pp. 67–68. Cf. the discussion of faith as essentially "unfounded" in "Abraham and Socrates," *Athens and Jerusalem*, pp. 396–397.
86. *In Job's Balances*, p. 218.
87. "Foreword," *Athens and Jerusalem*, p. 54.
88. *In Job's Balances*, p. XXVII.
89. "Foreword," *Athens and Jerusalem*, p. 67.
90. *In Job's Balances*, p. 82.
91. "The One Thing Necessary," *Athens and Jerusalem*, p. 435.
92. *Loc. cit.*
93. *In Job's Balances*, p. 141.
94. *Ibid.*, p. 230.
95. *Loc. cit.*
96. See above, p. 19.
97. *Ibid.*, p. 221.
98. *Ibid.*, p. 201.
99. *Ibid.*, p. 199.
100. *Loc. cit.*
101. *Ibid.*, p. 200.
102. Above, pp. 32–33.
103. *In Job's Balances*, p. 177.
104. *Ibid.*, p. 231. Cf. "Change and Time," *Athens and Jerusalem*, p. 406.
105. *In Job's Balances*, p. 232.

106. *Loc. cit.*

107. See Shestov's very remarkable essay "The Last Judgment: Tolstoy's Last Works," *In Job's Balances*, pp. 83–138.

108. *In Job's Balances*, p. 146.

109. *Ibid.*, p. 240.

110. *Loc. cit.*

111. *Ibid.*, p. 241.

112. *Loc. cit.*

113. *Ibid.*, p. 83.

114. "Foreword," *Athens and Jerusalem*, p. 69.

115. *In Job's Balances*, p. 171.

116. Above, Preface.

117. Heidegger, to be sure, has denied that he is an existentialist and insisted that his *Sein und Zeit* is ontology, not existentialist anthropology. Nevertheless, his description of human existence or *Dasein* has been generally regarded by critics as one of the major existentialist efforts of our time. It is interesting to note that though Heidegger seems to have had virtually no influence on Shestov, he was in Shestov's audience when the Russian philosopher lectured in Germany under the auspices of the *Nietzsche-Gesellschaft* in the 1920's.

118. One does not, however, often find in Shestov that willful and absurd word-play to which Kierkegaard himself, though he so deplored it in Hegel, frequently succumbed.

119. Cf. "Truth and the Recognition of Truth," *Athens and Jerusalem*, pp. 400–401.

120. Above, p. 33.

121. "The Maximum of Metaphysics," *Athens and Jerusalem*, pp. 389–393.

122. *Was ist Metaphysik?* 5th ed., Frankfurt-am-Main, Vittorio Klostermann, 1927, p. 10.

123. See especially Kierkegaard's *The Concept of Dread*, translated by Walter Lowrie, Princeton University Press, 1957.

124. *Sein und Zeit*, Halle, Max Niemeyer Verlag, 1931, p. 269. Heidegger here writes: "Der Gewissensruf hat den Charakter des Anrufs des Daseins auf sein eigenstes Selbsteinkönnen und das in der Weise des Aufrufs zum eigensten Schuldigsein."

125. See his *L'Etre et le Néant*, Paris, Librairie Gallimard, 1943.

126. *Introduction to Existentialism*, Chicago, Phoenix Books, 1959, p. 54.

127. Above, p. 36.

128. "Parmenides in Chains," *Athens and Jerusalem, passim.*

129. "Abraham and Socrates," *Athens and Jerusalem*, pp. 396–397; "Commentary on That Which Precedes," *Ibid.*, p. 442.

130. Above, pp. 38–39.

131. "Nature and Man," *Athens and Jerusalem*, p. 386.

Selections from
Shestov's Writings

•••——————◗◉◖————•••

ATHENS AND JERUSALEM

I

"Athens and Jerusalem," "religious philosophy"—these expressions are practically identical; they have almost the same meaning. One is as mysterious as the other, and they irritate modern thought to the same degree by the inner contradiction they contain. Would it not be more proper to pose the dilemma as: Athens *or* Jerusalem, religion *or* philosophy? Were we to appeal to the judgment of history, the answer would be clear. History would tell us that the greatest representatives of the human spirit have, for almost two thousand years, rejected all the attempts which have been made to oppose Athens to Jerusalem, that they have always passionately maintained the conjuction "and" between Athens and Jerusalem and stubbornly refused "or." Jerusalem and Athens, religion and rational philosophy, have ever lived peacefully side by side. And this peace was, for men, the guarantee of their dearest longings, whether realized or unrealized.

But can one rely on the judgment of history? Is not history the "wicked judge" of popular Russian legend, to whom the contending parties in pagan countries found themselves obliged to turn? By what does history guide itself in its judgments? The historians would like to believe that they do not judge at all, that they are content simply to relate "what happened," that they draw from the past and set before us certain "facts" that have been forgotten or lost in the past. It is not the historians who pronounce "judgment"; this rises of itself or is already included in the facts. In this respect the historians do not at all distinguish themselves, and do not wish to be distinguished, from the representatives of the other positive sciences: the fact is, for them, the final and supreme court of judgment; it is impossible to appeal from it to anyone or anything else.

Many philosophers, especially among the moderns, are hypnotized by facts quite as much as are the scientists. To listen to them, one would think that the fact by itself already constitutes truth. But what is a fact? How is a fact to be distinguished from a fiction or a product of the imagination? The philosophers, it is true, admit the possibility of hallucinations, mirages, dreams, etc.; and yet it is rarely recognized that, if we are obliged to disengage the facts from the mass of direct or indirect deliverances of the consciousness, this means that the fact by itself does not constitute the final court of judgment. It means that we place ourselves before every fact with certain ready-made norms, with a certain "theory" that is the pre-condition of the possibility of seeking and finding truth. What are those norms? What is this theory? Whence do they come to us, and why do we blithely accord them such confidence? Or perhaps other questions should be put: Do we really seek facts? Is it facts that we really need? Are not facts simply a pretext, a screen even, behind which quite other demands of the spirit are concealed?

I have said above that the majority of philosophers bow down before the fact, before "experience." Certain among the philosophers, however—and not the least of them—have seen clearly that the facts are at best only raw material which by itself furnishes neither knowledge nor truth and which it is necessary to mold and even to transform. Plato distinguished "opinion" (*doxa*) from "knowledge" (*epistêmê*). For Aristotle knowledge was knowledge of the universal. Descartes proceeded from *veritates aeternae* (eternal truths). Spinoza valued only his *tertium genus cognitionis* (third kind of knowledge). Leibnitz distinguished *vérités de fait* from *vérités de raison* and was not even afraid to declare openly that the eternal truths had entered into the mind of God without asking His permission. In Kant we read this confession, stated with extraordinary frankness: "Experience, which is content to tell us about what is that it is but does not tell us that what is is necessarily, does not give us knowledge; not only does it not satisfy but rather it irritates our reason, which avidly aspires to universal and necessary judgments." It is hard to exaggerate the importance of such a confession, coming especially from the author of *The Critique of Pure Reason*. Experience and fact irritate us because they do not give us knowledge. It is not knowledge that fact or experience brings us. Knowledge is something quite different from experience or from fact, and only the knowledge which we never succeed in finding either in the facts or in experience is that which reason, "our better part," seeks with all its powers.

There arises here a series of questions, each more troubling than the other. First of all, if it is really so, wherein is the critical philosophy distinguished from the dogmatic? After Kant's confession, are not Spinoza's *tertium genus cognitionis* and Leibnitz's *vérités de raison* (those truths which entered into the mind of God without His permission) confirmed in their hallowed rights by a centuries-old tradition? Did the critical philosophy overcome that which was the content, the soul even, of the pre-critical philosophy? Did it not assimilate itself to it, having concealed this from us?

I would recall in this connection the very significant conflict, and one which the historians of philosophy for some unknown reason neglect, between Leibnitz and the already deceased Descartes. In his letters Descartes several times expresses his conviction that the eternal truths do not exist from all eternity and by their own will, as their eternity would require, but that they were created by God in the same way as He created all that possesses any real or ideal being. "If I affirm," writes Descartes, "that there cannot be a mountain without a valley, this is not because it is really impossible that it should be otherwise, but simply because God has given me a reason which cannot do other than assume the existence of a valley wherever there is a mountain." Citing these words of Descartes, Bayle agrees that the thought which they express is remarkable, but that he, Bayle, is incapable of assimilating it; however, he does not give up the hope of someday succeeding in this. Now Leibnitz, who was always so calm and balanced and who ordinarily paid such sympathetic attention to the opinions of others, was quite beside himself every time he recalled this judgment of Descartes. Descartes, who permitted himself to defend such absurdities, even though it was only in his private correspondence, aroused his indignation, as did also Bayle whom these absurdities had seduced.

Indeed, if Descartes "is right," if the eternal truths are not autonomous but depend on the will, or, more precisely, the pleasure of the Creator, how would philosophy or what we call philosophy be possible? How would truth in general be possible? When Leibnitz set out on the search for truth, he always armed himself with the principle of contradiction and the principle of sufficient reason, just as, in his own words, a captain of a ship arms himself on setting out to sea with a compass and maps. These two principles Leibnitz called his invincible soldiers. But if one or the other of these principles is shaken, how is truth to be sought? There is something here about which one feels troubled and even frightened. Aristotle would certainly have declared on the matter of the Cartesian mountain without a valley that such things may be said but cannot be thought. Leibnitz could have appealed to Aristotle, but this seemed to him insufficient. He needed proofs but, since after the fall of the principles of contradiction and of sufficient reason the very notion of proof or demonstrability is no longer anything but a mirage or phantom, there remained only one thing for him to do—to be indignant. Indignation, to be sure, is an *argumentum ad hominem*; it ought then to have no place in philosophy. But when it is a question of supreme goods, man is not too choosy in the matter of proof, provided only that he succeeds somehow or other in protecting himself.

Leibnitz's indignation, however, is not at bottom distinguished from the Kantian formulas—"reason aspires avidly," "reason is irritated," etc. Every time reason greatly desires something, is someone bound immediately to furnish whatever it demands? Are we really obliged to flatter all of reason's desires and forbidden to irritate it? Should not reason, on the contrary, be forced to satisfy us and to avoid in any way arousing our irritation?

Kant could not resolve to "criticize" reason in this way, and the Kantian critique of reason does not ask such questions, just as the pre-critical philosophy never asked them. Plato and Aristotle, bewitched by Socrates, and, after them, modern philosophy—Descartes, Spinoza, Leibnitz, as well as Kant—seek, with all the passion of which men are capable, universal and necessary truths—the only thing, according to them, which is worthy of being called "knowledge." In short, it would hardly be extravagant to say that the problem of knowledge, or more exactly, knowledge as a problem, not only has never drawn the attention of the most notable representatives of philosophical thought but has repelled them. Everyone has been convinced that man needs knowledge more than anything else in the world, that knowledge is the only source of truth, and especially—I emphasize this particularly and insist upon it—that knowledge furnishes us with universal and necessary truths which embrace all being, truths from which man cannot escape and from which there is consequently no need to escape. Leibnitz said that the "eternal truths" are not content to constrain but do something still more important: they "persuade." And it is not, of course, only Leibnitz personally whom they persuade but all men; Leibnitz would not have ascribed any value to truths capable of persuading him but incapable of persuading others or even of constraining them.

In this respect there is hardly any difference between Leibnitz and Kant. The latter has told us that reason avidly aspires to necessary and universal judgments. It is true that, in the case of Kant, the element of constraint seems to play a decisive and definitive role: even if there should be men whom the truths do not persuade, whom they irritate as experience irritates Kant, this would be no great misfortune; the truths would nevertheless constrain them and thus fully succeed in justifying themselves. And, in the last analysis, does not constraint persuade? In other words, truth is truth so long as it has demonstrative proofs at its disposal. As for indemonstrable truths, no one has any need of them and they appear to be incapable of persuading even a Leibnitz.

It is this that determines Kant's attitude towards metaphysics. It is known that according to Kant, who speaks of this more than once in his *Critique of Reason*, metaphysics has as its object three problems—God, the immortality of the soul, and freedom. But suddenly it appears that the final result of the Kantian critique is that none of these three metaphysical truths is demonstrable and that there can be no scientific metaphysics. One would have thought that such a discovery would have shaken Kant's soul to its deepest foundations. But it did nothing of the sort. In his Preface to the Second Edition of *The Critique of Pure Reason*, Kant declares calmly, almost solemnly: "I had to renounce knowledge (*Wissen*) in order to make room for faith (*Glauben*)." So Kant speaks in this same Preface, where we read the following lines: "It will always be a scandal for philosophy and human reason in general that we must accept the existence of things outside ourselves merely *on faith* and that, if someone should take it into his head to doubt it, we would be incapable of setting before him any sufficient proof." It is impossible to prove the existence of God, the immortality of the soul, or free will, but there is nothing offensive or disturbing in this whether for philosophy or for human reason; all these will get along without proof and will content themselves with faith, with what Kant and everyone call faith. But when it is a question of the existence of objects outside ourselves, then faith does not suffice, then it is absolutely necessary to have proof. And yet, if one admits Kant's point of departure, the existence of objects outside ourselves is hardly in a more enviable situation, as far as proof is concerned, than God, the immortality of the soul, or free will. At best, the existence of objects outside ourselves can be postulated or be an object of faith. But it is this that Kant cannot endure, just as Leibnitz could not endure Descartes' mountain without a valley. And Kant, not having at his disposal any convincing demonstration, just like Leibnitz, did not recoil before the use of an *argumentum ad hominem*, before indignation: if we do not succeed in knowing that things exist outside ourselves, then philosophy and reason are forever covered with shame; it is a "scandal! . . ."

Why did Leibnitz so passionately defend his eternal truths, and why was he so horrified at the idea of subordinating them to the Creator? Why did Kant take to heart the fate of objects outside ourselves, while the fate of God, of the soul and of freedom left him untouched? Is it not just the opposite which should have happened? The "scandal" of philosophy, one would think, consists in the impossibility of proving the existence of God. One would also think that the dependence of God on the truths would poison man's mind and fill it with horror. So one would think; but in reality it was the contrary of this that occurred. Reason, which aspires eagerly to necessity and universality, has obtained all that it wished, and the greatest representatives of modern philosophy have expelled everything which could irritate reason to the region of the "supra-sensible" from which no echo comes to us and where being is confounded with non-being in a dull and dreary indifference.

Even before *The Critique of Pure Reason* Kant wrote to Marcus Herz that "in the determination of the origin and validity of our knowledge the *deus ex machina* is the greatest absurdity that one could choose." Then, as if he were translating Leibnitz's objections to Descartes, "To say that a supreme being has wisely introduced into us such ideas and principles (i.e., the eternal truths) is completely to destroy all philosophy." It is on this that all of the critical philosophy, just like the pre-critical philosophy, is built. Reason does not tolerate the idea of what Kant calls a *deus ex machina* or "a supreme being"; this idea marks the end of all philosophy for reason. Kant could not forgive Leibnitz for his modest "pre-established harmony" because it conceals a *deus ex machina*. For once one accepts the existence of a *deux ex machina*—that is to say, a God who, even though from afar and only from time to time, intervenes in the affairs of the world—reason would be obliged to renounce forever the idea that what is is necessarily just as it is, or, to use Spinoza's language, that "things could not have been produced by God in any other way or order than that in which they were produced."

Kant (in this, also, agreeing with Leibnitz) was very unhappy when he was compared with Spinoza. He, like Leibnitz, wanted people to consider him (and they did indeed consider him) a Christian philosopher. But for all his piety, he could not accept the idea that God can and must be placed above the truths, that God can be sought and found in our world. Why was this idea unacceptable to him? And why, when he spoke of the "dogmatic slumber" from which his "critiques" had permitted him to escape, did it not occur to him to ask whether the certitude with which he affirmed the autonomy of the truth, as well as his hatred for "experience," did not flow from the "dogma" of the sovereignty of reason, a dogma devoid of all foundation and one which is an indication not of slumber but of profound sleep, or even—perhaps—the death of the human spirit? It is a terrible thing to fall into the hands of the living God. But to submit to impersonal Necessity which (no one knows how) has been introduced into being—this is not at all terrible, this calms and even rejoices! But then, why did Kant need to distinguish himself from Leibnitz, and why did both Kant and Leibnitz need to distinguish themselves from Spinoza? And why, I ask once more, do the historians of philosophy —one might almost say, does the history of philosophy— continue up to our own day to guard so carefully that boundary which Kant drew between himself and his immediate predecessors, between his philosophy, on the one hand, and the medieval and ancient philosophy, on the other hand? His "critiques," in fact, have not at all shaken the foundations on which the investigative thought of European man has rested. After Kant, as before Kant, the eternal truths continue to shine above our heads like fixed stars; and it is through these that weak mortals, thrown into the infinity of time and space, always orient themselves. Their immutability confers upon them the power of constraint, and also—if Leibnitz is to be believed—the power of persuading, of seducing, of attracting us to themselves, no matter what they bring us or what they demand of us, while the truths of experience, whatever they may bring, always irritate us, just as does the "supreme being" (that is to say, *deus ex machina*) even when he wisely introduces into us eternal truths concerning what exists and what does not exist.

II

The critical philosophy did not overthrow the fundamental ideas of Spinoza; on the contrary, it accepted and assimilated them. The *Ethics* and the *Tractatus Theologico-Politicus* remain alive, though implicitly, in the thought of German Idealism quite as much as in the thought of Leibnitz: the Necessity which determines the structure and order of being, the *ordo et connexio rerum*, does not constrain us but persuades us, draws us along, seduces us, rejoices us, and bestows upon us that final contentment and that peace of soul which at all times have been considered in philosophy as the supreme good. "Contentment with one's self can spring from reason, and that contentment which springs from reason is the highest possible." Men have imagined, it is true—and certain philosophers have even supported them in this—that man constitutes in nature a kind of state within a state. "After men have persuaded themselves that everything that happens happens for their sakes, they must consider as most important in everything that which is for them most useful, and they must value most that by which they would be best affected." Consequently, *flent, ridunt, contemnunt vel quod plerumque fit, detestantur* (they weep, laugh, scorn or—what happens most of the time—curse). It is in this, according to Spinoza, that there lies the fundamental error of man—one could almost say man's original sin, if Spinoza himself had not so carefully avoided all that could recall the Bible even if only externally.

The first great law of thought which abolishes the biblical interdiction against the fruits of the tree of knowledge is *non ridere, non lugere, neque detestari, sed intelligere* (not to laugh, not to lament, not to curse, but to understand). Everything is then transformed before our eyes. In contemplating life "under the aspect of eternity or necessity," we accept whatever we encounter on our road with the same tranquility and the same feeling of good will. "Even if these things are inconvenient, they are nevertheless necessary and have determinate causes through which we seek to understand their nature, and the mind rejoices just as much over their true contemplation as over the knowledge of those things that are pleasing to the senses."

In contemplating the necessity of everything that happens in the universe, our mind experiences the highest joy. How does this differ from the statement of Kant, who says that our reason aspires eagerly to universal and necessary judgments? Or from Leibnitz's affirmation that the truths not only constrain but persuade? Or even from the famous Hegelian formula, "All that is real is rational"? And is it not evident that for Leibnitz, Kant and Hegel— quite as much as for Spinoza—the pretensions that man makes of occupying a special, privileged place in nature are ungrounded and absolutely unjustified, unless recourse is had to a "supreme being" who does not exist and has never existed? It is only when we forget all "supreme beings" and repress, or rather tear out of our soul, all the *ridere, lugere, et detestari*, as well as the absurd *flere* which flows from them and which comes to the ears of no one, it is only when we recognize that our destiny and the very meaning of our existence consist in the pure *intelligere*, that the true philosophy will be born.

Neither in Leibnitz nor in Kant do we find, to be sure, the equivalent of the *Tractatus Theologico-Politicus* which established what is now called "biblical criticism," but this does not mean that they had taken any less care than Spinoza to protect themselves from the biblical contamination. If everything that Kant said about *Schwärmerei* and *Aberglauben* (fanaticism and superstition) or that Leibnitz wrote on the same subject were brought together, one would completely recover the *Tractatus Theologico-Politicus*. And conversely, all the effort of the *Tractatus* is bent to ridding our spiritual treasury of the ideas which Scripture had introduced there and which nothing justifies.

The *non ridere, non lugere, neque detestari, sed intelligere* of Spinoza, who abrogated the ban placed by the Bible on the fruit of the tree of knowledge, constitutes at the same time a reasonable reply to the *De profundis ad te, Domine, clamavi* (out of the depths I cried unto Thee, O God) of the Psalmist. The Psalmist could cry to God, but the man *qui sola ratione ducitur* (who is led by reason alone) knows well that it is absolutely useless to cry to God from the depths. If you have fallen into an abyss, try to get out of it as best you can, but forget what the Bible has told us throughout the centuries—that there is somewhere, "in heaven," a supreme and omnipotent being who is interested in your fate, who can help you, and who is ready to do so. Your fate depends entirely on the conditions in which chance has placed you. It is possible, in some measure, to adapt yourself to these conditions. You may, for example, prolong your earthly existence by working to earn your bread or by taking it away from others. But it is a question only of prolongation, for it is not given anyone to escape death. An ineluctable eternal truth says: "Everything that has a beginning has also an end." The man of the Bible was unwilling to accept this truth; it did not succeed in "persuading" him. But this shows only that he did not allow himself to be led "by reason alone," that he was deeply bogged down in *Schwärmerei* and *Aberglauben*. The man who has been enlightened—a Spinoza, a Leibnitz, a Kant —thinks quite otherwise. The eternal truths do not simply constrain him; they persuade him, they inspire him, they give him wings. *Sub specie aeternitatis vel necessitatis*— how solemnly these words resound in Spinoza's mouth! And his *amor erga rem aeternam* (love for the eternal)— does not one feel ready to sacrifice for this the entire universe, created (if one may believe the doubtful, or rather, quite frankly, false teachings of this same Bible) by God for man? And then there is Spinoza's "we feel and experience that we are eternal," and the statement which crowns his *Ethics:* "Happiness is not the reward of virtue but virtue itself." Are these words not worth our abandoning all the passing and changing goods which life promises us?

We touch here precisely upon that which deeply distinguishes the biblical philosophy, the biblical thought—or, better, the mode of biblical thought—from the speculative thought that the vast majority of the great philosophers of historic humanity represent and express. The *ridere, lugere,* and *detestari* along with the accompanying *flere* that are rejected by Spinoza, the most audacious and sincere of these philosophers, *constitute that dimension of thought* which no longer exists, or more accurately, which has been completely atrophied in the man "who is led by reason alone." One could express this still more strongly: the prerequisite of rational thought consists in our willingness to reject all the possibilities that are bound up with *ridere, lugere, et detestari* and especially with *flere.* The biblical words "And God saw that it was very good" seem to us the product of a fantastic imagination, as does the God who reveals Himself to the prophet on Mount Sinai. We, enlightened men, put all our trust in autonomous ethics; its praises are our salvation, its reproofs our eternal damnation. "Beyond" the truths which constrain, "beyond" good and evil, all interests of the mind come, in our opinion, to an end. In the world ruled by "Necessity" the fate of man and the only goal of every reasonable being consist in the performance of duty: autonomous ethics crowns the autonomous laws of being.

The fundamental opposition of biblical philosophy to speculative philosophy shows itself in particularly striking fashion when we set Socrates' words, "The greatest good of man is to discourse daily about virtue" (or Spinoza's *gaudere vera contemplatione*—"to rejoice in true contemplation") opposite St. Paul's words, "Whatsoever is not of faith is sin." The precondition of Socrates' "greatest good," or of Spinoza's "true contemplation," is the willingness of the man "who knows" to renounce God's "blessing" by virtue of which the world and everything that is in the world were destined for man's use. The ancients already had seen the "eternal truth" that man is only one of the links of the chain, without beginning or end, of phenomena; and this eternal truth—constraining, of course, and coming from the outside—in antiquity already had at its disposal the power of constraining the philosophical intelligence and also of seducing it, or, as Leibnitz puts it, persuading it. And it is here that there arises the essential philosophical question, which unfortunately did not attract the attention of philosophers—neither of Leibnitz nor of all those who, before or after him, considered *implicite* or *explicite* that the eternal truths not only constrain but also persuade. It is the question of knowing what is essential in our relationship to the truths: is it the fact that they constrain or the fact that they persuade? To put the matter in another way: *if the truth which constrains does not succeed in persuading us, does it thereby lose its status as truth?* Is it not enough for the truth to have the power of constraining? As Aristotle says of Parmenides and the other great philosophers of antiquity, they are "constrained by the truth itself" (*hyp' autês alêtheiâs anankazomenoi*). It is true that he adds, with a sigh, *tên anankên ametapeiston ti einai,* "Necessity does not allow itself to be persuaded," as if he were replying in advance to Leibnitz, who said that the truth does more than constrain, that it persuades. But Aristotle ended by repressing his involuntary sigh and began to glorify the constraining truth, as if it were not content to constrain but also persuaded.

In modern philosophy, such expressions as Leibnitz's "persuasion" or Spinoza's *vera contemplatione gaudere* constitute, in a way, a substitute for the *flere* and for the biblical "God blessed," a substitute smuggled into the domain of objective thought which seemed to have been so carefully and once for all cleansed of all the *Schwärmerei* and *Aberglauben* to be found in the neighborhood of Scripture and its revelations.

But this was not enough for philosophy, or, more precisely, for the philosophers; they wished, and still wish, to think, and they try by all means to suggest to others, to make them think, that their truths possess the gift of persuading all men without exception and not only themselves who have uttered them. Reason recognizes as true only these truths. They are the truths that it seeks. It is these alone that it calls "knowledge." If someone had proposed to Spinoza, Leibnitz or Kant that they limit their pretensions, in the sense of recognizing that the truths are true only for those whom they persuade and cease to be truths for those whom they do not succeed in persuading, would the truths of Leibnitz, Spinoza and Kant have retained their earlier charm in the eyes of these philosophers? Would they have continued to call them truths?

Here is a concrete example (the fundamental opposition between Hellenistic and biblical thought bursts forth fully only in concrete examples): The Psalmist cries to the Lord out of the depths of his human nothingness, and all his thought is oriented—just as the truths that he obtains are determined—not by what is "given," by what "is," by what one can "see" be it even by means of the eyes of the mind (*oculi mentis*), but by something quite different—something to which what is given, what is, remains, despite its self-evidence, subordinate. Thus, the immediate deliverances of consciousness do not circumscribe the goal of the Psalmist's searchings; the facts, the given, experience—these do not constitute for him the final criterion which serves to distinguish truth from falsehood. A fact is for him something which rose one day, which had a beginning, and consequently may, if not must, have an end. We know from history that almost twenty-five hundred years ago Socrates was poisoned in Athens. "The man who is led by reason alone" must bow down before this "fact," which not only constrains but also persuades him; he will feel calm only when reason will have guaranteed that no force in the world could destroy this fact, i.e., when he will have perceived in it the element of eternity or necessity. It seems to him that by succeeding in transforming even that which happened only once into an eternal truth, he acquires knowledge, the true knowledge which concerns not what begins and ends, what changes and passes, but what is forever immutable. Thus he elevates himself to the understanding of the universe *sub specie aeternitatis vel necessitatis.* He attains, with a flap of his wings, the regions where truth lives. And what this truth brings with it is then altogether indifferent to him, whether it be the poisoning of the wisest of men or the destruction of a mad dog. The important thing is that he obtain the possibility of contemplating eternal, immutable, unshakable truth. The mind rejoices over the eternity of truth; as for its content, to this it remains quite indifferent. *Amor erga rem aeternam* fills the human soul with happiness, and the contemplation of the eternity and necessity of everything that happens is the greatest good to which man can aspire.

If someone had taken it into his head to tell Spinoza, Leibnitz, or Kant that the truth "Socrates was poisoned" exists only for a definite term and that sooner or later we shall obtain the right to say that no one ever poisoned Socrates, that this truth, like all truths, is in the power of a supreme being who, in answer to our cries, can annul it—Spinoza, Leibnitz and Kant would have considered these words a sacrilegious attack on the sacred rights of reason, and they would have been indignant, just as Leibnitz was when he recalled Descartes' mountain without a valley. The fact that on earth righteous men are poisoned like mad dogs does not at all trouble the philosophers, for they believe it in no way threatens philosophy. But to admit that a "supreme being" can rid us of the nightmare of the eternal truth "Socrates was poisoned"—this would appear to them not only absurd but revolting. This would not satisfy or persuade them but, on the contrary, irritate them to the last degree. Of course, they would have preferred that Socrates had not been poisoned but, since he was poisoned, it is necessary to submit and to be content with thinking up some theodicy; this, even if it does not make us completely forget the horrors which fill human existence, will perhaps succeed in somewhat weakening their impression. To be sure a theodicy—Leibnitz's or anyone else's—must rely on some eternal truth which, in the final analysis, reduces itself to Spinoza's *sub specie aeternitatis vel necessitatis.* It will be said that everything that is created cannot be perfect by reason of the very fact that it was created and that, consequently, the world that was created can only be the "best of all possible worlds"; we must then expect to find in it many bad things, even very bad things.

Why should creation not be perfect? Who suggested this idea to Leibnitz, who imposed it on him? To this question we will not find any answer in Leibnitz, just as we will not find in any philosopher an answer to the question how a truth of fact is transformed into an eternal truth. In this respect, the enlightened philosophy of modern times is hardly to be distinguished from the philosophy of the "benighted" Middle Ages. The eternal truths constrain and persuade all thinking beings equally. When in the Middle Ages the voice of Peter Damian rang out, proclaiming that God could bring it about that that which had been had not been, it seemed like the voice of one crying in the wilderness. No one, neither of our time nor even of the Middle Ages, dared to admit that the biblical "very good" corresponded to reality, that the world created by God had no defect. Even more: it may be said that medieval philosophy, and even the philosophy of the Church Fathers, was the philosophy of people who, having assimilated Greek culture, thought and wished to think *sub specie aeternitatis vel necessitatis*. When Spinoza says, in ecstasy, "the love for the eternal and infinite feeds the mind with joy alone, and this itself is free from every sorrow, which is greatly to be wished and striven after with every power," he is only summing up the teaching of the philosophers of the Middle Ages who had passed through the severe school of the great Greek thinkers. The only difference is that Spinoza, in order to trace the way which would lead him to *res aeterna et infinita*, believed that it was his duty as a thinker to sharply separate himself from Scripture, while the scholastics made superhuman efforts to save for the Bible the authority which belonged to it as a divinely inspired book.

But the more men occupied themselves with the authority of the Bible, the less they took account of the content of the sacred book; for, indeed, authority demands finally nothing but respect and veneration. Medieval philosophy never stopped repeating that philosophy is only the handmaid of theology and always referred to biblical texts in its reasonings. And yet as competent a historian as Gilson is obliged to recognize that the medieval phi-

losopher, when he read Scripture, could not fail to recall
Aristotle's words about Homer, "The poets lie a great
deal." Gilson also cites the words of Duns Scotus: "I
believe, Lord, what your great prophet has said, but if it
be possible, make me understand it." So the *doctor sub-
tilis*, one of the greatest thinkers of the Middle Ages,
speaks. When he hears the words, "Rise, take up your
bed and go," he replies, "Give me my crutches that I
may have something upon which to lean." And yet Duns
Scotus surely knew the words of the Apostle, "Whatsoever is not of faith is sin," as well as the biblical account
of the fall of the first man, who renounced faith in order to
attain knowledge. But, just as later on in the case of Kant,
there never occurred to him the thought of seeking in
the biblical legend the "critique of reason," the critique
of the knowledge which pure reason brings to man. Is it
possible that knowledge leads to the biblical "you shall
die" while faith leads to the tree of life? Who will dare
admit such a "critique?" The truth that knowledge is
above faith, or that faith is only an imperfect kind of
knowledge—is not this an "eternal truth," a truth to which
Leibnitz's words, "it not only constrains but also persuades," could be applied *par excellence?* This truth had
already seduced the first man, and ever since, as Hegel
very rightly says, the fruits of the tree of knowledge have
become the source of philosophy for all time. The constraining truths of knowledge subdue and persuade men,
while the free truth of revelation, which has not and does
not seek any "sufficient reason," irritates men, just as
experience irritates them. The faith which, according to
Scripture, leads us to salvation and delivers us from sin
introduces us, in our view, into the domain of the purely
arbitrary, where human thought no longer has any possibility of orienting itself and where it cannot lean upon
anything.

And even if the biblical "critique" of reason is right,
even if knowledge, by introducing itself into being, leads
inevitably to all the horrors of existence and to death—
even then, the man who has once tasted the forbidden
fruits will never consent to forget them and will not
even have the power to do so. Such is the origin of
Spinoza's rule: *non ridere, non lugere, neque detestari,
sed intelligere.* To "understand" we must turn away from

all the things to which our joys, our sadnesses, our hopes, our anxieties, and so on are bound. We must renounce the world and that which is in the world. "Constrained by the truth itself," Spinoza, following the example of antiquity and of the Middle Ages, turns away from the world created by God; everything that exists in the world is reduced for him to "wealth, honors and sensuality." Everything that exists in the world passes away, is condemned to disappear. Is is worth the trouble to hold on to such a world? Were not the ancient and medieval philosophers, who preferred the ideal world created by human reason to the world created by God and who saw in the former the "greatest good" of man, right? *Amor erga rem aeternam* is the only thing that can be called "very good," that is, capable of justifying being in the eyes of man.

There is then, on the one side, Socrates with his "knowledge" who has withdrawn into his ideal world and, on the other side, the biblical legend of the fall of the first man and the Apostle who interprets this legend by declaring that "whatsoever is not of faith is sin." The task which I have set for myself in . . . *Athens and Jerusalem* consists in putting to proof the pretensions to the possession of truth which human reason or speculative philosophy make. Knowledge is not here recognized as the supreme goal of man. Knowledge does not justify being; on the contrary, it is from being that it must obtain its justification. Man wishes to think in the categories in which he lives, and not to live in the categories in which he has become accustomed to think: the tree of knowledge no longer chokes the tree of life.

In the first part, "Parmenides in Chains" (*Parmenidês desmôtês*), I try to show that, in pursuing knowledge, the great philosophers lost the most precious of the Creator's gifts—freedom; Parmenides was not a free man but one enchained. The second part, the most difficult, "In the Bull of Phalaris," reveals the indestructible bond between knowledge, as philosophy understands it, and the horrors of human existence. The immoralist Nietzsche glorifies unpitying cruelty and swears eternal fidelity to fate with all its ineluctabilities; and he rejoices and prides himself on the bargain of his submission to fate, forgetting his "beyond good and evil," his "will to power," and all that he had said about the fall of Socrates: the praises and threats of morality have seduced him also. In Kierkegaard mild Christianity loses its mildness and is impregnated with a ferocity which transforms it by ancient destiny—away from the moment where the "fact" has obtained the sovereign right of determining both the will of man and of the Creator. In the third part, *"Concupiscentia Invincibilis,"* the fruitless efforts of the Middle Ages to reconcile the revealed truth of the Bible with the Hellenistic truth are dealt with. The fourth part, "On the Second Dimension of Thought," begins by assuming that the truths of reason perhaps constrain us but are far from always persuading us and that, consequently, the *ridere, lugere, et detestari* and the *flere* which flows from them not only do not find their solution in the *intelligere* but, when they attain a certain tension, enter into a struggle against the *intelligere*—a terrible, desperate struggle—and sometimes overthrow and destroy it. Philosophy is not a curious looking around, not *Besinnung*, but a great struggle.

A similar purpose underlies all four parts of the book: to throw off the power of the soulless and entirely indifferent truths into which the fruits of the tree of knowledge have been transformed. The "universality and necessity" to which the philosophers have always aspired so eagerly and with which they have always been so delighted awaken in us the greatest suspicion; in them the threatening "you will die" of the biblical critique of reason is transparent. The fear of the fantastic no longer holds us in its power. And the "supreme being," transformed by speculation into a *deus ex machina*, no longer signifies for us the end of philosophy but rather that which alone can give meaning and content to human existence and consequently lead to *the true philosophy*. To speak as did Pascal: the God of Abraham, the God of Isaac, the God of Jacob, and not the God of the philosophers. The God of the philosophers, whether he be a material or ideal principle, carries with him the triumph of constraint, of brutal force. That is why speculation has always so obstinately defended the universality and necessity of its truths. The truth spares no one, no one can escape it; it is this, this alone, that has enticed the philosophers. Leibnitz's "persuasion" was only a hypocritical mask behind which the longed-for "constraint" hid itself. It is said in Scripture, "You shall receive according to your faith." Would Leibnitz or any other philosopher have ever had the audacity to say, "You shall receive according to your truth"? Athens could not bear such a truth. It does not constrain, it does not constrain at all; it will never obtain ethical approval. How could human reason be enticed by it?

But Jerusalem holds only to this truth. The constraining truths, and even the truths which seek the approbation and fear the reprobation of autonomous ethics—those eternal truths which, according to Leibnitz, were introduced into the mind of God without asking His permission—not only do not persuade Jerusalem but are, on the contrary, the abomination of desolation. Within the "limits of reason" one can create a science, a sublime ethic, and even a religion; but to find God one must tear oneself away from the seductions of reason with all its physical and moral constraints, and go to another source of truth. In Scripture this source bears the enigmatic name "faith," which is that dimension of thought where truth abandons itself fearlessly and joyously to the entire disposition of the Creator: "Thy will be done!" The will of Him who, on his side, fearlessly and with sovereign power returns to the believer his lost power: . . . "what things soever ye desire . . . ye shall have them."

It is here that there begins for fallen man the region, forever condemned by reason, of the miraculous and of the fantastic. And, indeed, are not the prophecy of the 53rd chapter of Isaiah, "the Lord hath laid upon him the iniquity of us all," and what the New Testament tells of the fulfillment of this prophecy, fantastic? With a sublime daring and unheard of power Luther says of this in his *Commentary on the Epistle to the Galatians:* "All the prophets saw this in the spirit: that Christ would be the greatest robber, thief, defiler of the Temple, murderer, adulterer, etc.—such that no greater will ever be in the world." The same thought was expressed by Luther in a still plainer, more naked, and truly biblical fashion in another passage of the same commentary: "God sent his only begotten son into the world and laid upon him all the sins of all men, saying: 'Be thou Peter, that denier; Paul, that persecutor, blasphemer and doer of violence;

David, that adulterer; that sinner who ate the apple in paradise; that thief on the cross—in sum, be thou the person who committed the sins of all men.'"

Can we "understand," can we grasp, what the prophets and the apostles announce in Scripture? Will Athens ever consent to allow such "truths" to come into the world? The history of humanity—or, more precisely, all the horrors of the history of humanity—is, by one word of the Almighty, "annulled"; it ceases to exist, and becomes transformed into phantoms or mirages: Peter did not deny; David cut off Goliath's head but was not an adulterer; the robber did not kill; Adam did not taste the forbidden fruit; Socrates was never poisoned by anyone. The "fact," the "given," the "real," do not dominate us; they do not determine our fate, either in the present, in the future or in the past. What has been becomes what has not been; man returns to the state of innocence and finds that divine freedom, that freedom for good, in contrast with which the freedom that we have to choose between good and evil is extinguished and disappears, or more exactly, in contrast with which our freedom reveals itself to be a pitiful and shameful enslavement. The original sin—that is to say, the knowledge that what is is necessarily—is radically uprooted and torn out of existence. Faith, only the faith that looks to the Creator and that He inspires, radiates from itself the supreme and decisive truths concerning what is and what is not. Reality is transfigured. The heavens glorify the Lord. The prophets and apostles cry in ecstasy, "O death, where is thy sting? Hell, where is thy victory?" And all announce: "Eye hath not seen, nor ear heard, neither have entered into the heart of man the things which God hath prepared for them that love Him."

The power of the biblical revelation—what there is in it of the incomparably miraculous and, at the same time, of the absurdly paradoxical, or, to put it better, its monstrous absurdity—carries us beyond the limits of all human comprehension and of the possibilities which that comprehension admits. For God, however, the impossible does not exist. God—to speak the language of Kierkegaard, which is that of the Bible—God: this means that there is nothing that is impossible. And despite the Spinozist interdictions,

fallen man aspires, in the final analysis, only to the promised "nothing will be impossible for you"; only for this
does he implore the Creator.

It is here that religious philosophy takes its rise. Religious philosophy is not a search for the eternal structure
and order of immutable being; it is not reflection (*Besinnung*); it is not an understanding of the difference between good and evil, an understanding that falsely promises
peace to exhausted humanity. Religious philosophy is a
turning away from knowledge and a surmounting by faith,
in a boundless tension of all its forces, of the false fear of
the unlimited will of the Creator, that fear which the
tempter suggested to Adam and which he has transmitted
to all of us. To put it another way, religious philosophy
is the final, supreme struggle to recover original freedom
and the divine "very good" which is hidden in that freedom and which, after the fall, was split into our powerless
good and our destructive evil. Reason, I repeat, has ruined
faith in our eyes; it has "revealed" in it man's illegitimate
pretension to subordinate the truth to his desires, and it
has taken away from us the most precious of heaven's
gifts—the sovereign right to participate in the divine "let
there be"—by flattening out our thought and reducing it
to the plane of the petrified "it is."

This is why the "greatest good" of Socrates—engendered
by the knowledge that what is is necessarily—no longer
tempts or seduces us. It shows itself to be the fruit of
the tree of knowledge or, to use the language of Luther,
bellua qua non occisa homo non potest vivere (the
monster without whose killing man cannot live). The old
"ontic" critique of reason is re-established: *homo non
potest vivere*, which is nothing but the "you will die" of
the Bible, unmasks the eternal truths that have entered
into the consciousness of the Creator, or rather of the
creation, without asking leave. Human wisdom is foolish-
ness before God, and the wisest of men, as Kierkegaard
and Nietzsche, however unlike each other, both perceived,
is the greatest of sinners. Whatsoever is not of faith is
sin. As for the philosophy that does not dare to rise above
autonomous knowledge and autonomous ethics, the philosophy that bows down will-lessly and helplessly before
the material and ideal "data" discovered by reason and

that permits them to pillage and plunder the "one thing necessary"—this philosophy does not lead man towards truth but forever turns him away from it.

(From *Athens and Jerusalem*, pp. 47–71)

MORALITY AND PESSIMISM

Whence came good, whence evil? Anaximander, the first Hellenic philosopher, thought that evil began when individual things escaped from the womb of single Being and insisted impiously on beginning a separate, independent existence. So the Pythagoreans thought also. The same idea runs more or less distinctly through the whole philosophy of antiquity. The last great Hellenic philosopher, Plotinus, is of the same conviction. He says that the individual souls tore themselves audaciously free from the One and live in evil so far as they maintain their independence. Plotinus, of course, is expressing Anaximander's thought more accurately. One can, of course, only speak with qualifications of individual things. Only living beings, and not things, are normally individuals.

Can one describe a stone, a mountain, a river, a piece of iron, as individuals? Have they escaped from the womb of the One? So, too, with the house, the table, the clock, the pen, the statue, etc. All these are "things" and "individuals" only for us, for men. For nature, this or that form assumed by iron, marble, or plaster, has no meaning. Marble in the block or marble in the statue of Apollo is for nature only marble; nature preserves or destroys it with equal indifference, whether it received its shape in "natural" wise or through the artist's hand. In earthquakes, landslides, fires, works of nature crumble or burn equally with works of art, one and the other accepting their fate with equal readiness and passivity. Consequently one cannot say of things that they have asserted themselves audaciously or impiously; things stand beyond (or this side of) good and evil. Only living creatures assert themselves. They want to "be" and revolt against every attack on their individuality or their "ego."

It is here that questions of good and bad begin, as of

good and evil. Individuals which assert themselves meet with some resistance. They want, let us say, to eat—but there is no food there; they want to drink—there is nothing to drink there; they want to warm themselves—they cannot. And conversely, sometimes food, drink, and warmth are there in abundance. Why is this so, why is there sometimes everything in abundance, and sometimes too little? Further: all these beings which assert themselves want to "be," while nature, without heeding their wishes, arbitrarily sets a limit to their being by sending them death. And then these creatures revolt and declare that if they are refused food, drink, and warmth, or their lives suddenly are cut short without asking them, that this is bad, but if they are given superfluity and a long life, and particularly such a life that the thought of death does not even enter their minds, so that they think there is not and never will be any death, then this is good. In a word, for nature, for that which we call nature, there is neither a good nor a bad. Only for individuals is there a good and a bad, particularly, of course, for man, precisely for the thinking man who remembers the past and imagines the future vividly. And thus man, through his thousand years of experience, has come to the conviction that life holds too much that is insuperably bad. Man must constantly fight and yield. For a moment one can arrange one's life, but only for a moment. To none is it granted to escape death. Even the students sing, "*nemini parcetur.*" The fool, the sage, the serf, the prince, all must pay tribute to death. Before the inevitable man must bow, and accept passively the blows and gifts of fate.

Most men, the overwhelming majority, bear this lot patiently. But there are also some who think, who seek to reach the heart of things. Why is Nature indifferent to that which seems to us supremely important? Nature is infinitely powerful, surely she is right? Perhaps we are wrong. Perhaps we cannot succeed in understanding Nature, in raising ourselves to her level? I think it was thus that the question posed itself to Anaximander and thus to Plotinus, and that it was taken over in the same form by later philosophy and religious consciousness. When man had to choose between the mutually conflicting and irreconcilably opposed endeavours of the insignificant atom-individual, and the vast, infinite universe, it seemed to him quite clear that he could not be right and that the universe was right. An infinitely small part cannot hope for its cause to be of greater import than the cause of the colossal whole. What men hold for good and bad is in reality neither good nor bad. Before the supreme judgment it is one whether a man is full or hungry, warm or cold, sick or sound. It is even one whether he is alive or not. The only thing that is not "one" is that which is specially guarded from the first and for ever. In contrast to the good and bad, i.e. to the valuable from the point of view of the individual, there arose the autonomous, ethical values—the idea of good and the idea of evil. They are autonomous—that is to say, they have no connection with the usual conceptions of good and bad; indeed, they exclude them. In the light of these new ideas of good and evil, the very existence of the individual was revealed as audacity and impiety. What wonder if nature is indifferent to its "good" and "bad"? On the contrary, one may wonder that these bold and impious creatures have so much good provided for them on earth. Nourishment, drink, and much else is, at least, there for them. If one looks rather closer, one may perhaps soon come to the conclusion that all these blessings are only supplied in order that the individuals should pay the fitting penalty for their sin. They must first be given the opportunity to assert themselves to their heart's desire—then the disappointment will be all the more painful and torturing. However this may be, the contrast between good and bad on the one hand and good and evil on the other can be expressed and explained in this way. Good and bad is what individuals need or do not need. But if the individual comprehends the secret of existence, it must renounce both itself and also its needs, forget good and bad and strive only after the general good. For its own "good" is precisely the fundamental arch-evil, while the real arch-good is the complete renunciation of self, self-annihilation.

This, I repeat, is the fundamental idea of Hellenic philosophy, from Anaximander to Plotinus. It is also the point of departure of modern philosophy. With Schopenhauer this idea assumes, for the first time, an entirely new form, that of pessimism. For Schopenhauer too the *principium individuationis* is the beginning and the source of evil. All that is born must perish, all that begins must end.

The individual begins, consequently it must perish. In this Schopenhauer differs in no wise from his predecessors. But his attitude to life, his evaluation of life, is different. He might have said with Plotinus, that death is the fusion of the individual with the original One. And he almost does say so. Only—and here is the difference between him and Plotinus—he sees in this neither something beautiful, nor something bad. Existence—whether as an empirical individual or as a metaphysical principle—seems to him equally pitiable and valueless. Or, to put it better, the "will" (as Schopenhauer calls the metaphysical principle), although eternal and real, does not, in its superhuman being, attract Schopenhauer's attention. With all its reality will remains absolutely strange to him. He esteems supreme human creative achievement—philosophy, religion, art— solely because he is convinced that it kills the will to live. It teaches man to raise himself above the good and bad in which life has its only hold, and to aspire towards the real *good* which denies life.

In no single philosopher is the link between morality and pessimism so clearly expressed as in Schopenhauer. Not only has man no need to be—there is no need for anything empirical, and far less metaphysical, to be. Schopenhauer rejects suicide, in the name of supreme morality, of the supreme good. For with him good requires more than this. It is not the individual entity that must be killed, annihilated, but the will itself, the metaphysical principle: that is the last task of philosophy and of those religions, such as Buddhism and Christianity, which are sufficiently advanced.

And now, when Anaximander and Plotinus created their "life," when they exalted their "One" and spurned all that was individual, were they not doing just what Schopenhauer did in our days? Were they not expressing pessimism and the negation of the will to live, only in a less frank and consequently a more dangerous form? The Greeks work out the contempt of the individual, the illusory and senseless character of the existence of the individual human being, as consistently as Schopenhauer himself. They do so, indeed, only in the name and to the glory of the One. But this is precisely the heart of the riddle: what is the point of the whole world-comedy? Why does the One, which is so self-satisfied, so peaceful, so all-comprehensive, need to split itself into myriads of souls, to throw them out into the world, to lodge them in these mysterious, alluring body-cells, if it turns out afterwards that the best that souls could do would be to leave their bodies and return to the One whence they came? It is impossible, with the worst will in the world, to conceive anything more senseless—and the One of the Greeks, in face of all this, is primarily a rational principle. Both in Plato and in Plotinus we find suggestions of an answer to this question, but they are so clumsy that it is not worth while discussing them. It looks as though they had no answer of any sort ready. But if they spoke—not spoke, but sang, and how nobly they sang!—of their joy at the possibility of returning to "that world," so Schopenhauer, too, exalted with no less joy, and often with real enthusiasm, the philosophy of renunciation. Now, enthusiasm, delight and even ecstasy are psychologically comprehensible to us, especially in men like Plotinus who felt so bitterly the degrading necessity of abiding in the burdensome, despised body.

(From *In Job's Balances*, pp. 161–165)

WHAT ARE QUESTIONS MADE OF?

We are told that it is natural for man to ask questions, and that the innermost essence of the soul expresses itself in the ability to ask questions and find answers. Animals ask few questions, plants and inanimate things none at all, but this is precisely why man is so audacious: because he is no animal, no plant, and no inanimate thing. And further, questions are not thought out; they arise in some fashion of themselves in natural wise: it is impossible for a reasonable creature not to ask. Let us assume this to be true. But then that means that a reasonable creature can be nothing else but limited. For he alone asks, who does not know and who lacks knowledge. "None of the gods," says Plato, "philosophizes and seeks to become wise." It is obvious that the reasonable creature's desire for knowledge is born of his limitations. Consequently reasonableness is itself limitation. Of course if one compares man with a plant or a stone, the natural conclusion will be that to be reasonable is the same thing as to be more highly perfected.

But who forces us to compare ourselves with stones? Why should we not follow the example of the ancients and direct our eyes to the gods? That is to say, why should we not add to all our questions one more: what are questions made of? For I hope that it is now clear that questions are *made*, and always by the same limited, intimidated, preoccupied human being and, of course, of the material which lies directly to its hand. These conditions also determine the result achieved. We have before us a stone, a plant, an animal, man. Question: How did man become so reasonable, seeing that he is composed of the same material as stones, plants, and animals? It seems unthinkable not to pose such a question. It seems that even a god might ask it. And the answer is taken from the same source as the question: from usual, normal, daily experience. We know that we can accomplish nothing at one blow. To create a statue out of stone we must slowly and painfully chisel small pieces of it out until the formless block is turned into a beautiful work of art. And here we have already the theory of evolution, of slow, imperceptible changes. *Imperceptibly* the plant turns into the animal, the animal into man, and even into civilized man. Since it happens imperceptibly, since no one can notice it, one need not look at it. Consequently there is no exciting surprise and we are content: we think that we have freed ourselves from our limitations and no one is disturbing the natural course of life. I repeat once again: it seems to us that question and answer both originated spontaneously, that no one interfered in this—neither we, nor any other beings. We only registered objectively something which originated spontaneously, as though it was not we but some ideal registering apparatus.

But answer and question alike are purely human. God could never have asked such a question, and He would never have accepted such an answer. And precisely the thing which distresses us most, the thing which we first reduce to an infinite number of infinitely small changes, and then painfully try to make into something unnoticed and more or less non-existent—precisely that, far from distressing God, far from seeming to Him something which ought not to be, something intrusive, unnatural, is, on the contrary, in His eyes, the beneficent essence both of His own life and of life in general.

We are terrified by every creative fiat, by every inexplicable miracle, we are afraid of discovering a break in the course of historical phenomena. We devote all our efforts to banishing out of life everything "sudden," "spontaneous," "unexpected." We describe all such things as chance, but chance in our tongue means something which, strictly speaking, cannot exist. If in any theory, not only scientific but also philosophic (meaning by this a theory which rejects in advance all presuppositions), we discover anything "sudden" or "all at once," we consider our theory irretrievably ruined. And we hold our conviction of the faultiness of everything "sudden" for no premise, but the very truth made word. It cannot be that stones and plants were, and that then "suddenly" beasts appeared, much less men.

Nor can it be that man should "suddenly," "for no reason," "precipitately" take some decision or feel some desire; if he took a decision or felt a desire, he had "grounds" for it. Free will in its pure form is a myth, which has come down to us from the distant ages of humanity's prehistoric existence. Not only the determinists, but also the opponents of determinism, who maintain that man is a free creature, yet hold it necessary to reduce freedom into an infinite number of infinitely minute elements, of which the decision which determines our action is then composed *imperceptibly*.

The cult of the imperceptible has permeated our whole being to such a degree that there is in fact much, very much, that we now do not notice. And we dream, as of an ideal, of that blessed age in which no one will any more ask any questions. This will be the final triumph of theoretical reason. Man will cease to ask; he will himself be as God. But this is just where the fatal self-deception is hidden.

Man will ask nothing because he will see nothing, because he will transform everything into the "imperceptible." By plucking the fruit off the tree of knowledge man became as God—but only in his negative attributes, or rather, in one of his negative attributes, in that which God has not. But the object was not to possess one or more of God's negative attributes. We are as God in having no horns, hoofs, tails, etc.—is that a reason for gratification? What we have to aim at is to possess what God has. Consequently we must not be anxious to transform the perceptible into the imperceptible, but rather to make visible even the barely perceptible. We must accordingly throw ourselves greedily upon each "sudden," "spontaneous," "creative fiat," each absence of purpose and motive, and screen ourselves with the utmost care from that emasculator of thought, the theory of gradual development.

The dominant of life is audacity, $\tau \acute{o} \lambda \mu a$, all life is a creative $\tau \acute{o} \lambda \mu a$ and therefore an eternal mystery, not reducible to something finished and intelligible. A philosophy which has let itself be seduced by the example of positive science, a philosophy which endeavours, and believes its essential task to be, to differentiate everything problematic and surprising into infinitely minute quantities, is not only bringing us no nearer the truth, it is leading us away from it. And I wish to repeat once again what I said before: the Fall of philosophy began with Thales and Anaximander. Thales proclaimed that All is One. Anaximander saw in multiplicity, that is, in the eternal problematical, an impiety, a something which ought not to be. After them philosophers began systematically to eschew multiplicity and to esteem uniformity. The comprehensible and the uniform became synonymous with the real and with that which ought to be. The individual, the independent, the different were looked on as unreal and audacious. Some qualification, of course, is necessary. Interest in the mysterious has always lived on in philosophy, particularly in ancient philosophy. Plato and Plotinus lent a shuddering ear to mysteries, knew the meaning of initiation, were themselves initiates. They honoured with reverence the memory of the great sages of the past. At the same time, however, they wanted to be lords over the spirit of man. That is, the esoteric and the exoteric attracted them equally. Aristotle alone forsook the esoteric. But precisely for that reason history left the victory with Aristotle. Even the Middle Ages, which sought so greedily after the mysterious and guessed at it everywhere, took Aristotle for guide.

Modernity has now broken altogether with antiquity.

Descartes is generally looked on as the father of modern philosophy. The true father of modern philosophy was, however, Spinoza. Spinoza's whole philosophy was imbued with the thought that God's reason and will differ *toto caelo* from human reason and will, that God's reason and will have as little in common with human reason and will as the dog-star has with the dog, the barking animal: that is, only the name. Hence he drew the conclusion that what we call beautiful, perfect, good, etc., has no relationship with God. Consequently one has not to laugh, nor weep nor be wroth, but to understand; that is, to ask no questions relating to the things which mean most to us, and to give answers which are totally unnecessary to us. Thus Spinoza taught, and his commandments were received as a new revelation. And no one noticed (men prefer not to notice) that Spinoza himself acted, both as man and philosopher, in the diametrically opposite way. He asked no questions which he did not need, and found no answers which did not concern him. *"Omnia praeclara tam difficilia quam rara sunt"*—with these words he closes his *Ethics.* That is, the "beautiful" which, if one bears Spinoza's earlier words in mind, stands in no relationship to God, is restored to its divine rights precisely because human reason and human will are so loyally devoted to it. And it is towards the beautiful alone, although it is so difficult to attain and is found so rarely, that Spinoza's soul aspires. Further, his *"amor Dei intellectualis,"* the intellectual love of God—why, it consists simply of *"ridere, lugere et detestari,"* and has as little in common with the scientific *"intelligere"* as the dog-star has with the dog, the barking animal. That is to say, Spinoza, like so many of his ancient predecessors, held that the *"intelligere"* was only there for the crowd, for "everyone." It was an outer decoration: when one mingles with men, one must wear the appearance of an understanding, quiet, composed man, untroubled with doubts. To the crowd one must always speak in the tone of a man in whom power reposes. But for himself and for the initiated Spinoza used quite another language.

Modern philosophy, which has made herself the handmaid of science, has only taken from Spinoza what he kept for the crowd, for the uninitiated: only his *"intelligere."* It is convinced that questions ought to be made of indifferent, worthless material. It sweeps away beauty, good, ambition, tears, laughter, and curses, like dust, like useless refuse, never guessing that it is the most precious thing in life, and that out of this material and this alone, genuine, truly philosophic questions have to be moulded. Thus the prophets questioned, thus the greatest sages of antiquity, thus even the Middle Ages. Now only rare, lonely thinkers comprehend this. But they stand aside from the great highway, aside from history, aside from the general business of philosophy. Official, recognized philosophy, which aims at being science, does not go beyond the *"intelligere,"* and is, moreover, quite genuinely convinced that it alone is seeking the truth. But precisely it should halt and ask itself: Of what are questions made? Perhaps it would then renounce the idea of transforming all that is important into the imperceptible, which is so imperceptible that it cannot be seen. And then, instead of a world which always and in all its parts remains the same, instead of a process of development—then before man's eyes would arise a world of sudden, wonderful and mysterious transformations, each of which would mean more than the whole process of to-day and all its natural development.

Such a world, cannot, it is true, be "comprehended." But such a world *need* not be comprehended. In such a world comprehension is superfluous. Comprehension is necessary for the natural world from man, who came in natural wise into it. But in a world of wonderful transformations, in an eternally unnatural world, comprehension is only an ugly, crude extra, a meagre and wretched gift of the pauper world of limitation. So it was felt by the best representatives of humanity in moments of inspiration and of spiritual ecstasy. But humanity has not been granted to think thus. *Omnia praeclara tam difficilia quam rara sunt.* How much divine laughter, how many human tears and curses are needed to learn how to live in such a world, to penetrate into such a world! But we want peace, first and last, we want to count, measure, and weigh automatically, and we assume that this is lofty science and that such science will reveal to us all secrets! And we even hesitate to ask ourselves of what questions are made, being convinced in advance that all questions are made of one and the same material and that the

justified questions are simply those which arise from untroubled spirits and can be solved through self-satisfied
comprehension.

(From *In Job's Balances*, pp. 156–161)

CUR DEUS HOMO?

A man has toothache and he is incapable of anything.
He sees nothing, he hears nothing, he thinks only of the
pain and his tooth. Neither contemplation nor proofs of
reason can convince him that it will all be over to-morrow.
The cursed pain absorbs his last strength, clothes the
whole world, the whole universe, in its grey, torturing, dull
colours. Even the idea of eternity can awake in him no
enthusiasm, for even eternity seems to him a product of
the tooth and the pain. Perhaps it was under such conditions that Spinoza's *"Deus sive natura,"* the "One" of
Plotinus and the mediaeval mystics, was born, and also
that repulsion against all creation of which philosophers
speak so much. It is possible that contempt of what
Spinoza called *"divitiae, honores, libidines"* and of our
empirical ego arose out of some obstinate, enduring pain
which men could not remove and which took the name
of supreme truth, mounted the throne and rules im-
periously over the living and the dead.

Even in Plato, as some of his warmest admirers sur-
mise, the idea of the ideal world may have arisen in
connection with Socrates' execution. According to tradition Plato did not visit Socrates in prison, sickness pre-
venting him. Perhaps it was not sickness at all; it was
certainly not sickness. The pupil could not look on the
impotence of the honoured teacher. And, therefore, he
brooded all his life long how it could have come about that
Anytus and Meletus, the despicable Athenian judges, the
dirty prison jailer, and the cup with the repulsive poison,
could have shown themselves mightier than the very truth
that was incorporated in Socrates. Plato turned his whole
genius to banishing this fearful, never-ceasing, intolerable
pain which he felt when he remembered the wretched

death of the "best of men." His philosophy and his poetry were struggle and victory over this pain.

The whole Greek philosophy which followed him sought, now consciously, now unconsciously, for the words which might have freed man from the mad power of senseless necessity. Mediaeval philosophy continued the work of the great Hellenes and went on seeking with equal enthusiasm and excitement. It is only the modern, or rather, the most modern philosophy, which found the solution of the question in positivism *à la* Kant and Comte; to forget plagued and poisoned truth and live for the positive necessities of the next day, year or decade. This terms itself "Idealism." It is, of course, also Idealism of the purest water which has so possessed the spirit of modern man. The idea is the only god which has not yet been cast down from its pedestal. Scientists worship it no less than philosophers and theologians. If one reads the latest Catholic apologists one will convince oneself of this.

But perhaps it will be objected: "Pain is a condition of the apperception of truth. Truth is truth only because, and only in so far as, it is nailed to the cross." Possibly, certainly. But why, then, Idealism? Why bedew the prose, the dirt and blood of the life beyond with the fragrant blooms of earthly poesy? Let it come before us in all its hateful nakedness! Or can this be just the function of creation—any creation, artistic as well as philosophic and religious—to cause lovely flowers of Here to burgeon from the ugly truth of Beyond? And is not man's task, whatever the ancients say, not to return to the original "One" but to move as far away from it as possible? So that in that case, the individual, in escaping from the womb of the One, would have committed no crime by its audacity ($\tau\delta\lambda\mu a$), but rather an achievement, the supreme achievement! And was Protagoras, who taught that man is the measure of all things, modest and timid? A new commandment must be created: man shall be the measure of all things, therein lies his supreme purpose.

The beginning has been made. Man has escaped from the womb of the One. Now a great battle awaits him. Not yet have nearly all the fetters which bound him when he still lived in "the womb" been broken asunder. He is still tempted away by memories of his earlier contemplative, almost unreal existence, to the blissful, unperturbed peace of super-individual being. "Reason" still affrights him through the unlimited possibilities and difficulties which await the single, independent being in its new life.

Philosophy—mundane as well as religious—which also draws wholly from reason, obstinately contrasts the untroubled peace of past being in the One, with the eternal unrest, tension, tortures and doubts of multiple existence. And yet there are already men who no longer believe the whisperings of reason. "Instinct," or something else in them, resists such persuadings. Men resist, resist with all the forces of their nature, the worship of unfleshly ideals, even the loveliest. Even the philosophers, the professional preachers of the godhead of the ideal principle, strive in their lives in every way to shake off its yoke from them. It is as though they, like Socrates, had besides reason a second daemon for guide, which in decisive cases interposes its incomprehensible but imperious final veto. So in the Russian sect of the self-immolators the "ideal" leaders, when they led the herd of common believers as sacrifice to the flames, used themselves unobtrusively to leave the burning building through a previously prepared exit. Neither Socrates nor Plato, nor Plotinus himself let his being be absorbed in the "One." The Stoics, meanwhile— witness Epictetus and noble Marcus Aurelius—the Sceptics, Epicureans, and all the numerous schools descended from Socrates and his pupils, immolated themselves conscientiously at stakes of their own driving.

Socrates, Plato, and Plotinus, and Spinoza in modern times, developed in the shadow of their philosophic constructions. When they cried, "Back to the One," they advanced—away from the One. Never yet—after, of course, the first break with the One—have men so dared to document their "ego" as Socrates did. And how marvellously! Listen with what reverence Alcibiades speaks of Socrates. But follow him?—no, that he does not do; his daemon forbids. It is not for nothing that the astute poet Ovid said, "*Video meliora proboque, deteriora sequor.*" ("I see the better and approve it, I follow the worse.") Behind these words lies hidden the vast, final, and perhaps most fateful riddle of our being. Alcibiades was a frivolous, unrestful, ambitious man. And he had many "shortcomings"—I do not wish to speak of them. I do not at all wish to "justify" him, especially as that is quite unnecessary; history and the historians have already passed judgment on him. But equally indubitable is this: Socrates, too, had his shortcomings, but Alcibiades was an unusually gifted man, almost a genius. "*In hoc natura quid efficere potest videtur experta,*" says Cornelius Nepos—in him nature tried to see what she could create. What else, then, is genius but *the great gift of audacity* sometimes granted to mortals who are frightened by their "anamnesis" of laws and imperatives accepted in their earlier existence (of the "synthetic, a priori judgments," to express it in modern terms)? Even so Alcibiades saw these imperatives no less plainly than Socrates, and approved them as the "better," but owing to some mysterious commandment (he too, like Socrates, had his own particular daemon and protector) dared to do the "worse," i.e. his own—even as Socrates acted, though he taught otherwise.

Ovid remarked this "antinomy" and expressed it with "antique simplicity" in the words I quoted. How often have men repeated Ovid's verses (we find them even in Spinoza and the Early Fathers) and yet interpreted them as though to aim at "one's own," at the "worse," were weakness, and to follow the "better," the common course, were strength. Why did they choose this interpretation? Ordinary, daily, average experience imposed it on them. In everyday reality the commandments of reason do in fact protect us from disaster, as Socrates always made admirably plain in his dialogues. An overheated man longs for cold water. Reason forbids: if you drink it will do you harm, you will fall ill. He who, seeing and approving the "better," which means the dictates of reason, yet follows the "worse," his own immediate wish, will naturally suffer for it. From this, from a series of similar examples which could be multiplied indefinitely, Socrates concluded: Reason is the source of all knowledge, its truths are unalterable, etc. But here, precisely, lay the mistake; Socrates *forgot* his daemon.

The might of reason has and must have a bound. Precisely because reason is destined to guide man in his empiric existence, to protect him here on earth, it is essentially unable to guide us in our metaphysical wanderings. Reason can tell the carpenter, the smith, the cook, the doctor, the statesman, what is "good" and what "bad."

But the "good" and "bad" of the cook and smith, the doctor or builder, are by no means the universal "good" and "bad," as Socrates maintained in his Meditations, and Plato after him. Here there is a genuine μετάβασις εἰς ἄλλο γένος (transition into another field). In the field of metaphysics there are neither cooks nor carpenters, neither their "good" nor "bad." There rules the daemon of whom we are not even entitled to assume that he is interested in any "norm" at all. Norms arose among the cooks and were created for cooks. What need is there then to transfer all this *empiria* thither whither we flee to escape *empiria*? . . .

The whole art of philosophy should be directed towards freeing us from the "good and evil" of cooks and carpenters, to finding that frontier beyond which the might of general ideas ceases. But philosophy has been unable to free itself from "theorizing" Socrates. Kant himself in his *Critique of Practical Reason* restored to reason all the unlimited rights and privileges of infallibility taken from it by the *Critique of Pure Reason*. Alcibiades and with him all audacity are condemned in advance and without examination as eternally unlawful, dangerous, and harmful. The anamnesis, the innate ideas—Kant calls them the "a priori ideas"; that is, of course, more correct, safer and less questionable—which man brought with him from the epoch of his pre-mundane Babylonian captivity, have got the upper hand. And one must admit that appearances and proofs, rational and empiric, are altogether on the side of Kant and his Idealism. For audacity is only audacity because it has no guarantee of success. The audacious man advances boldly, not because he knows what awaits him, but because he is audacious or—if the theological way of putting it be preferred—*sola fide*. It often, indeed generally, happens that he does not reckon on success at all and indeed may not do so. On the contrary, he plainly envisages a failure and assumes with the utmost horror a responsibility for actions the consequences of which neither he nor any one else can foresee.

I suppose that the first entity which escaped from the womb of the One suffered the greatest tortures, if it possessed consciousness at all. Most probably it possessed no consciousness, if it took such a mad resolve. How heavy was the punishment of Prometheus simply because he stole fire from the gods! There we have it again: *"video meliora proboque, deteriora sequor."* For philosophic purposes one only has to alter the poet's way of putting it just a little; one should not decide in advance what is better and what worse. One must say: my reason leads me to the one, but my whole being yearns for another. But where, on which side is "truth"? In the forward movement away from the "One" from which we have succeeded in escaping after such indescribable efforts, or in the movement back to the One, in the consciousness that the first audacity was a primal sin? Certainly, if the first audacity was sin, then there is nothing else left but to humble ourselves and to return again to the One in order to expiate that sin. But what if, on the contrary, the first audacity was a great human achievement? If it was the beginning of life? If the "One" which is a "Nothing" is death, and escaping its power means not straying from God but moving towards God?

The whole Christian Middle Ages tortured themselves with the riddle: *"Cur Deus homo?"* It was answered in different ways. Always, indeed, in the spirit of Plotinus, for the Middle Ages were exposed through Augustine and Dionysius the Areopagite to the influence of Hellenism. But however the explanations may run, the fact then acknowledged universally and even to-day very widely, is this: there was a moment in history in which God assumed human form and thereby took on Himself all the tortures and difficulties which are the lot in this life of the most unfortunate and miserable man. But why? *Cur Deus homo?* Why, to what purpose, did He become man, expose Himself to injurious mistreatment, ignominious and painful death on the cross? Was it not in order to show man, through His example, that no decision is too hard, that it is worth while bearing anything only in order not to remain in the womb of the One? That any torture whatever to the living being is better than the "bliss" of the rest-satiate "ideal" being?

I think that my suggestion has a right to compete with other answers to the question *"Cur Deus homo?"* It is not at all necessary to think, in conformity, with the wrongly interpreted views of the Hellenic self-immolators, that God assumed human form in order that man should cease to be himself and become an ideal atom of the intelligible

world. This end could have been attained in "natural"
wise, whatever the mediaeval theologians might argue.
Supernatural interference was only necessary because man
had to be supported in his mad endeavour, in his incredible and unreasonable audacity of self-affirmation. God
became man in order that man, shaken in his original
resolve—this was expressed in the Hellenic philosophy—
should again be confirmed in it. But man would not understand God. The mediaeval philosophers and theologians
interpreted the "glad tidings" in the spirit of their "phi-
losophus" Aristotle. And our contemporaries continue to
interpret it in the same way, even the Catholic and
Protestant theologians. Can one hope to convince man
differently, or must one wait for the Second Coming?

Or—the last and most overwhelming, most appropriate
reply: Are Plato and Plotinus, the mediaeval theologians
with their disputes why God became man, and the "glad
tidings" which God incarnate brought to earth—are they
no more than empty chatter which one may pardon in
young men, but for which, as Callicles said to Socrates,
aged and venerable men must be beaten? This objection is
very reasonable. With Plato, Plotinus, Anselm, Thomas
Aquinas, one may argue. But how is one to argue with a
positivist whose self-assurance and complacency surpass
even the idea of peace itself? Is one to remind him of the
events of recent years? But he has seen it all—and what he
has seen has not enriched his knowledge any more than
it has awakened in him the doubts which he so much
hates.

(From *In Job's Balances*, pp. 171–178)

DE NOVISSIMIS

You have probably not seen it with your own eyes but
you have undoubtedly heard that sometimes a man's hair
turns white in one night: someone who had black hair on
lying down to sleep finds himself completely white on
waking. We have grounds to believe that the opposite at
times also happens: old men are transformed overnight

into young people—only their hair does not regain its original color. But if this is so, if such transformations are possible on earth, how can we speak of the immutable principles of thought? Of what value then are the foundations on which Kant's famous postulates rest? Kant explains that he cannot renounce his postulates, "for in that case my moral principles would be overthrown—those principles which I cannot renounce without becoming contemptible in my own eyes."

Here the Russian proverb is proven true: "Do not ask an old man but one who has experienced much." Kant was almost sixty years old when he published his *Critique of Pure Reason*, but it seemed to him impossible that his moral principles could ever be shaken and he could, consequently, become an object of hatred and disgust to himself. But if he had read the lives of certain saints— the writings of St. Theresa, St. Bernard—or even looked at Luther's works, he would have become convinced that what appeared to him unbelievable, inconceivable even, nevertheless actually happened. St. Theresa, St. Bernard, and Luther many times recognized themselves in their own consciousness as the least, the vilest, the most miserable of human beings. And if Kant had been able to read Nietzsche or had reflected on the epistles of St. Paul, he would have discovered that his moral principles were not at all as solid as he imagined: it requires only a strong subterranean shock for any earthly stability to be thrown down completely. But Kant did not in the least suspect this. A page further he repeats that his postulate is so strictly bound to his moral disposition that, just as he runs no danger of losing the latter, so he does not fear that the former can ever be taken away from him. (*Kr. d. R. V. 857, II Aufl.*) Whence comes this unconcern of Kant's? This scholar par excellence, accustomed to extraordinary caution in his judgments, who advanced his reflections with extreme deliberateness, and who permitted himself to take a step forward only after having first carefully studied the terrain on which he proposed to set his foot, suddenly showed an almost child-like trust. And his case is not unique. Look, for example, at Plato. Having established that the soul which aspires to unity and universality in the human and divine scorns all pettiness, he asks: "Do you think that the great soul which is the spectator of all time and all existence can think much of human life?" (*Republic 486 A*)

To his own question Plato responds negatively and with the same assurance with which Kant responds to his. And—what is particularly important—Plato's question and Kant's play a decisive role in the systems of the two philosophers. If it turns out that Kant's morality is not at all as solid as it seemed to its author or if, despite Plato, a great soul which has long wandered in the most distant realms of cosmic being discovers that a single human life has no less value than all human lives together—what will remain of Plato's and Kant's systems?

I have already said, in speaking of Kant, that if he had consulted men who had lived and experienced much, they would have made him see that there are many things on earth and in heaven of which the most learned of the scholars do not even dream. And he would then have felt what appeared to him entirely inconceivable—he would have felt a great disgust for himself! But may it not be that it is not necessary to fear this feeling so greatly and to avoid it? May it not be that it is the condition of important revelations? St. Theresa, St. Bernard, Luther, Shakespeare, Dostoevsky, Tolstoy—I could continue the list indefinitely—all felt a disgust for themselves and all repeated with terror the words of the psalmist: *de profundis ad te clamavi, Domine*. Why then did Kant conclude that everything that leads man to a horror of himself must be rejected? Why consider respect for oneself the sign of truth and the reward of truth?

Note that Plato's statement is also based on the assumption that the normal and natural attitude of the soul toward itself is respect and not disgust. Plato speaks of a great soul—that is, of a soul that respects itself and for which the whole world must have respect, respect that it obtains not as *gratia gratis data* but for its merits. One can even generalize and say that every philosopher proceeds from the assumption that the soul, if it wishes, can obtain its own respect as well as that of others. Without this supposition no philosophical system could subsist even for a moment. It is the dogma *stantis et cadentis philosophiae*.

But just here it would be well to recall the testimony of

those men of different type that I have set opposite Plato and Kant. Through the mouth of his Hamlet, Shakespeare admits that if one acted toward people according to their merits, no one could avoid a box on the ear. Notice that Hamlet himself did not always speak thus. There was a time when Hamlet declared, and with no less assurance than Plato or Kant, that he would never put himself in the situation of feeling disgust for himself. I think that it is not necessary to prove what I put forward, i.e., to quote passages of Shakespeare's work prior to *Hamlet*. Anyone who has read even only his historical chronicles will easily remember the phrases. For a long time Shakespeare knew contentment and mental equilibrium and believed that it was perfectly natural and normal for man to love and respect himself. The point of departure for his philosophy prior to *Hamlet* was the conviction that equilibrium of the soul is the supreme good for man. However, the word "conviction" is not altogether exact. It may be, it is certain even, that Shakespeare did not even guess that he had this conviction, just as a strong and healthy man has no idea that health and strength are precious. He learns this only later, after having lost them. But this does not change the situation in the least. Man may not realize the importance he ascribes to equilibrium of the soul and yet strain all his powers to secure it for himself.

Of course, at the first threats of fate reason will become excited and do all that its nature prescribes to avoid the misfortunes preparing to break over man. When the natural ground begins to disappear under our feet, reason tries to create through its own powers an artificial ground. And this is what is ordinarily called "philosophy." Man asks himself: "How can I bring it about that fate return to me what it has taken away from me?" He does not doubt in the least that it is absolutely necessary to obtain the return of what has been taken away from him. To entrust his existence to fate, to admit that the fate which has taken away his equilibrium is just as righteous as the fate which only a while ago granted him this "supreme good"—this, man, especially the man of reason who is persuaded that he knows everything better than anyone else, is incapable of doing. He knows that equilibrium of the soul is happiness, a good, and that its loss is unhappiness, an evil. He knows this through his own experience, you will say. Yes, certainly, but there is something else here besides. For if it were a question only of experience, neither Kant nor Plato could have clothed their statements in the form they did. They could have spoken only of themselves and, moreover, of the past. That is, Kant could have said: "When I happened to think for a moment that my moral principles could be proven false or stripped of their value, I experienced a feeling of disgust for myself of which I tried to get rid." This confession would have been the statement of a fact, nothing more. But Kant's pretensions extend infinitely further. He assures us that not only he, Kant, but every man, every reasonable being, is aware and will always be aware of an indissoluble relationship between his existence and his moral principles, and that every man wishes to respect himself and is afraid above everything else of feeling disgust for himself. I ask, who gave Kant the right to proceed to all these generalizations and anticipations which constitute, as is known, the very essence of his critiques? How does he know what every man feels? How does he know what he himself will feel tomororw? May it not be that tomorrow he will experience disgust for these very feelings of his worthiness whose sweetness he savors today? Is it not possible that he could be forced to say, like Antisthenes, μανείην μαλλον ἤ ἡσθέιην (I would prefer losing my reason to experiencing pleasure) and go still further than Antisthenes by understanding ἡσθέιην as including not only physical pleasures (eating, drinking, etc.) but also moral pleasures? Or even to realize that the most repugnant and vilest pleasures are not at all those which eating and drinking give but precisely those that are aroused by a good conscience, the feeling of moral worth, of acting well—the things of which he speaks as the foundation of his philosophy and his ethical system? This, you will say, cannot be. I expected this answer. For we must finally uncover the invisible prompter who whispers such categorical statements to man. Who says this cannot be? Obviously, our reason—that reason which proudly considers itself capable of guiding us in all the difficult circumstances of life, that reason which has convinced us that it "enlarges" our poor and miserable experience. But consider for once exactly what it does. With all its generalizations and its anticipations it does not en-

large but, on the contrary, infinitely restricts our already
sufficiently impoverished experience. Reason knows the
single case of Kant and from it immediately "concludes"
that it knows all possible cases. And it does not any longer
itself wish or permit us to see, to hear, to seek. Kant was
frightened by the idea that he could come to feel disgust
for himself, and he cried out pathetically, "Hold fast to
the pillars of your morality, else you will perish!" It is as
if one tried to restrain Christopher Columbus at the moment of his departure upon unknown seas by conjuring him
not to abandon his familial hearth, for it is only in the
bosom of his own family and under the roof of his own
house that he can be happy, while the seas hide terrible
dangers. Certainly it is dangerous to roam the seas—no
one denies it. But Christopher Columbus did not listen to
the objections of his familial Kants and threw himself
into his adventure. And likewise ὁ ἀνθρώπινος βιός—the
individual human soul—does not listen to Plato. It aspires
to freedom, it wishes to escape, to throw itself into infinite space, far from the familial *penates*, the work of
famous philosophers with clever hands. Often it has not
the time even to think of this. It does not recognize that
reason, which transformed its poor experience into a
doctrine of life, has deceived it. The gifts of reason—calm-
ness, peace, pleasures—suddenly disgust it. It aspires to
what reason is not even capable of imagining. It can no
longer live according to the general rules established for all.
All knowledge is painful to it precisely because it is knowledge, i.e., a generalized poverty. It does not wish to
know, it does not wish to understand, in order not to find
itself bound and limited. Reason is a siren; it knows
well to speak of itself and its works in such a way that
it seems its doctrines and its knowledge do not bind but
deliver. It speaks only of freedom. And it heaps up the
most amazing promises. It promises everything except
what it cannot conceive, what it cannot even suspect. But
we already know what it can conceive and foresee. It
promises us all the postulates—those of which Kant spoke,
and Plato's also—on condition that we prostrate ourselves
before it and worship it. But it does not go beyond promises. If this is enough for you, take reason for your
guide, generalize and anticipate experience and continue
to believe that this is a most important and useful thing.

If not, abandon your calculations and generalizations and go daringly, without looking backward, toward the unknown where God will lead you—and then, come what may! You have no desire for this? That is your affair.

(From *Potestas Clavium*, pp. 72–83)

PENSÉES FROM *ATHENS AND JERUSALEM* AND *POTESTAS CLAVIUM*

IGNAVA RATIO

Can reason be anything but lazy? Laziness is of its very essence, as is cowardice. Open any manual of philosophy and you will soon be convinced that reason even boasts of its submissiveness, its humility, its cowardice. Reason must "servilely" reproduce what is "given" to it, and it reproaches as the greatest of crimes every attempt at free creation. As for us human beings, we in turn must servilely obey all that reason dictates to us. And this is what is called "freedom." For he only is free who is "guided by reason alone." So Spinoza taught, so the ancients taught, so think all those who wish to learn and teach. And since almost everyone either learns or teaches, "lazy reason" (*ignava ratio*) becomes, in fact, the sole master of the world.

(From *Athens and Jerusalem*, p. 375)

THE INTELLECTUAL VISION

Essentially the intellectual vision aspires to discover, behind living beings, the eternal and immutable principles which govern the universe. The "freest" human thought ceases to search and is satisfied when it thinks (or, as people prefer to say, when it is convinced) that, having transcended the limits of the individual, the arbitrary and the changing, it has penetrated into the domain of immutable laws. That is why all metaphysical systems begin with freedom and end with necessity.

But since necessity in general does not enjoy a very good reputation, one usually tries to demonstrate that this final and supreme necessity to which the intellectual vision aspires is in no way distinguishable from freedom or, to put it otherwise, that reasonable freedom and necessity are one and the same thing. Now, in reality, they are not at all the same. Reasonable or not, necessity is always necessity. But people ordinarily call "reasonable" every necessity that cannot be overcome—a thing which they carefully dissimulate. And that is quite understandable. The indestructible need to live "according to one's own will" is inherent in the human soul; nothing will make it renounce its eternal dream. But a reasonable will, and what is more, a necessary will, is not "my own will"; the latter is something altogether different. What is more important to man than anything else in the world is to "act according to his own will," even if that will be unreasonable or foolish. And the most eloquent and convincing arguments remain useless in this matter.

Certainly it is not difficult to force man to silence, be it even by the blows of arguments (although there are much more powerful means); and, as history shows, reasonable arguments have always accepted all alliances. But silence is by no means a sign of acquiescence. It often happens that we are silent because we realize the uselessness of speech. Many people, moreover, are not at all lovers of argument. The philosophers (or at least the most intelligent of the philosophers) know this well. That is why they detest the mob so much (they "scorn" it, they say—this sounds more noble), although the mob only very rarely permits itself to contradict them. Men listen, nod in approval, and finally act as if they had heard nothing. Sometimes they even repeat what has been said to them. They repeat it continually, but they live and act as they please. "I see the better and approve of it, but I follow the worse."

Is it not strange? Freedom and necessity are identical; the systems which subordinate reality to ideal laws are true. Man recognizes all this, but when he passes on to action, one might truthfully say that the intellectual vision and its ideal essences never existed. Who, then, is right—the metaphysicians who seek ideal principles, or the simple mortals to whom their instinct whispers that ideal principles are of the devil, just as are all mechanistic explanations of the universe and of life?

(From *Athens and Jerusalem,* pp. 378–380)

ON THE TRUTH WHICH CONSTRAINS

One person asks how knowledge is possible, how it can be that something which differs essentially from us enters into us. Having put this question, he will be satisfied only when he will have proved, or imagine himself to have proved, that the subject and object of knowledge do not differ and are at bottom one and the same thing and that, consequently, the impossible does not exist. Why should the thought that the impossible exists trouble him so much, and why should he find so reassuring the thought that the impossible does not exist. And again, why should he yearn so strongly for tranquility, as if tranquility were the greatest of human goods? I do not undertake to answer these questions, and I am inclined to believe that he cannot answer them either.

Another person has other concerns. He would be very happy to learn that not only what is possible exists, but that it happens sometimes that the impossible also exists. But reality forces him to recognize, on the contrary, not only that the impossible does not exist, but that many things that are possible do not exist either. There would be nothing finally impossible in the fact that men should love one another; now, in reality, *homo homini lupus est.* There would be nothing impossible either if men, like certain animals, lived for several centuries or if they died when they themselves wished and not on a day and at an hour fixed no one knows by whom or by what. Still many other things of this kind appear to experience unrealizable. And the thirst for absolute knowledge that torments mankind is also unrealizable: we know very little, and what we do know is relative. The final truth hides itself behind impenetrable darkness, though there would be nothing impossible if the truth did not remain hidden to men who long for it so greatly.

But it happens that the theorist of knowledge at times feels other disturbances as well: Why does that which *is* in no way correspond to that which we wish would be? I shall be told that this is not an appropriate question for the theory of knowledge. But, yes, it is, much more so than that of which we spoke above—how it is possible that what is not similar to us becomes the object of our knowledge. This question appears fundamental and essential only because we are superstitiously convinced that the possible alone exists. But that is a prejudice which daily experience contradicts. This experience shows us that if one combines in a certain proportion oxygen with hydrogen, one obtains water—oxygen with nitrogen, air. Now this is something that is clearly impossible. Why should oxygen and hydrogen produce water? Why should they combine and give birth to a new product, or rather, why is not the result of their combination air? All this is perfectly arbitrary; all this is groundless and, consequently, impossible. Chemistry is the science of the absolute arbitrariness that rules in nature. Chemistry takes its rise from the principle that anything one wishes may arise from anything else one wishes, but with this restriction— that it is not a question of our wish or that of other men who study chemistry, but of the wish of someone or of something that we are incapable even of naming. We are constrained, whether we will it or not, to study chemistry, that is, to recognize the wish of this someone or something which acts as it pleases.

But one is then justified in asking: Whence does it come that this someone or something (at bottom everyone is convinced that it is not a living being) commands and we are constrained to obey? To put the matter otherwise, whence comes the *constraining* power of knowledge? Why should oxygen and hydrogen combining produce water, and not bread, gold, or a musical symphony? Or why is water the product of oxygen and hydrogen, and not of sound and light? Whence comes the irresistible *force* of scientific truths or even of simple empirical truths? And how does it happen that men who are so disturbed at the idea that the least impossibility might steal into reality establish with indifference that that reality contains many things inadmissible to us? It is, for example, much easier to admit Pygmalion's statue, Joshua's sun, and all the rest, than to accept the fact that the Athenians poisoned Socrates. And yet we are *constrained* to affirm the opposite.

Joshua did *not* stop the sun, Pygmalion did *not* animate his statue—but the Athenians *did* poison Socrates.

Now, to admit this would be only half a misfortune. But the most incomprehensible thing of all is that philosophers should glorify and bless this constraint which knowledge exercises and demand that everyone else do the same (the theory of knowledge is in fact nothing else than knowledge raised to the level of the ideal, identified with truth). Those who are so agitated at the thought that any impossibility might be introduced into reality consider the constraint which knowledge exercises perfectly reasonable and legitimate. Why? There is here something that is incomprehensible. Should not one ask himself, before everything else, whence this *constraint* comes? And who knows: if the philosophers were to make the impossible more of their business, if this constraint were to trouble them, if they were to resent it as an offense—perhaps many judgments considered today as necessary and consequently obligatory for everyone would appear absolutely foolish and ridiculous. And the greatest of absurdities would then be found to be this very idea of a truth which constrains.

(From *Athens and Jerusalem*, pp. 382–384)

THE ABSOLUTE

The mortal sin of the philosophers is not the pursuit of the absolute. Their great offense is that, as soon as they realize that they have not found the absolute, they are willing to recognize as absolute one of the products of human activity, such as science, the state, morality, religion, etc. Obviously the state, just like science, morality and religion, has very great value—but only so long as it does not pretend to occupy the throne of the absolute. Religion itself, no matter how profound and sublime it be, is, in the last analysis, only a vessel intended to contain the absolute—the vestment, so to speak, of the absolute. And it is necessary to know how to distinguish the sacred treasure from the vessel which contains it; otherwise one risks falling into idolatry. But men do not know how, or rather, do not wish, to make this distinction. Idols are to them—why, one does not know—nearer, more comprehensible, than God. Holy Scripture speaks much of these things. Idols seduced even the Jewish people, which was called to reveal God to half the human race, and it was only thanks to the prodigious efforts of its prophets that it succeeded in attaining the heights where eternal truth is discovered.

(From *Athens and Jerusalem*, pp. 385–386)

FREEDOM OF THOUGHT

According to Kant, our thought—our excellent and only guide in the labyrinth of existence—leads us finally to regions where it becomes powerless and useless, where the principle of contradiction, which never deceives and which always furnishes answers that have an unambiguous meaning, no longer rules but where, instead, antinomies which exclude all possibility of answer rule. What, then, is to be done? Kant says we must stop, for here there is nothing any longer to interest us. Where questions remain necessarily without answer, man has nothing more to do, nothing more to search.

Now, one obviously can stop, and the majority of people do stop. But is it really necessary to do so? What if it is not necessary? What if it is found, on the contrary, that man is capable of "re-learning," of transforming himself, of re-educating himself in such a way as to free himself from the need of obtaining unambiguous answers to all questions? What if man ever succeeded in coming to feel that such answers, though they had formerly consoled him and even made him rejoice, are in reality the curse of his existence, that vanity to which the creatures are subject, despite themselves, groaning and as in travail to this day? (Romans 8:20–22.)

Kant forgot Holy Scripture when he meditated on the relationships between science and metaphysics. That is a pity! If he had remembered, he would perhaps have been able to answer differently the questions he raised. Perhaps it would not have seemed to him that metaphysics loses its *raison d'être* if it does not lead us to general and necessary judgments. Perhaps he would even have been led to

recognize that the *raison d'être* of metaphysics is precisely
to return to man his primordial freedom and to break
forever the bonds in which general and necessary truths
have fettered us.

Kant, like his successors—Fichte, Schelling, Hegel—
speaks of freedom often and enthusiastically. But when
these men found themselves face to face with true freedom,
they were terrified. They were petrified, as if they had seen
not freedom but the head of Medusa surrounded by
serpents. The scientist cannot get along without necessary
judgments; how should metaphysics be able to renounce
them? One can, in fact, neither discuss nor prove anything
if there is not an obligatory norm. Even relationships
between men become impossible if they do not submit
to a single principle equally constraining for all. But all
this only proves one thing: our thought has arrogated
rights which do not belong to it. From the fact that, in
the empirical domain, the idea of constraining truth is
the condition of knowledge, one cannot in any way conclude that it must be the same in the domain of metaphysics—just as the fact that the possibility of communication between men presupposes, according to our observations in a great number of cases, the recognition of one or
several fundamental principles that are common to all,
does not at all justify the conclusion that communication
between men is possible only if they agree to recognize the
absolute power of a *single* truth.

Exactly the opposite is the truth. Such a demand often
destroys all possibility of communication. The Eastern
Church separated from the Western Church precisely because of *filioque*. Catholics have in fact no communication
with Eastern Orthodox believers; they even hate them—
even though Catholicism and Eastern Orthodoxy are both
Christian religions. I do not even speak of the abyss which
separates Christianity from Islam or Buddhism. Not only
does communication become impossible, but the supposed
necessity of bowing down before a single truth leads to
an eternal hatred. The Crusades still exist in our day.
Men who live side by side detest and despise each other.
They do not dream of "communicating" with their neighbors, but each wishes to subordinate the other, to oblige
him to forget himself, to renounce everything which he
needs and is important to him. Obviously we can declare

that there is no salvation outside our truth. But we cannot anticipate in any case that, armed with a single truth, we shall find the way to all human souls. Here again our thought deceives us with illusory promises. In this way, on the contrary, all avenues of approach are cut off and one obtains unity among men not by communication but by the destruction of all who think, feel, or desire differently than we.

It will be said that it is dangerous to grant "freedom" to men. Meister Eckhardt taught that he who has succeeded in entering into communion with God has no need of dogmas, but freedom proved to be fatal for Eckhardt. Without realizing it, he slipped from the summit that he had apparently succeeded in attaining to the plane of current thought and substituted an abstract idea for God. As for German Idealism, which owes much to Eckhardt, it denied God completely. All this is perfectly correct. But if Eckhardt did not know how to stay at the altitude he had attained, if the German Idealists slipped back to positivism, it was precisely because their ultimate aim was to attain a single truth for all and because they did not believe in freedom.

(From *Athens and Jerusalem*, pp. 394–396)

ABRAHAM AND SOCRATES

When God says to Abraham, "Leave your country, your friends and your father's house, and go to the land that I will show you," Abraham obeys and "leaves without knowing where he is going." And it is said in Scripture that Abraham believed God, Who imputed it to him for righteousness. All this is according to the Bible. But common sense judges quite otherwise. He who goes without knowing where he is going is a weak and frivolous man, and a faith which is founded on nothing (now faith is always founded on nothing, for it is faith itself that wishes to "found") cannot be in any way "imputed for righteousness." The same conviction, clearly and neatly formulated and raised to the level of method, reigns in science, which was born of common sense. Science, in fact, is science only so long as it does not admit faith and always demands of man that he realize what he is doing and know where he is going. Scientific philosophy, or to put it another way, the philosophy which utilizes in its search for its truths the same methods that science employs in its search for its truths also wishes to know where it is going and where it is leading its adherents. It follows from this that faith is distinguished from science, above everything else, by its methods.

The believer goes forward, without looking to the right or to the left, without asking where he is going, without calculating. The scientist will not take a step without looking around him, without asking, and is afraid to budge from his place. He wishes to know beforehand where he will arrive. Which of these two methods leads us to "truth?" One can discuss this matter, but it is beyond doubt that he alone will be able to attain the promised land who, like Abraham, decides to go forward without knowing where he is going. And if philosophy wishes to attain the promised land (Kant himself, you will recall, said that metaphysics must reveal for man God, freedom and the immortality of the soul), it must adopt the method of Abraham and not that of Socrates and teach men at all events to go forward without calculating, without seeing anything beforehand, without even knowing where they are going.

Is it possible that such a philosophy should become the philosophy of the future? Or is this rather the philosophy of a far-off, forever lost past—the philosophy of the ancient and blessed wise men who (to recall once more the terms of Plato) were better than we and lived closer to God?

(From *Athens and Jerusalem*, pp. 396–397)

FAITH AND PROOFS

Heinrich Heine says that when he was a child he used to amuse himself by teasing his French teacher. When the latter, for example, asked him how one said *"la foi"* in German, Heine would answer: *"der Kredit."* And still today many very serious people, without the least intention of amusing and in all sincerity, identify faith and credit. It seems to them, indeed, that faith is nothing other than knowledge—with this single difference: that he who has faith takes proofs on credit under the verbal promise that they will be presented in time. You cannot convince anyone that the essence of faith and its most admirable, its most miraculous, prerogative consists precisely in that it does not feel the need of proofs, that it lives "beyond" proofs. This privilege is sometimes considered a *privilegium odiosum*, sometimes—still worse—as skepticism badly dissimulated. For what is a truth that cannot be imposed by means of proofs?

(From *Athens and Jerusalem*, p. 400)

ON THE SOURCES OF "CONCEPTIONS OF THE WORLD"

The appearance of man on earth is an impious audacity. God created man in His own image and likeness and, having created him, blessed him. If you accept the first of these two theses, your philosophical task will be *catharsis* (purification) or, to put it another way, you will try to kill in yourself your particular being, your so-called "ego," and aspire to be dissolved in the "supreme" idea. The fundamental problem for you will be the ethical problem, and ontology will be in a way a derivative of the ethical. Your ideal will become the kingdom of reason to which all who are prepared to renounce the primordial *jubere* (the right to command) and to see the destiny of man in the *parere* (obedience) have free access.

If, on the other hand, you accept the second thesis, the fruits of the tree of knowledge of good and evil will cease to tempt you; you will aspire to that which is "beyond good and evil." The anamnesis, the remembrance of that which your ancestor Adam contemplated in paradise, will not stop troubling you. Hymns to the glory of reason will appear tiresome, and in the midst of your self-evidences you will feel yourself as if in prison. Plato felt himself shut up in a cave; Plotinus was ashamed of his body; the men of the Bible were ashamed and afraid of their reason.

There is every reason to believe that Nietzsche turned away from Christianity because the Christians, taught by Aristotle and the Stoics, completely forgot the primordial *jubere* and remembered only the *parere* which follows it.

That is why Nietzsche spoke of the morality of slaves and the morality of masters. He could have, he should have, spoken as well of the *truth* of masters (of men to whom it is given to command) and the *truth* of slaves (of those whose destiny is to obey).

I could also mention in this connection Dostoevsky, but no one will believe me. Everyone is convinced, in fact, that Dostoevsky wrote only the several dozen pages devoted to the *starets* Zossima, to Alyosha Karamazov, etc., and the articles in the *Journal of a Writer* where he explains the theories of the Slavophiles. As for *Notes from the Underground*, as for *The Idiot*, as for *The Dream of a Ridiculous Man*, as for the nine-tenths of all that constitutes the complete works of Dostoevsky—all that was not written by him but by a certain "personage with a regressive physiognomy" and only in order to permit Dostoevsky to cover him with shame.

So profound is our faith in the *parere* (that is what we express in affirming that everything happens "naturally"), so great is our fear of everything, no matter what it may be, that recalls even from afar the *jubere* (the miraculous, the supernatural)!

(From *Athens and Jerusalem*, pp. 404–406)

ON THE USEFULNESS OF PHILOSOPHY

Men believe so little in the possibility of participating, no matter how partially, in the final truth that the deepest thirst to know, the most sincere searches—when they pass beyond certain limits—only excite their irritation and danger. Before you no one has found anything and, after you, no one will find anything either; why, then, disturb yourself and trouble the equilibrium of others? For every search begins with disquietude and ends with the loss of equilibrium.

One can, of course, interest himself in metaphysical problems and occupy himself with them, but on the condition of not connecting them with our own fate or that of humanity. Metaphysical systems must be constructed in such a way that they do not irrupt into life and do not shake the established order of existence, or, better yet, in a way such that they bless and sanctify the established order. And when a man arises to declare that metaphysics can discover a new truth and completely transform life, the whole world together throws itself upon him. Metaphysics must be useful to society, just like science and art and religion. A useless metaphysics, a useless religion— has anyone ever thus characterized the object of his final aspirations? And yet all those who seek have always known, and without the least doubt, that metaphysics *cannot* be useful and that there is nothing more terrible than to fall into the hands of God. But people do not speak of this, or only very rarely. Even the religion of the crucified God tries to imitate metaphysical systems, and Christians almost always forget, even though they wear a cross on their breasts, that the saviour of the world cried out from the height of the cross, "My God, my God, why hast Thou forsaken me?" They believe that the saviour must know this terrible despair, but that men may escape it. Men need a metaphysics which consoles and orders existence, and a religion which also consoles and orders existence. But no one cares for a truth of which he does not know beforehand what it will bring, nor for a religion which leads us into unknown territory. Even more than very rare, I repeat, are those who admit that religion and metaphysics may lead us ultimately toward anything worth-while. Everyone demands that religion and metaphysics be visibly and indubitably useful right here, on the shores of time.

(From *Athens and Jerusalem*, pp. 408–409)

THE LIMITS OF THE POWER OF THE PRINCIPLES OF IDENTITY AND OF CONTRADICTION

If we take it into our heads to say that "sound is heavy," the principles of identity and of contradiction immediately become involved in the matter and oppose their veto. It is impossible, they declare. But when we say that Socrates was poisoned, these two principles do not intervene. May it be that there is a reality in which the principles of identity and of contradiction would remain indifferent and inactive when sounds become heavy but

rise up in rebellion when one kills the just? If such a
reality is possible, these principles are not principles but
simply "executive organs" and their role is completely
different from that which people ordinarily ascribe to
them.

It will be asked, "How is one *to know* if such a reality
is possible or impossible, and if it is given us to penetrate
into this reality?" Yes, this is just it: how is one to know.
Obviously, if you ask, "Is such a reality possible?" people
will answer you that it is impossible, that the principles
of identity and of contradiction have always reigned autocratically and will always reign over the world, that there
will never be heavy sounds, and that people will continue
to kill the just. But try not to ask anything of anyone!
Will you thus be able to realize the free will which the
metaphysicians promise you? Or, to put it better, do you
want this free will? It seems, indeed, that you would
hardly have any desire at all for it, that "sacred Necessity"
would be nearer and dearer to you, and that, after the
manner of Schelling, you would see in *Herrschaft* the
source of all *Herrlichkeiten*.

(From *Athens and Jerusalem*, pp. 409–410)

THE POSSIBLE

Everything that has a beginning has an end, everything
that is born must die: such is the unshakeable law of
existence. But what about truths? For there are truths
which have not always existed, which were born in time.
Such are all truths that state matters of fact. Four hundred
years before Christ the truth, "the Athenians poisoned
Socrates," still did not exist; it was born in the year 399.
And it still lives, although it took place almost 2,500
years ago. Does this mean that it will live eternally? If
it must disappear like everything that is born, if the general law that we apply with such assurance to everything
that exists does not—as a truth a priori—admit of any
exception, then there will come a moment when the truth
about the poisoning of Socrates will die and cease to
exist. And our descendants will then have the possibility
of affirming that the Athenians did *not* poison Socrates, but

that, quite simply (or, on the contrary, not "simply" at all) men lived a certain time, a very long time even, in an illusion which they took for an eternal truth because they forgot, through chance or intentionally, the law of birth and death and its ineluctable character.

(From *Athens and Jerusalem*, pp. 411–412)

THE TRUTHS THAT CONSTRAIN

The great majority of men do not believe in the truths of the religion they profess. Plato already said, "Unbelief is proper to the mob." Thus they demand that those around them profess the very truths which they themselves officially believe and say the same things as they: that alone supports them in their "faith"; it is only from their environment that they draw the force of their convictions. And the less convincing the revealed truths appear to them, the more important it is to them that no one doubt these truths. It is for this reason that people who believe the least are ordinarily the most intolerant. While the criterion of ordinary, scientific truths consists in the possibility of making them binding upon all, there is room to believe that the truths of faith are true insofar as they are able to do without the consent of men, insofar as they are indifferent to recognition and demonstrations. However, the positive religions do not hold truths of this kind in very high esteem. They maintain them, for they cannot get along without them, but they rely on other truths, on those which constrain men; and they seek to place under the protection of the principle of contradiction even the revealed truths in order that these shall in no wise yield to ordinary truths.

As is known, the protection of the principle of contradiction appeared insufficient to Catholicism and it invented the Inquisition, without which it would not have been able to accomplish its immense historical work. It defended itself by means of "intolerance" and even made a virtue of its intolerance. It never occurred to the mind of Catholicism that that which requires the protection of the principle of contradiction or of executioners and jailers is outside the divine truth, and that what truly saves men is precisely that which, according to our human reckoning, is feeble, weak, and devoid of all protection. The truths of faith are to be recognized by this sign: that, contrary to the truths of knowledge, they are neither universal nor necessary and, consequently, do not have the power of constraining human beings. These truths are given freely, they are accepted freely. No one officially certifies them, they do not justify themselves to anyone, they do not make anyone afraid, and they themselves fear no one.

(From *Athens and Jerusalem*, pp. 424–425)

THE EMPIRICAL PERSONALITY

How are the rare moments when the "self-evidences" lose their power over man to be used for philosophy? These moments presuppose the existence of a very special kind of inward state wherein that which ordinarily appears to us as the most important, the most essential, and even as the only reality becomes suddenly insignificant, useless, fantastic. But philosophy wishes to be objective and despises "states of the soul." If, then, one runs after objectivity, one inevitably falls into the clutches of self-evidences; and if one wishes to rid himself of self-evidences he must, before everything else and contrary to tradition, disdain objectivity. Certainly no one will decide to do that. Everyone flatters himself that he has obtained a truth which, no matter how little, no matter how very little, will be a truth for all. It is only when we are alone with ourselves, under the impenetrable veil of the mystery of the individual being (the empirical personality), that we decide occasionally to renounce the real or illusory rights and privileges which we possess from the fact of our participation in the world common to all. It is then that there suddenly shine before our eyes the ultimate and the penultimate truths—but they appear more like dreams than truths. We forget them easily, as we forget dreams. And if it happens that we do retain a vague memory of them, we do not know what to do with it. And, to tell the truth, one cannot do anything with these truths. At the very most, one can try to translate them by means of a certain verbal music and listen to what those who, acquainted with these visions only by having heard others speak of them and not by their own immediate experience, transform them into judgments and, having thus killed them, make them necessary always and for everyone, that is, comprehensible and "evident." But they will then be truths quite different from those that were revealed to us in our solitude. It is no longer to us that they will belong, but to everyone, to that "omnitude" which Dostoevsky so hated and which his friend and disciple, Soloviev, for the sake of traditional philosophy and theology, made the basis of his system under the less odious name of "ecumenicity." It is here that there clearly appears the fundamental opposition between the thought of Dostoevsky and that of the school out of which Soloviev arose. Dostoevsky fled from "omnitude" to himself; Soloviev fled from himself to "omnitude." The living man, whom the school calls the "empirical personality," was for Soloviev the major obstacle on the road to the truth. He thought, or, to put it better, he affirmed (who can know what a man thinks?) that one cannot see truth as long as one has not completely rid himself of his "ego" (in other words, as long as one has not overcome and destroyed his empirical individuality). Dostoevsky, however, knew that truth is revealed only to the empirical personality.

(From *Athens and Jerusalem*, pp. 429–430)

LOGIC AND THUNDER

Phenomenology, the faithful disciples of Husserl declare, ignores the difference between *homo dormiens* (sleeping man) and *homo vigilans* (waking man). This is true. It does ignore this difference, and herein lies the source of its power and persuasive force. It exercises all its efforts towards preserving its *docta ignorantia*. As soon, indeed, as phenomenology feels that not only *homo vigilans*, the man who has been awakened (it seems there has never yet been any such person on earth), differs from the man who is asleep, but that the man who is only beginning to awaken also differs from him *toto coelo*—it will be at the end of its success. Consciously and unconsciously, the man who is asleep tends to consider the conditions from which his dreams flow as the only possible conditions of existence. That is why he calls them "self-evidences" and guards and protects them in all kinds of ways (logic and the theory of knowledge: the gifts of reason). But when the moment of awakening comes (the rumbling of the thunder is heard: revelation), one will begin to doubt the self-evidences and to put up a struggle against them that is completely unreasonable—that is to say, one will do precisely what, for the man who is asleep, is the height of absurdity. Can there, indeed, be anything more absurd than to answer logic with claps of thunder?

(From *Athens and Jerusalem*, pp. 432–433)

THE CLASSICAL ARGUMENT

Since the most ancient times philosophers have been divided into two quantitatively unequal groups. The first —and these always form the large majority—wished to believe and did believe that they knew a great deal. The others believed that they knew very little. It will be recalled that Socrates declared that he knew nothing. But this was only a pretense on his part, a methodological trick similar to Descartes' *de omnibus dubitandum*, a pretext to establish the propositions destined forever to deliver us from all doubts. In any case, it is precisely from Socrates on that the philosophers began to claim the capacity of omniscience. Even the skeptics, as becomes evident when we carefully examine the problems they raised, never renounced knowledge entirely. They said only that our knowledge was probable, not certain. But they were nevertheless convinced that they possessed criteria permitting them to distinguish the probable from the improbable. Further, if we examine the matter more closely, skepticism with its probable judgments does not differ so very much from dogmatism with its certain judgments. When it is a question of choosing between two probable judgments that are opposed to each other, the skeptic relies on a determinate criterion. But from where did he take it? Does not the totality of his criteria finally form a certain system of knowledge that is very little distinguished from the systems of the dogmatists? We could establish a series of judgments as acceptable to skeptics as to dogmatists, but it seems hardly necessary. In the domain of empirical knowledge you will not find any more profound divergences between the representatives of two points of view as different as those of the skeptics and the dogmatists than between the diverse representatives of one and the same point of view. The certain judgments of the dogmatists will be accepted by the skeptics, but qualified by the latter as probable. And then there is this also: the dogmatist, having attained certitude, feels calm and declares that he has achieved the supreme goal, for tranquility of mind is the highest goal of every reasonable being in general and of the philosopher in particular. But the skeptic will not make any different use of his probable knowledge. He celebrates his ἀταραξία which, if one does not show a philological scrupulousness that would be here inappropriate, can be translated by the term "tranquility of mind." In brief, certain knowledge and probable knowledge are hardly distinguishable from one another.

But when it is a question of ignorance, it is quite different. When the dogmatists attacked the skeptics, they set out from the supposition that their adversaries did not admit any knowledge. And then they pushed forward their classical argument like a destructive battering ram: he who says that knowledge is impossible contradicts himself, for he knows that he does not know; therefore, knowledge is possible. And he arrives at his knowledge that knowledge is impossible by employing the same methods of judgments that everyone else employs. Why, then, does this man who recognizes the methods of searching for truth acknowledged by all, after arriving at a certain limit, suddenly renounce and reject them as useless? Why cannot the method which served to obtain the knowledge that one can not know furnish the knowledge that one can know? These arguments, as you see, are irresistible. As the dogmatists have loved to put it since the most ancient times, they silence the most obstinate of opponents. The dogmatists have always triumphed over their opponents, for an opponent reduced to silence is no longer dangerous, no longer an opponent.

This naturally holds only so long as we set ourselves the modest aim of getting rid of an opponent. But what if we admit the possibility of other aims? What if we aim not at confusing our opponent in the eyes of the mob but at convincing him? Or what if we trust our opponent, respect him, and do not assume that he involves himself in contradictions because he is foolish or blind or—what is still worse—because, unlike us, he is indifferent to the truth and sets for himself only "practical" or "finite" goals—what, I say, if we admit this? The opponent is as intelligent, clear-headed, sincere and conscientious as we or—*horribile dictu*—even surpasses us in all these respects; and if he expresses judgments whose contradictory character he himself perceives, it is because they impose themselves upon him with that necessity which, according to our own judgment, is inherent in truth. Yes, it was and still is so. In the reality of the everyday contradictions are absent, or they are less conspicuous. A is always equal to A, the whole is greater than its parts, there is no action without a cause, each of us sees what the others see, *Deus impossibile non jubet,** etc. One can employ general methods that are obligatory upon all, and these methods yield excellent results. And our opponent himself, as has been said, uses these methods so long as, together with other men, he stands in full light. But there are places where the light of the sun does not penetrate—under the earth, at the bottom of the sea. There, there is no light, there darkness rules, but are life and the truth of life impossible there? May it not be that our opponent, who has lived in those regions where few beings have ever descended, tries to reveal to us the deepest, most unknown secrets? And that it is precisely because that rigorous logic to which we have become accustomed here is unknown there, in those obscure regions, that he embroils himself in contradictions and his tongue stammers? We can certainly force him to silence. We can, like Aristotle, say that he is only pronouncing empty words that have no sense even for him. This will surely give us peace, the supreme good, or ἀταραξία (tranquility) which is also the supreme good. For shall we not thus be certain of possessing the final truth?

In this respect the classical argument is above all praise. But what if our curiosity awakens, what if life shakes in

* God does not command the impossible.

us the Aristotelian assurance, and we ask ourselves: may not this man who contradicts himself be in communion with some mysterious reality? May not this confusion, this mass of inextricable contradictions hide in themselves that precisely which is indispensable, most significant, and most meaningful for us? Will it not then occur to us that the pride of the conqueror is less desirable than the humility of the conquered? And that our classical argument, like all mechanical means of constraint, is not at all as seductive as it seems to us? All the more so since those who have perceived the contradictory nature of reality are not ordinarily very disputatious. There is no need to force them to silence by means of the classical argument, for they do not generally attach any very great importance to the triumph of their "truths." If you wish them to be silent and not contradict you, you need not demonstrate anything to them. Tell them simply that you do not wish to listen to them and that you wish to be conquerors. This will act on them as effectively as your arguments. They will of themselves be silent, depart and leave you a free field.

(From *Potestas Clavium*, pp. 43–46)

THE POWER OF THE GOOD IN PLATO

Meletus did a great wrong to Socrates, accused him falsely before the judges, and had him condemned. And Socrates answered with only one word: he called him "unrighteous." If Plato is to be believed, of the two adversaries confronting each other the loser was not Socrates but Meletus. If one accepts the judgment of the crowd, τῶν πολλῶν, Meletus did not suffer at all and it was Socrates who was overcome. And then the question arises: which is the stronger—the hemlock that poisoned Socrates, or the word "unrighteous" with which Socrates struck Meletus and Anytus?

When we today, twenty-five hundred years after the death of Socrates and his enemies, read the *Apology* or the *Phaedo* we see clearly that the moral condemnation is more powerful than the hemlock. Anytus and Meletus are quite as dead as Socrates, they survived him by only a few years. If he had not been condemned to death,

Socrates would in any case have died several years later and nothing would be changed today: we would say that he died twenty-five hundred years ago. But Anytus and Meletus are forever nailed to the pillory, while the image of Socrates is surrounded with a halo. Is moral condemnation therefore stronger than poison? And is Plato right when he declares that the idea of the good is the most powerful force that exists in the universe? Did Anytus and Meletus therefore miscalculate and were they, like short-sighted and weak minds, deceived?

Let us now go further. Two thousand years more will elapse, or even twenty-five thousand years. It may be that a day will come when the earth will no longer exist or even our solar system, when time itself will no longer be. Eternity will then engulf the pillory on which Plato and history nailed Anytus and Meletus. What will then happen to the power of the good? It will be said that Socrates counted on the immortality of the soul. But he declared that even if death were complete destruction, he would nevertheless remain as he was. Was he right? It is fortunate, indeed, that the inspired Plato took up his defense and that the tribunal of history condemned Anytus and Meletus. But, in millions of cases a legal action between the good and the wicked in no way attracts the attention of history. The wicked harms the good, he does him wrong, and that is the end of the matter. For his part the good man will, in a weak voice, call his offender "wicked": but his voice will be smothered by the loud voices of the offender's friends and flatterers and his word of condemnation will never even reach his enemy's ears. The good and its verdicts do not always have the power Plato wished to see in them. In Socrates' "case" it was history that conquered and not the good, which triumphed only accidentally. But Plato and his readers imagined that the good must always, by its very nature, triumph. No, "by nature," victory can be given to anything whatsoever—to physical force, to talent, to intelligence, to science—but not to the good.

Why do I say this? First, because it is the truth, that is, because it corresponds to reality. And secondly—but I would answer this question with another: Why must it not be spoken of, why must it be passed over in silence? To save Plato's reputation? Not to offend his disciples? Do you perhaps believe that it would be "better" to be silent? But then you believe many things. And what kind of "better" is it that may have misled you? Contemporary science is much too sure of itself, and it would do no harm to take away some of its pride.

(From *Potestas Clavium,* pp. 122–124)

THE ENIGMAS OF LIFE

In several of his dialogues (*Gorgias 523, Phaedo 107, Republic 614*) Plato speaks to us in detail about the fate of souls after death. We shall all have to pass in our new life the tribunal of the sons of Zeus—Minos, Rhadamanthus, and Aeacus. In order that their judgments not be mistaken and that the judges not allow themselves to be led astray by the position of the souls on earth, Zeus ordained that the souls should appear in the other world not only without clothing but also without bodies. According to Plato, the naked soul would not be able to dissemble its sins in any way. He who has lived virtuously will have preserved his soul clean of all blemish; the soul of him who has sinned much will be broken, battered, covered with repugnant marks and sores—just as a body which has borne many illnesses becomes ugly and deformed. So thought Plato, who, as far as is known, never saw any souls naked and deprived of their bodies but only guessed what they would look like when their fleshly envelop fell off.

I believe that the sons of Zeus, who had to judge the dead and who saw the naked souls, would have smiled if they had somehow been able to hear Plato's conjecture. They saw the souls with their own eyes and did not need to have recourse to guesses or to judge by the analogy which holds that if sicknesses deform the body, sins likewise deform the soul. Indeed, from the very beginning, the analogy is far from flawless: certain persons become handsomer after sickness. Furthermore, it is very probable that wicked men and precisely those who have the most abdominable vices, those who do not distinguish and do not wish to distinguish good from evil, possess souls that are very clean and very smooth, as if highly polished. Whatever they do, they always feel that they are in the right. The inward struggles that so painfully torment the souls of sensitive and anxious people by imposing upon them a constant tension—these are alien to them. Ideally pure souls are the property of ordinary, normal people who in their way know what is good and what bad, avoid the great evils, do good in small measure, and sleep with a tranquil conscience. The soul of a bourgeois or rentier is much cleaner and smoother than that of Socrates, Tolstoy, Pascal, Shakespeare, or Dostoevsky, just as a rentier's face is rounder and more placid, and his gaze more carefree. If Minos followed Plato's rules he would send Dostoevsky and Shakespeare to hell and populate the Field of Elysium with French rentiers and Dutch peasants. This is clear as day. Plato should not have spoken with such assurance of what he did not know.

But there is still another extremely important thing: if someone had pointed out in time to Plato that he was wrong, that it is not evil and vices but rather good and inward struggles—which in any case cannot be considered "bad"—that render the soul ugly and deformed, what would he have replied to this? The careful reader of Plato will understand the importance such a question must have for him. Indeed, let us assume that Plato could have convinced himself with his own eyes that the good does not beautify the soul but rather deforms it, that it introduces into it not harmony but disharmony—would he have, for all this, renounced the good? To put it differently, would he have advised men to wrong their neighbors or, at least, to think the least possible about justice and injustice, like those women who avoid all work and cares and refuse even to bring their children into the world in order not to lose their beauty?

But then he would have been obliged to renounce not only the λόγος but also his favorite idea of harmony: Φιλοσοφίας μεν οὔσης μεγίστης μουοίκῆς, ἐμοῦ δὲ τοῦτο πράττοντος (Philosophy is the supreme music and I follow it). He would even perhaps have been obliged to become a μισόλογος (hater of reason), though he considered this the greatest of dangers and warned his disciples against it. Only a μισόλογος, indeed, would be capable of advising the soul to do that which deforms it. Not to fear either ugliness of the body or of the soul! Not to fear them—without such fearlessness being justifiable on any grounds whatsoever! Plato, the Greeks in general, and perhaps even all men will never agree to this; everyone wishes to have "sufficient reasons." And yet it must be agreed to. Tolstoy and Dostoevsky had souls that were deformed and completely broken: I saw this with my own eyes, I could not be deceived. In the case of Socrates, likewise, his soul was no more beautiful than his body; we have on this matter the authoritative testimony of Zopyrus who was much more perceptive than Alcibiades and perhaps even than Plato.

It follows from this that all the enigmas of being are still not solved. I say this only because it seems to me that it is always forgotten.

(From *Potestas Clavium,* pp. 119–121)

Franz Rosenzweig
1886-1929

I

Summarizing the results of a recently published symposium to which thirty-eight prominent American and Canadian Jewish theologians and scholars contributed statements of their personal faith as Jews, the editor of the collection concluded, "The single greatest influence on the religious thought of North American Jewry . . . is a German Jew—a layman, not a rabbi—who died before Hitler took power and who came to Judaism from the very portals of the Church."[1] The German Jew to whom he referred is Franz Rosenzweig, a thinker who has had a profound impact on Jewish theology not only in America but in Europe and Israel as well. Indeed, many competent students of Jewish thought would regard him as possibly the most seminal and significant Jewish theologian of the twentieth century.

The pre-eminent place occupied by Rosenzweig in modern Jewish thought is due, in no small measure, to the fact that he was a man thoroughly familiar with the best of Western culture and thought who, at one point in his life, was on the verge of a serious, religiously motivated conversion to the dominant faith of the Western world but who, nevertheless, decided that he must affirm the faith of his fathers, devoted the rest of his days to a sustained effort to appropriate that faith existentially, and made it the ruling passion of his life. That Rosenzweig was a *baal teshuvah*, a returnee to Judaism from both the pagan and Christian cultures that once so powerfully attracted him, and may hence be "a guide to reversioners,"[2] marginal Jews desiring to reappropriate their religious heritage, is no doubt a significant factor in the esteem accorded him in Jewish quarters. But that esteem, as well as the growing respect in which he is held in non-Jewish philosophical and theological circles,[3] is also strongly based on his substantive writings, his original and profound contributions to contemporary religious discussion.

In his works Rosenzweig presented a statement concerning the role of "speech thinking" and "common sense" in theology and philosophy that is of major import for both Judaism and Christianity. He also developed a unique doctrine of the relationship between these two faiths which, while not subsequently finding widespread acceptance among either Jews or Christians, has stimulated fruitful discussion of an age-old problem on which little of permanent value has yet been said. In elaborating his view of the essence and structure of Jewish faith, Rosenzweig pointed to a new conception of Judaism, transcending the sterile opposition between the literalism and fundamentalism of much of Orthodox Jewish thought, on the one hand, and the rationalism and liberalism of many Conservative and Reform Jewish positions, on the other, around which virtually all Jewish religious discussion in the nineteenth century and well into the twentieth revolved. For these and many other reasons Rosenzweig is assured of a place of continuing significance in Jewish religious thought.

As in the case of every major religious thinker, so in Rosenzweig's the general course of his life and the crucial events of his biography were decisive in molding his theological and philosophical outlook.

Born December 25, 1886, in Cassel, Franz Rosenzweig grew up in a well-to-do, cultured and, Jewishly speaking, assimilated environment that was not untypical of middle- and upper-class German-Jewish families of the time. His father, Georg, was a successful businessman and civic leader; his mother, Adele, an intelligent, well-read woman with a strong interest in the German literary classics. The Jewishness of the family was nominal and formal. To be sure, the young Rosenzweig celebrated his *bar mitzvah* at the synagogue, but the Jewish education he received in childhood was of the most elementary kind. The one strong and positive Jewish influence on the boy's life was the presence in his home of his great-uncle, Adam Rosenzweig (1826–1908), a man with a strong and knowledgeable interest in German culture but with a genuine attachment to his Jewish heritage as well.[4]

After graduating from a gymnasium in Cassel in 1905, Rosenzweig studied medicine for two years at the universities of Göttingen, Munich and Freiburg. In the winter of 1907, however, he abandoned his medical studies. The next five years, until the summer of 1912, were spent at the universities of Berlin and Freiburg, where he concentrated on history, philosophy, theology, art, literature and the languages of classical antiquity. In this period the teacher whom he most admired and who exerted the profoundest influence on him was the great historian and political theorist Friedrich Meinecke. In the fall of 1912, after having received his doctorate for a dissertation on Hegel's political theory, he was drafted into the German army and served briefly at Darmstadt before being discharged in December of that year because of a minor injury.

Rosenzweig spent the first part of 1913 at the university of Leipzig, where he took courses in jurisprudence. Here he encountered a friend, Eugen Rosenstock, who had converted to Protestantism from Judaism and who, while lecturing at the university on medieval constitutional law, was also deeply immersed in studying theology and church history. Rosenstock's conversion had been a matter of profound existential import to himself, and he felt constrained to bring others to the light he had found. The two men met daily for lunch and conversation. Apparently Rosenzweig was subjected to intensive intellectual pressure by his friend over a period of several months either to justify his remaining a Jew or to convert to Christianity. The thought of taking the latter course was not altogether new to Rosenzweig; indeed, some years earlier he had expressed the idea that he ought perhaps to be baptized, but had decided against doing so at the time out of what he described as the fear that his family and friends would disapprove and regard his act as motivated more by social than religious considerations. But now such a fear seemed irrelevant; impressed by the sincerity and religious zeal of his friend Rosenstock, for whom he had the profoundest intellectual respect, he felt that he had to make his decision on philosophical and theological grounds alone and disregard all other considerations.

The religious discussion between the two friends reached its climax in an all-night conversation on July 7, 1913, to which Rosenzweig later frequently referred in his correspondence and which clearly constituted a major turning point in his life. It was not so much as Jew and Christian that Rosenzweig and Rosenstock faced each other, but as a protagonist of "faith in philosophy" against a protagonist of "faith based on revelation." Rosenstock could not take seriously what passed for Judaism in his friend; he regarded it simply as "a kind of personal whim, or at best as a pious-romantic relic of the posthumous power of a dead great-uncle."[5] He forced Rosenzweig to face the theological and philosophical issues squarely and, on that July night, apparently defeated him. Several months later, Rosenzweig wrote:

In that night's conversation at Leipzig, in which Rosenstock pushed me step by step out of the last relativist position which I still held and forced me to take an absolute standpoint, I was inferior to him from the start, because I had to affirm for my part, too, the justice of this attack. If I could then have buttressed my dualism between revelation and the world with a metaphysical dualism between God and the Devil,[6] I should have been unassailable. But the first sentence of the Bible prevented me from doing this. This piece of common ground forced me to face him. This has remained the immovable point of departure even later in the weeks that followed. Every relativism of world-outlook is now impossible for me.[7]

When Rosenzweig capitulated to Rosenstock and declared his intention to become baptized as a Christian, he made only one condition, namely, that he would enter the Church "as a Jew," as the earliest Christians had done, not as a "pagan," i.e., out of a previously irreligious or rationalistic position.[8] He would convert in the way in which the New Testament Epistle to the Hebrews speaks of the final conversion of the entire Jewish people, observing the Torah until the moment of conversion frees him, as in the view of the Church it does, from the duty to perform its *mitzvot* (commandments). Acting on this condition, he decided to attend Rosh Hashanah services in the synagogue at Cassel. These services affected him as little as similar services had in his youth. Ten days later, on Yom Kippur, however, he found himself in Berlin and went to a small Orthodox synagogue there. What happened to Rosenzweig on that Yom Kippur he always kept a closely guarded secret; he never spoke of it even to his most intimate friends, and there is no reference to it in his writings. But it is clear that some inner transformation took place in him in the little synagogue on that day that made it the decisive turning point of his life. For twelve days later, on October 23, 1913, we find him writing a long letter to his mother in which he discusses Judaism and Christianity and concludes, "You will have gathered from this letter that I seem to have found the way back about which I had brooded in vain for almost three months."[9] And a week after that, in a letter to his cousin Rudolf Ehrenberg, who had himself converted to Christianity some time before, he explicitly announces that he has changed his mind about becoming a Christian: "I must tell you something that will distress you and at least at first seem incomprehensible to you; after prolonged and, I believe, thorough reflection I have reversed my decision. It no longer seems necessary to me, and therefore, in my case, no longer possible. I will remain a Jew."[10]

Whether or not Rosenzweig had a sudden "conversionary experience" in the synagogue is a matter on which the evidence permits no decision, but it is fairly obvious that he found on that Yom Kippur a sense of the reality of God and of personal communion with Him which he had been seeking so ardently and had come to believe he would find only in the church. Years later, lecturing at the *Freie Jüdische Lehrhaus* in Frankfurt-am-Main, he said:

> Anyone who has ever celebrated Yom Kippur knows that it is something more than a mere personal exaltation (although this may enter into it) or the symbolic recognition of a reality such as the Jewish people (although this also may be an element)—it is a testimony to the reality of God which cannot be controverted.[11]

And in his major theological work, *The Star of Redemption* (*Der Stern der Erlösung*), he wrote of Yom Kippur:

> All sins, even those committed against and forgiven by man, are sins before God, sins of the solitary individual, sins of the soul, for it is the soul that sins. And God lifts up His face to this united and lonely pleading of

men in shrouds, men beyond the grave, men of souls—
the God who loves man both before and after his sin,
the God whom man, in his need, may call to account,
asking why He has forsaken him . . . And so man, to
whom the divine face has been lifted up, shouts with
joy the profession: He, this God of love, He alone is
God! Everything earthly lies so far behind the transport
of eternity in this profession that it can hardly be imagined how a way may be found back from here into
the circuit of the year.[12]

This passage is from an important section of *The Star of
Redemption* devoted to a theological exposition of the
structure of the festivals of the Jewish year and of the
synagogue liturgy. It can hardly be doubted that the
centrality of these aspects of Judaism in Rosenzweig's understanding of Jewish faith and his profound interest in
them stemmed from his experience in the synagogue in
Berlin on that Yom Kippur of 1913.

Having made his decision to remain a Jew, Rosenzweig
further decided that he would have to undertake a serious
study of the religious tradition which he had inherited and
now wished to make his own. From the fall of 1913 to
the fall of 1914 he remained in Berlin reading Jewish
religious texts and sources. Here he met Hermann Cohen,
the great neo-Kantian philosopher who, after retiring from
his prestigious chair at the university of Marburg in 1912,
had come to Berlin to teach Jewish philosophy at the
liberal rabbinical seminary. Cohen, for whom Rosenzweig
came to cherish both great intellectual regard and personal
affection, had a pronounced influence on the development
of his philosophical and theological perspectives. It was
at this time that he also met in Berlin Martin Buber, who
was to become his lifelong friend and later his collaborator
in the enterprise of translating the Hebrew Bible into
German. At Buber's invitation Rosenzweig wrote, in the
spring of 1914, an article which he entitled "Atheistische
Theologie" (Atheistic Theology). This, his first essay on
religious thought, was a critique of certain tendencies in
contemporary theology, both Christian and Jewish, that
wished to do away with the concept of divine revelation.[13]
As such, it was a forerunner of his later contention, devel-

oped at length in *The Star of Redemption*, that revelation is one of the three indispensable foundations of the structure of Jewish faith.

Along with his new-found interest in Judaica Rosenzweig continued his previous studies in the history of philosophy. Besides working on the preparation for publication of his two-volume work, *Hegel und der Staat*, which finally appeared in 1920 in Munich and Berlin, he discovered at this time in Hegel's handwriting a brief document which he identified as Schelling's first outline for a complete system of Idealistic philosophy. His interpretation of this document was published in 1917 by the Heidelberg Academy of Sciences under the title *Das älteste Systemprogramm des Deutschen Idealismus.*

The outbreak of the First World War put an abrupt end to Rosenzweig's scholarly life in Berlin. In September 1914 he joined the Red Cross and worked for several months in German-occupied Belgium as a male nurse. Early in 1915, believing that he would in any case soon be drafted, he volunteered for service in the regular German army. After receiving his military training in artillery at Cassel he was sent in January 1916 to the Distance Measuring (Ballistics) School at La Fére in France. Shortly thereafter he joined an anti-aircraft unit which in March was transferred to the Balkans, where he remained most of the time until virtually the end of the war in 1918. Military service and the war seem to have had no great effect at first on Rosenzweig's life. In a letter to his cousin Hans Ehrenberg, dated October 1916, he wrote: "The war itself does not in any way mean a break for me. In 1913 I had experienced so much that 1914 would have had to produce the world's collapse to make any impression on me . . . Thus I have not experienced the war . . . I carry my life through it like Cervantes his poem."[14]

While the conditions under which he had to live were quite primitive, Rosenzweig's military duties during much of this period were apparently not overly demanding, for he was able to undertake a regimen of very extensive reading and study in many of the fields in which he had become interested. In May of 1916 he also began a correspondence, which was to last until the end of the year, with Eugen Rosenstock, who was with the German army on the Western front. Now it was no longer as a hesitant seeker, overwhelmed by the learning and theological subtlety of his friend, that he confronted the latter, but as a faithful Jew speaking frankly and sincerely to a faithful Christian and trying to define the areas of agreement and disagreement between themselves.

Rosenzweig's concern with the meaning of Jewishness had been growing ever since 1913 and now began to focus on the problem of Jewish religious education in Germany. The fruit of his wartime reflection in the Balkans on this question was an article "Zeit ist's" (It Is Time) in the form of an open letter addressed to Hermann Cohen.[15] Remembering his own very superficial and inadequate Jewish education, Rosenzweig here presented the outline of a detailed, graded curriculum which would not teach the young "about Judaism" but rather concentrate their attention on the study of Hebrew and bring them to a direct confrontation with the basic literary sources of Judaism—the Bible, the Mishnah, the Aggadah, and other fundamental documents of the tradition. In addition he proposed a program for the preparation of a cadre of theologically trained "scholar-teachers," either at a new academy which would be associated with one of the German universities or in conjunction with the Jewish seminaries already in existence.

It was in the spring of 1917 that Rosenzweig in Üsküb, Yugoslavia, first encountered Sephardic Jews, whose Jewishness was far more natural, integral and all-embracing than that of the marginal, half-assimilated, middle- and upper-class Jews he had known in Germany. He relates how he met a ten-year-old boy named Emanuel Noah, who became his close friend and guide and who, when Rosenzweig once explained to him that at home he wrote historical books for both Jews and non-Jews, asked him: "Pourquoi ne fais-tu pas tout pour les Israelites?"[16] It was a question that was to haunt him for a long time afterward and to play a part in his eventual decision to devote himself exclusively to Judaism and the Jewish people.

In the spring of 1918 Rosenzweig was assigned to an officers' training course in Rembertow near Warsaw, where he first came into contact with East European Jews. Here again he was deeply impressed by the vitality and strength of their Jewish existence. In a letter to his mother from Rembertow, dated May 23, 1918, he wrote:

The Jewish boys are splendid, and I experienced something I rarely feel, true pride in my race, in so much freshness and liveliness. Driving through the town, too, I was greatly impressed by the masses of Jews . . . In general what among us are only (or again) qualities of the intellectual upper stratum are here typical qualities: absolute alertness, the ability to place every trivial detail in interesting contexts. If you tease a tiny fellow by telling him that he is crafty, he answers you with a whole diatribe on craftiness that could have come straight out of Shakespeare. I well understand why the average German Jew no longer feels any kinship with the East European Jew: *actually* he has lost it; he has really become philistine, bourgeois; but I and people like me must feel it keenly.[17]

On August 22, 1918, after having spent some weeks in a military hospital in Leipzig, Rosenzweig began to work on what was to be his magnum opus, *Der Stern der Erlösung* (*The Star of Redemption*). Few, if any, theological or philosophical works have been composed under odder circumstances. Rosenzweig wrote the first draft of his book in trenches in the Balkans, in barracks, on trains and in military hospitals largely on postcards and letters which he sent to his mother, who collected them so that he might expand and systematize them on his return home. At the end of September, during the retreat of the German troops from the Balkans, he was hospitalized in Belgrade with a malarial infection, but he continued his writing. In December he was discharged from the army and returned to Cassel. There and in Berlin he continued to work on his book uninterruptedly for the next few weeks, and on February 16, 1919, wrote its final sentences. The book was published in Frankfurt-am-Main in 1921.

The Star of Redemption is an exceedingly complex work, bearing signs of the haste and the heat of enthusiasm in which it was written, but it is an immensely rich and profound book. In it Rosenzweig presented a criticism of the history of philosophy through Hegel and developed his own method of philosophical and theological thinking, which he was later to characterize as "absolute empiricism"[18] and as based on "common sense" and "speech thinking." He also sketched in it systematic theologies of

Judaism and Christianity, built around the central themes which the two religions stress in common—Creation, Revelation and Redemption—and elaborated a theory of the nature of the Jewish people and of Jewish history. Rosenzweig later insisted that what he had written was an essentially "Jewish book" but not one based on Jewish dogmatic presuppositions. In an essay entitled "Das neue Denken" (The New Thinking), which he wrote in 1925 as a kind of commentary to *The Star of Redemption*, he characterized the book as a "system of philosophy" in which he, as a Jew, could present "the New Thinking" in no other way than in the "old words" of his faith; a Christian would have used New Testament words to write it and a pagan would have done it with words perhaps entirely his own.

The Star of Redemption, which begins with an emphasis on the reality of death, concludes with the words *ins Leben*, "into life." With its completion Rosenzweig believed that an epoch of his life had come to an end. No longer would he devote himself primarily to scholarly and literary pursuits; instead, he would concentrate on the task of teaching and studying the sources of Jewish tradition with other serious adults who were seeking to find their way back to a genuine identification with their people and their faith. In April 1919 he was introduced to Dr. Nehemiah A. Nobel, the Orthodox communal rabbi of Frankfurt-am-Main, with whom he quickly developed a very close and warm relationship. With the help of Rabbi Nobel and several other leading Jews of Frankfurt, Rosenzweig succeeded in establishing that year the *Freie Jüdische Lehrhaus*, a unique institute for adult Jewish studies in which the teachers were not to be professional scholars in Judaica nor the students passive recipients of instruction; instead teachers and pupils alike would together explore the Bible, the Talmud, and other major sources of Judaism and, through free and open discussion, seek to learn from them how to be Jews in the modern world.

Nahum N. Glatzer, who took part in the work of the academy, reports that

. . . in the seven years of its activity, the *Lehrhaus* offered ninety lecture courses and conducted one hundred and eighty study groups, seminars, and discussion meetings. Sixty-four lecturers had participated in the programs, among them Martin Buber, Gershom Scholem, Ernst Simon, Leo Strauss, Erich Fromm. Enrollment reached its peak in 1922–23, with 1100 students out of a Jewish population of some 26,000.[19]

Though it lasted for only a few years (it was revived in 1933, when the Nazis came to power, by Martin Buber), the *Lehrhaus*, under Rosenzweig's leadership, was a significant factor in the minor renaissance that took place in German Jewry just before its tragic end, and some who were to become numbered among the foremost Jewish scholars and teachers of the century were involved in its work.

While at the height of his activities on behalf of the *Lehrhaus* and Jewish education in general, Rosenzweig was stricken with a strange paralysis. Late in 1921 the first symptoms of the disease, which was diagnosed in February 1922 as amyotrophic lateral sclerosis with progressive paralysis of the bulba, became noticeable. It was apparent that the disease would soon paralyze his limbs and vocal chords and cause death when it reached his vital organs. With his devoted wife Edith, whom he had married on March 29, 1920, Rosenzweig retired to his attic apartment on Schumanstrasse in Frankfurt which he was never to leave again after the summer of 1922.

Then began a seven-year period not of inactivity and gloomy waiting for death but of remarkable creativity and even of joy in life. His friends and disciples formed a *minyan* (quorum of ten adult males, required for a public prayer service in Judaism) which came together regularly in his room so that he might worship with them on Sabbaths and festivals. At the circumcision of his son, Rafael Nehemiah, born September 8, 1922, and named in honor of his devoted teacher and friend Rabbi Nehemiah Nobel, who had died some months before, Rosenzweig could no longer speak intelligibly and was able to move only with great difficulty, but he observed the ceremony joyfully in his room. A constant stream of friends continued to call on him then and, indeed, until almost the end of his life. The poet Karl Wolfskehl wrote after a visit to him:

Whoever stepped over the threshold of Franz Rosenzweig's room entered a magic circle and fell under a
spell, gentle yet potent—in fact, became himself a
charmed being. The solidity and the familiar forms of
every-day life melted away and the incredible became
the norm. Behind the desk, in the armchair sat, not as
one had imagined on climbing the stairs, a mortally
sick, utterly invalid man, almost totally deprived of
physical force, upon whom salutations were lost and
solace shattered; behind the desk, in the chair, Franz
Rosenzweig was throned. The moment our eyes met his,
community was established. Everything corporeal,
objects as well as voices and their reverberations, became
subject to a new order, were incorporated without strain,
conscious effort, or need for readjustment, into that
wholly genuine, primordially true kind of existence
irradiated by beauty. It simply couldn't have been otherwise, for what reigned here was not pressure and
duress, but utter freedom . . .[20]

At first it had appeared that Rosenzweig's disease would
quickly cause death. But in the fall of 1923, after the
paralysis had destroyed virtually all movement of his
limbs, the progress of the disease was halted before it
reached the organs essential for life. Rosenzweig, who
had looked forward to a speedy death, had to adjust himself to living indefinitely as a total paralytic.

The spring of 1923 brought Rosenzweig one deep satisfaction when Dr. Leo Baeck, a leading Liberal rabbi in
Berlin, carried out the plan, originally conceived by
Rabbi Nehemiah Nobel, of conferring on him the rabbinical title *morenu* (our teacher). This act was kept
secret and not made public until after Rosenzweig's death.

During the first months of his illness Rosenzweig continued to direct the work of the *Lehrhaus* and, indeed,
to lecture but, as speech became increasingly difficult and
finally impossible for him, he had to give up the latter
activity and turned to writing. At first he was able himself to work on the special typewriter that was constructed
for him, but later on he had to point out the characters
with his left hand while someone else, most often his wife,
operated the keyboard.

Even before his paralysis Rosenzweig had abandoned his

stated purpose to write no more books. Shortly after the
appearance in 1921 of *The Star of Redemption*, he was
invited by a German publisher to present the philosophy
of that massive and complex work in a more popular
fashion. Rosenzweig accepted the invitation and the
result was a manuscript, written in July 1921, which he
entitled *Das Büchlein vom gesunden und kranken Menschenverstand* (The Little Book of Healthy and Sick
Human Reason). In this work the follower of Idealist
philosophy is portrayed as a paralytic patient who is
cured by exposure to "the New Thinking" based on
"common sense" or healthy, uncorrupted reason. Having
completed the work, Rosenzweig, however, was not altogether happy with something that he had written not
out of inner compulsion but "to order," and after some
weeks of vacillation, decided to withdraw the manuscript,
at the same time giving carbon copies to a few friends.
It was not until 1954 that *Das Büchlein* was published in
English translation under the title *Understanding the Sick
and the Healthy*, with a fine introduction by Nahum N.
Glatzer.[21]

Illness drove Rosenzweig back to writing, despite the
agonizing difficulties entailed by his physical condition.
In 1922 and 1923 he worked on a translation, with notes
and an epilogue on the art of translating, of sixty hymns
and poems of Jehudah Halevi, the great eleventh century
Spanish-Jewish poet-philosopher.[22] In the summer of 1923
he wrote "Die Bauleute" (The Builders), an essay in the
form of an open letter to Martin Buber, on the place of
the law in Judaism. In this essay he took strong exception
to his friend's view of Halakhah and urged the adoption
of a more serious and responsible attitude toward the legal
tradition of Judaism. That same year he also wrote an
extensive introduction to the *Jüdische Schriften* (Collected
Jewish Writings) of his deceased teacher and friend
Hermann Cohen, and in 1925 the very important essay
"Das neue Denken" (The New Thinking).[23]

In the spring of 1925, when his paralysis had already
lasted three years and had long since destroyed his powers
of speech and bodily movement, Rosenzweig embarked on
the great enterprise of collaboratng with Martin Buber
on a new German translation of the Hebrew Bible which
would be faithful to the spirit and style of the original.

Buber later described their method of collaboration. "I translated and sent the sheets of the first version, mostly in chapters, to Rosenzweig. His replies comprised reservations, references, suggested changes. I immediately incorporated those that struck me at once as being good. We discussed the rest by correspondence, and whatever remained controversial we discussed during my Wednesday visits."[24] By the time of Rosenzweig's death, the two friends had finished the translation through the Book of Isaiah. The last books were later completed by Buber working alone. The entire work has been widely acclaimed as the greatest German translation of the Bible since Martin Luther's.

In the last months of 1929 Rosenzweig's life force was slowly ebbing away. On the afternoon of December 9 he managed painfully to communicate to his wife the unfinished sentence: ". . . and now it comes, the point of all points, which God had truly revealed to me in my sleep; the point of all points for which there . . ." He died at two o'clock the next morning and was buried in Frankfurt. Following his instructions, there was no eulogy at his funeral, but Martin Buber read the Seventy-Third Psalm, containing the verse which Rosenzweig had asked be inscribed on his headstone:

> Nevertheless I am continually with Thee;
> Thou holdest my right hand.

II

Rosenzweig regarded his philosophy as based on a new way of thinking, very different from the *philosophia perennia* of the Western tradition. In the introduction to *The Star of Redemption*, as well as in his essay "Das neue Denken" (The New Thinking), he described this philosophy as diametrically opposed to the whole philosophic tradition which was inaugurated by Thales in Greece in the sixth century B.C. and culminated with Hegel in Germany in the nineteenth century. Most of the great philosophers "from Ionia to Jena" were monists, concerned with discovering the one "essence" of all things, whether this be water, as Thales believed, or Spirit, as Hegel thought. As far as the three fundamental entities which,

according to Rosenzweig, sound "common sense" directly
perceives in experience—God, world and man—are concerned, philosophy has steadfastly declined to accept their
independent reality and distinctiveness. In its view, all
these "must 'really' be quite different from what they
seem." If this were not so, "if they were really only what
they are, then philosophy—God forbid!—would finally be
superfluous."[25] Thus the "cosmological" philosophy of
ancient Greece (and of modern naturalism) derived God
and man from the world; the "theological" Middle Ages
derived man and world from God, and the "anthropological" modern era, especially in the form of philosophical
Idealism, has tended to derive God and world from consciousness, hence from man.

Idealism, which is the culmination of this entire philosophic stream, posited, along with the unity of being, a
unity of thought which is capable of fully comprehending
all being because being is based upon thought. In the
completely developed Idealism of Hegel all reality is
founded upon consciousness, not the consciousness of
individual persons but "consciousness in general" (*Bewusstsein überhaupt*). Against this fundamental principle
of Idealism Rosenzweig's New Thinking represents a decisive rebellion. God, world and man, he insisted, are
three separate and irreducible entities, given in experience, which thought does not produce but which it must
rather accept as given and seek to understand.[26]

Rosenzweig also protested against the tendency of
Idealism to devaluate and, indeed, to deny the reality of
particular men in favor of "man in general" and of particular consciousness in favor of "consciousness in general." He recognized that a revolt had been brewing against
this tendency throughout the nineteenth century. Schopenhauer, in raising the question of the *value* of the world
to the individual man rather than its *essence*, dealt the
first blow to the traditional philosophy. Nietzsche followed
him in passionately defending the rights of the individual
soul. And Kierkegaard found the "Archimedean fulcrum"
to contest the sham Hegelian reconciliation of philosophy
and Christian revelation, and the inclusion of revelation in
the Whole, in his own personal situation: ". . . Sören
Kierkegaard's—or that of anyone else with a first name and

a surname—consciousness of his own sin and his own redemption, which neither required nor was capable of dissolution in the cosmos."27

Rosenzweig's own rebellion against the Idealist submergence of individual personality, however, appears to have been motivated primarily by his consciousness of the fact of death, a consciousness no doubt intensified by his personal experiences in the war. Death is the most particular of realities; only the single individual can die. Man is never more conscious of his individuality than when he is threatened by death with the loss of it. Idealist philosophy tries to quiet the individual's fear of death and to console him by assuring him that he is part of the Whole and that the Whole can never die. But this proffered consolation is felt by the particular person as worse than the fear it seeks to allay.

> Though man crawl like a worm into the folds of the naked earth before the whirring missiles of blind, inexorable death; though he there experience violently and inevitably what he otherwise never has experienced: that his *I* would become only an *It* if he died; and though he therefore protest his *I* with every cry still in his throat against the inexorable from which such unthinkable destruction threatens him—philosophy smiles its empty smile at all this distress and points out with extended finger, for the creature whose members shake with anxiety for its *here*, a *beyond* of which it does not wish to know anything. For man does not at all wish to escape from any fetters; he wishes to remain, he wishes—to live. Philosophy, which extols death to him as its special protégé and as the grand opportunity of escaping the narrowness of life, appears only to mock him.28

Man cannot and does not wish to become free of the anxiety of death in this way; he must reject all theories which deny his individuality in order to still that anxiety. He, with his own experiences, with his particular sufferings and the threat of mortality that hangs over him, wishes to be and to live as a unique person, not as a part of the total world process.

From this Rosenzweig drew the conclusion that only that philosophy which derives from the unique, subjective thought and experience of the individual person is ultimately meaningful. As he put it in a letter to Rudolf Stahl in 1927:

I really think that a philosophy, if it wishes to be true, must be philosophized from the actual standpoint of the philosophizing person. There is no possibility of being objective other than by honestly proceeding from one's own subjectivity. The duty of being objective requires only that one really survey the whole horizon, not that one look out from a standpoint other than that on which he is standing, or even from "no standpoint at all." One's own eyes are certainly only one's own eyes; but it would be foolish to think that one must pluck them out in order rightly to see.[29]

Such subjectivism obviously laid Rosenzweig open to the charge that it would destroy the one universal truth *quod semper ubique et ab omnibus creditum est*. He did not flinch from accepting the charge. Ultimate truth may be one, but it is one only for God.[30] For men, truth must necessarily be various and manifold, and "the" truth must be one's "personal" truth. Human truth cannot be what "is" eternally and universally true, but rather what is "made truth," verified (*bewährt*) in the actual life of the person who professes it.

The concept of "making" truth true (*Bewährung*) is the fundamental concept of the new theory of knowledge . . . and in the place of the static concept of objectivity a dynamic one is introduced . . . From those most unimportant truths, truths of the type "two times two are four," to which men agree easily without making more than a very small use of their brains—a little less for the simple multiplication table, a little more for the theory of relativity—the way leads to those truths for which man is willing to pay something, on to those which he cannot prove true (*bewähren*) except with the sacrifice of his life, and finally to those whose truth can be proven only by the staking of the lives of all the generations.[31]

This "messianic theory of truth," as Rosenzweig called it,[32] emphasizes decision, commitment, daring, the willingness to take great risks. It is, as Will Herberg has pointed out,[33] identical with what Emil Brunner meant when he spoke of "knowledge of faith" as being "not theoretical knowledge but 'existential' knowledge, that is, knowledge of such a kind that it is only fully realized as practical decision and wholly excludes the attitude of a mere spectator." Rosenzweig adds that his messianic theory of truth cannot lead beyond the forever irreconcilable hopes of Judaism and Christianity for the Messiah, the one awaiting a Messiah who is to come and the other one who is to return; the ultimate truth here can be verified only by God.[34] As far as individual human truths are concerned, these can be verified—and then only in part—at the time of death, which Rosenzweig elsewhere described as "the ultimate verification of life."[35]

Rosenzweig was aware, however, that his subjective and individualistic theory of verification, of "making true" by commitment and staking one's life on one's commitment, did not really answer the question of how one can pass from subjective truth to objective truth. "Where," he asked in *The Star*, "is to be found that connecting bridge between extreme subjectivity—one might say, deaf-blind selfhood—and the luminous clarity of infinite objectivity?"[36] And his answer there was that this bridge between supreme subjectivity and supreme objectivity is formed only by the theological idea of revelation, for only man as receiver of revelation has both of these in himself. The philosopher must simultaneously be a theologian in order to understand eternal truth, such as it is *in itself*, as truth for us.[37]

The New Thinking, as Rosenzweig described it, is distinguished from traditional philosophy not only by its theories of knowledge and truth but by the fact that it takes time seriously. At the head of his *Das Büchlein vom gesunden und kranken Menschenverstand*, Rosenzweig placed the well-known lines from Goethe's *Westöstlicher Diwan:*

> Why is truth so woefully
> Removed? To depths of secret banned?
> None understands in time! If we

> But understood betimes, how bland
> The truth would be, how fair to see!
> How near and ready to our hand![38]

Traditional philosophy has sought to understand reality independently of time, to comprehend the universe *sub specie aeternitatis*. This, Rosenzweig insisted, was a fundamental error. Cognition is strictly bound to time; it cannot make its past something that is not already over or its future something that is not yet to be. As Rosenzweig put it, "one cannot begin a conversation with the end, or a war with a peace treaty (as the pacifists would like) or life with death."[39] Strict attention to the sequences of temporality that are involved in any phenomenon and that are not interchangeable is of the essence in arriving at any adequate understanding of it. This is also true of those ultimate matters with which religion is concerned. "What God has done, what He is doing, what He will do; what has happened to the world and will happen to it; what has happened to man and what he will do—all this cannot be disengaged from its connection with time . . ."[40] God, man and the world cannot be grasped timelessly or independently of one another. They reveal their true being only in their temporal relationships to each other, those relationships which, as we shall see, Rosenzweig describes as Creation, Revelation and Redemption.

Since the New Thinking takes serious cognizance of time, it must, Rosenzweig held, follow that method which he characterized as "speech thinking" (*Sprachdenken*) or "grammatical thinking," as distinguished from "logical thinking." In logical thinking, which has been the method of traditional philosophy, the thinker has no genuine partner. He thinks for, and speaks to, "no one but himself" or "every one" (in this context, these are equivalent). But speech thinking means, Rosenzweig maintained, "speaking to some one and thinking for some one; and this some one is always a quite definite some one, and has not merely ears, like 'all the world' (*die Allgemeinheit*), but also a mouth."[41] Speech thinking is a genuine dialogue, not that kind of dialogue in the form of which Plato cast his philosophical essays but a real conversation with a real partner in which something unforeseen may happen.

The course of such a conversation cannot be anticipated; neither partner knows in advance all that he himself or the other may say. A speaker may find himself saying or discovering, in response to his partner in the dialogue, things he had not known before. This kind of speaking may thus be a form of revelation, and Rosenzweig urged that men speak and think in this way, especially, though not exclusively, about the ultimate problems of human existence.

When *The Star of Redemption* was written, this philosophy of "speech thinking" or "dialogue" was still little known. Rosenzweig himself[42] declared that it was Ludwig Feuerbach[43] who first discovered it. He found it also in Hermann Cohen's posthumously published *Die Religion der Vernunft aus den Quellen des Judentums*, in which the great philosopher, overcoming his Idealist orientation, outlined his concept of "correlation" between man and God and between man and man. The greatest influence on *The Star*, however, Rosenzweig admitted,[44] was his friend Eugen Rosenstock's *Angewandte Seelenkunde*, which he had read in draft form a year and a half before beginning his own work. Writing in 1925, Rosenzweig called attention to several other works which had appeared after *The Star* and expounded the same philosophy, among them Hans Ehrenberg's *Fichte* and Rudolf Ehrenberg's *Theoretische Biologie* and, most importantly, Martin Buber's *Ich und Du* and Ferdinand Ebner's *Das Wort und die geistigen Realitäten*.[45] Apparently some of the foremost figures in German philosophy of that generation were independently working along the same lines and tending toward similar conclusions.

Rosenzweig himself had applied the New Thinking to theological problems, and he recognized that his friends and colleagues who had been developing a similar methodology had also been motivated, at least in part, by religious concerns. It need not, however, he insisted, be restricted to theological problems; it can and does deal with general philosophical problems, the problems of logic, ethics and aesthetics. He himself rejected any exclusively theological method. Philosophy and theology both require regeneration through the New Thinking, and the two disciplines need each other.

Theology must not degrade philosophy to the part of a housemaid, but the role of charwoman which philosophy has become accustomed in recent times to assign to theology is just as degrading. The true relationship of these two renewed sciences is a sisterly one . . . and this must lead to a personal union of their bearers. Theological problems must be translated into human terms, and human problems brought into the theological. The problem of the name of God, for instance, is only a part of the logical problem of names in general; and an aesthetic that gives no thought to the question whether artists can be saved is a polite but incomplete science.[46]

From the outline here given of Rosenzweig's New Thinking, its affinity with the philosophical movement developing in his time and already beginning to be called existentialism, and particularly with the thought of Martin Heidegger, is apparent.[47] Heidegger's basic insistence that being in general (*Sein*) can only be approached from the radically isolated, definite and eminent being which is always I, myself,[48] and that general ontology requires a "fundamental" ontology, i.e., an analysis of actual existence (*Dasein*), is paralleled by Rosenzweig's contention that the true starting point for knowledge of the Whole or of being in general must be, not abstract thought, but something real and simple, "man in the plainest sense 'who still exists,'" a concept of "*pure factuality*" (*Tatsachlichkeit*),[49] or, as he also puts it, "I quite ordinary private subject, I first and last name, I dust and ashes, I am still in existence. And I philosophize . . ."[50]

Both thinkers also find in death the supreme manifestation of man's irreducible individuality. The awareness of death is, as we have seen, the starting point of *The Star of Redemption*, and it lies at the very heart of *Being and Time*. To be sure, Rosenzweig's philosophical theology does not end with death but moves through an understanding of Creation, Revelation and Redemption to "eternal life" and "eternal truth," while Heidegger's atheism recognizes only man's "freedom toward death" and temporal, existential truths, regarding belief in eternalities as the residue of an outmoded Christian theology. Nevertheless, both thinkers rebel against the Idealist disregard of the overwhelming reality of individual death.

Rosenzweig and Heidegger both further reject the traditional philosophic concern with timeless "essence" and seek to understand the meaning of the term "is" in temporal, historical terms. Both insist that everything, including thought, is inevitably time-bound. This being so, Rosenzweig urged, as we have noted, that the method of philosophy must be "grammatical" or "speech" thinking, which is sustained in time and nourished by time. Heidegger himself developed a whole new philosophical vocabulary based on temporality. Such terms as *alltäglich* (everyday), *jeweils* (at any given time), *schon immer* (already and always), *zunächst* (first of all), *im voraus* (beforehand) and many other temporal words are central in the analysis of *Being and Time*. But, whereas Rosenzweig emphasizes that "speech thinking" requires a real dialogical partner with whom one enters into a mutual relationship, Heidegger's philosophy, as Karl Löwith has pointed out, "knows the second person only in the levelled form of the 'other' person, but not as my partner or as the thou belonging to an I."[51] And, of course, Rosenzweig's contention that man's ego is in the beginning veiled in itself and dumb, waiting to be called into full being not only subsequently and indirectly by his neighbor but primordially and directly by the voice of God, in responding to which man expresses his awareness of having found his place in relation to both God and the world,[52] finds no parallel in Heidegger's thought.

III

Of the rich variety of subjects with which Rosenzweig dealt in *The Star of Redemption* space here permits only a brief discussion of the central themes of Creation, Revelation and Redemption. These theological categories are the names Rosenzweig gave to the processes whereby God, world and man (which, as we have seen, are for him the three fundamental and irreducible entities discovered in experience) enter into mutual relationships with each other. The two triads, God-World-Man and Creation-Revelation-Redemption, when combined, form the figure of a six-pointed star, the figure which suggested to Rosenzweig the title for his major work.

In the view of the ancient Greeks, whose thought represents the highest intellectual achievement of the pagan world, each of the three basic elements encountered in experience was regarded, according to Rosenzweig, as a separate entity, entirely independent of the two others. For the Greeks the world was a plastic cosmos, self-caused and self-subsistent, without beginning and without end, and having no intrinsic relationship either to the gods or to man. Man himself was portrayed in the Greek theater as the tragic hero, whose greatness lies in his existing in his special nature and whose fate is the alienation and isolation in which he is enclosed. And the gods of Greek mythology were conceived as living apart in a separate realm of their own, venturing only occasionally to intervene in the affairs of the world and of men.[53] This pagan view of the world was, according to Rosenzweig, a true one, but in a veiled, unrevealed state. Only the revolutionary proclamation of Biblical faith, which came to be incorporated in Judaism and Christianity, binds the three entities together, for it views the world as the creation of God, brings man and God into relationship in the act of revelation, and connects man and the world in the process of redemption.

Creation, for Rosenzweig, is not only an event of the past but an ongoing process whereby God, as the Jewish Prayer Book puts it, "renews every day the works of creation."[54] This does not mean that the world is an emanation, in the neo-Platonic sense, of an impersonal Godhead, or that its existence is renewed at every single moment; it means rather that the world is not self-subsistent but has its ground in God. With the Biblical affirmation of creation, the world, according to Rosenzweig, awoke to a consciousness of its creatureliness. It became aware that it was not a completed being but a continuous becoming and that the general causality of nature—its immanent *logos*, as Rosenzweig puts it—requires the external actuality of God to preserve it in being. In God's eternal creative activity Rosenzweig saw a manifestation of His non-arbitrary will. God's power is such that it must express itself in creation, but in this power God's freedom is contained.[55]

Just as the world as a whole becomes aware of its creatureliness and total dependence upon God, so does man, who, in his natural existence, is part of the world. Man, however, experiences not only his dependence upon God but God's love for him, and out of this comes to understand God as simultaneously omnipotent Creator and loving Father.[56] Rosenzweig's strong emphasis on human creatureliness, it may be noted, did not lead him to any view of man's depravity or worthlessness in the sight of God. Though God is infinite and eternal and man finite and transient, man experiences himself not as nothing before God but as one whom God regards as worthy of His love and concern.

Creation, for Rosenzweig, is fulfilled in revelation. God's bringing the world into existence and sustaining it does not immediately relate Him to his human creatures. This occurs only in His turning toward men in love, and this turning on God's part and man's knowledge of it is, in Rosenzweig's understanding, the essence of revelation. Revelation, while completing creation, is itself grounded in it. The experience of God's love would be only the experience of single, isolated individuals, if it were not that God is the Creator upon whom all existence depends. Awareness that he is the object of divine love saves man from his primordial loneliness and breaks down the isolation in which he, as an individual ego, is originally enclosed by awakening in him the urge to love God in return. Julius Guttmann correctly interprets Rosenzweig's conception of the effect of revelation on man when he writes:

> Thus the primary religious experience brings about a fundamental change in the nature of man. The man of faith is different from what he was before the encounter of faith. Despite the apparent similarity, the nature of this change in man by reason of his encounter with God is totally different from the conversion process of Pauline Christianity. The change does not lie in the freeing of man from the bondage of sin; and it does not demand that man fight continually against the grain of his natural impulses. The selfhood of man; the rigorous obligation that man's ego determine his character—are not sins; and the change in man does not include the

fact that he must battle against the tendencies and impulses of his nature, but that he direct them toward new goals. The rebellion of man's ego is transformed by divine love into faithfulness, which man gives as a response to God, and he maintains his love of God with all his strength.[57]

Through God's love for him and his answering love for God man overcomes his isolation and dumbness and becomes a true person capable of speaking and of responding to God's first commandment, which is to love others. Man's experience of the divine love releases in him the power to love his fellowman and to perform for him the works of love in fulfillment of this commandment.[58] And it is, Rosenzweig emphasized, a *commandment*, felt as addressed directly to the individual in the experience of divine love, and not a *law*, understood as an objective, universally binding obligation. Man responds to it authentically not by considering with his reason, as a philosophic ethic would prescribe, whom he should love and how and what the results may be, but rather by doing spontaneously what is demanded by the situation of the person whom he has encountered at this given moment and whom God has prepared for him to love.

Revelation, for Rosenzweig, is not, then, an event of the past in which God is believed to have delivered moral or ritual prescriptions to some person or group of persons. It is rather the individual's experience, which may occur at any moment, of the divine love and of the sense of responsibility toward his fellowmen that flows from it. The content of revelation is nothing more and nothing less than the presence of God. As Rosenzweig put it in a note on a poem by Jehudah Halevi,

All that God ever reveals in revelation is—revelation. Or, to express it differently, He reveals nothing but Himself to man. The relation of this accusative and dative to each other is the one and only content of revelation. Whatever does not follow directly from this covenant between God and man, whatever cannot prove its direct bearing on this covenant, cannot be a part of it. The problem has not been *solved* for the visionary who beheld the vision; it has been *dissolved*.[59]

It must, however, be noted that once Rosenzweig had married, established a home of his own, and committed himself to the fullest possible observance of the traditional law of Judaism, that law which orthodoxy held to be divinely revealed, he came to have a somewhat broader understanding of revelation than he had when he was elaborating the philosophical theology of *The Star of Redemption*. The law itself, he made clear in his famous letter of 1923 to Martin Buber which he entitled "Die Bauleute," had become of immense importance in his own religious life, as it had been in the life of the Jewish people throughout history. He described it as

the law of millennia, studied and lived, analyzed and rhapsodized, the law of every day and of the day of death, petty and yet sublime, sober and yet woven in legend; a law which knows both the fire of the Sabbath candle and that of the martyr's stake; the law Akiba planted and fenced in, and Aher trampled under, the cradle Spinoza hailed from, the ladder on which the Baal Shem ascended, the law that always rises beyond itself, that can never be reached—and yet has always the possibility of becoming Jewish life, of being expressed in Jewish faces.[60]

To be sure, Rosenzweig agreed with Buber that God is not a law-giver, but he insisted that God does command and that the precepts of the Halakhah are to be seen as the historical product of His commandment to the people of Israel that they love Him and their fellowmen. More specifically, Rosenzweig saw observance of the Halakhah as the "acting-out" by the Jew of his belief in the divine election of Israel and its "separation," to employ the terminology of the Bible, "as a kingdom of priests and a holy nation" (Exodus 19:6). "The law as a whole," he wrote, "is connected with being chosen, the law whereby divine election is transformed into human electing, and the passivity of being called and set apart is transformed into the activity of performing the deed which sets apart."[61]

Rosenzweig did not share the orthodox view that the traditional 613 precepts of the Torah are the eternal prescription of God, given to Israel through Moses on Mount Sinai. The law, in his view, was not meant to be unchanging and eternal; it was to be a living, growing process. Orthodoxy had erred in congealing the Halakhah into the fixed paragraphs of the *Shulhan Aruch* and other legal codes. For the Jew of today, Rosenzweig urged, observance of the traditional law must become a personal, existential, freely chosen act. The corpus of the Halakhah confronts the Jew as *Gesetz*, as law, but to be religiously meaningful, its particular prescriptions must become *Gebot*, that is, commandment felt as personally addressed to the individual. God commands, but "in his inertia or indolence (*Trägheit*) man changes the commandments (*Geboten*) by the way he observes them, into law (*Gesetz*), into something systematized, without the realization that he stands under God's commandment, without the awareness that 'I am the Lord,' without 'fear and trembling.' "[62] This process, Rosenzweig held, must be reversed. "Law (*Gesetz*) must again become commandment (*Gebot*) which seeks to be transformed into deed at the very moment it is heard. It must regain that living reality (*Heutigkeit*) in which all great Jewish periods have sensed the guarantee for its eternity."[63]

For this to happen, the individual Jew must choose. He must discover what precepts of the traditional law he, as an individual, is able to fulfill.

> What counts here . . . is not our will but our ability to act. Here . . . the decisive thing is the selection which our ability—without regard to our will—makes out of the wealth of the possible deeds. Since this selection does not depend on the will but on our ability, it is a very personal one . . . whether much is done, or little, or maybe nothing at all, is immaterial in the face of the one and unavoidable demand: that whatever is being done shall come from that inner power. As the knowledge of everything knowable is not yet wisdom, so the doing of everything do-able is not yet deed. The deed is created at the boundary of the merely do-able, where the voice of the commandment causes the spark to leap from "I must" to "I can."[64]

Though one person can and should teach another in this realm, he cannot decide for another what the latter can do, nor may he reproach him for his inability to do something. "Only *I* know what *I* can do . . . And perhaps another's nonability does more for the upbuilding of both teaching and law than my own ability."[65] For himself, Rosenzweig, once embarked on the responsible quest (which he urged all Jews to undertake) of discovering what elements of the traditional Halakhah were personally do-able, found that more and more of them were and that through them he could sense the presence of the self-revealing God who not only loves man in general and commands him but also loves Israel in particular and commands it to be a holy people, consecrated to this service.

While Rosenzweig eventually so broadened his concept of revelation as to include in it the historical experience of the Jewish people as a community of love and also, in some sense, the traditional law of Judaism, he never changed his conviction that revelation yielded no knowledge of God's essence or of the nature of the divine life. As far as he was concerned, it provided only the assurance of God's existence in its relation to man, "That God loves, this we experience, not that God is love . . . Only that He is God do we experience in His love, but not what He is. The what, the essence, remains hidden."[66]

The human power to love, which, as we have seen, was held by Rosenzweig to be aroused in man by the awareness that he is the beloved of God, is the instrument of redemption in its first stages. Following the affirmation of the Song of Songs, "For love is strong as death," Rosenzweig ascribed to love and to the deeds of love a capacity for transcending the finitude and mortality which are the heritage of man as a temporal creature. In the deed of love the passing moment is endowed with the quality of eternity.

Love, Rosenzweig held, is a redemptive power not only in the life of the individual but also in the associations which the individual enters or in which he finds himself, such as marriage, or the family, or the state. Marriage, for example, is reducible either to a relationship based on biological urges or to a legal, contractual relationship; but when the association of two persons in marriage is filled with love, it becomes something of an altogether different order, a relationship in which the partners experience the highest degree of closeness possible for human beings.

Into other associations as well, even those with an economic or political basis, love may enter, generating new powers within men. Essentially, human redemption is the intensification of the power to love and the application of it to every realm of human existence.[67]

But it is not only man who is redeemed by love; the world as a whole, according to Rosenzweig, is similarly redeemed. In his pan-psychic view, the world, though not actually everywhere alive, is potentially so, and it is love that is charged with changing the potentiality into actuality. "The world must become wholly alive. Instead of merely individual burning points of life, like raisins in a cake, the entire world must come alive. Existence must be alive at every one of its points. That it is not yet so means no more than that the world is still not finished."[68] Man, through his deeds of love, can affect the world and bring its dormant life into activity only because both he and the world are the creatures of God.[69]

In its preliminary stages redemption means the progressive improvement of the quality of human life and society, as well as the natural world, through the power of man's love. But in redemption in its final stage, Rosenzweig believed (strangely enough), the existence of man and the world is negated and God alone is left to perfect Himself. "Man and the world disappear in Redemption, but God completes Himself. Only in Redemption does God become that which the carelessness of human thought has always everywhere sought, everywhere affirmed, and yet nowhere found, because it was still nowhere to be found, since it did not yet exist: the All and the One."[70] In redemption at the end of time God the Creator and the Revealer becomes, for Rosenzweig, the pantheistic God in whom all things are included and who has no relationships to man and the world. "Redemption frees Him (God) from the work of creation . . . Redemption is His day of rest, His great Sabbath . . ."[71] Then God is "freed from His own Word; He is silent."[72] Redemption thus means, according to Rosenzweig, the completion of the flowing circle of reality. Reality now becomes an undifferentiated unity of being; everything is swallowed up in the one absolute God.

It is odd that Rosenzweig, who began *The Star of*

Redemption with such a powerful polemic against the Whole (*das All*) of Idealism and who always insisted so strongly on the separate reality of man, world and God and the irreducibility of the first two of these to the third, should have conceived the final redemption in this way. Apparently here, as in other aspects of his thought, the Hegelianism in which he had been so deeply steeped in his youth, but against which he consciously struggled, crept in disguised and unnoticed form into his mind.

IV

Having once been so deeply attracted by Christianity that he was on the point of accepting it as his personal faith, Rosenzweig never abandoned his concern with understanding the Christian faith and with defining its relationship to Judaism. Major stages in the development of his thought on this subject are reflected in his letter to Rudolf Ehrenberg, written in 1913 to communicate his decision to remain a Jew, and in his correspondence with Eugen Rosenstock in 1916.

Already by 1913, as a result of his historical and philosophical studies, Rosenzweig had adopted the view that the history of Europe from the early fourth century (Constantine) on was the history of its progressive Christianization, and this not only in the political and sociological sense but in the spiritual and intellectual as well. Philosophy, the legacy of pagan Greece, had been absorbed into Christianity. Medieval scholasticism had adopted it and transformed it to Christian uses. The founders of modern philosophical thought, Descartes, Spinoza and Leibnitz, were no longer pagans outside the Church but heretics within it, and Kant, Fichte, Schelling and Hegel in fact considered themselves (rightly so, in Rosenzweig's view) Christian philosophers. Indeed Hegel, for Rosenzweig, was at one and the same time the last of the philosophers and the first of the new Church Fathers, i.e., of that Church which, following the tradition of Joachim of Floris and of nineteenth century German Idealism, he called the Church of the Holy Spirit or the Johannine Church. The emergence of this Church he saw as coinciding with the French Revolution and its movement as tending toward the development of a free, undogmatic, humanitarian, universalist Christian society.[73]

On this view, the question which Rosenzweig had to face in his discussions with Rosenstock in 1913 was, What place is there for Judaism in a world in which Christianity has been the fundamental motive force for centuries and is now (as he believed) on the verge of its universal triumph? For a time, apparently, he believed the answer was, none; and it was then that he reached his decision to be baptized. But once he found himself affirming his inherited religious tradition, he had to justify the continued existence of Judaism and the Jewish people.

In his letter to Rudolf Ehrenberg announcing that he was and would remain a Jew, Rosenzweig used the symbolism of the medieval sculptured figures of the Church and Synagogue, such as those found in the cathedrals at Bamberg, Freiburg and Strasbourg, to present his conception of the continuing function of the Synagogue and of its relationship to the Church. In these figures, to which repeated reference is made in his letters, the Synagogue is portrayed with her eyes covered with bandages and carrying a broken staff, while the Church, with a crown on her head and a scepter in her hand, has "her eyes open to the world, a fighter certain of triumph." The Church is, indeed, triumphant and on its way to ultimate victory in its mission of bringing the pagan peoples to God, Rosenzweig explained, but it needs the Synagogue, whose people already know God and have known Him from the beginning, for it is only the Synagogue, uninvolved in history and its ambiguities, stubbornly living its inner and separate life, and with a covering over its eyes, that can see "with the prophetic eye of inner vision the last and most distant things." The Synagogue already knows the *eschaton*, the final fulfillment to which divine Redemption will ultimately bring the entire world, and it serves the Church by warning it against mistaking any partial and preliminary fulfillment for the final one. Furthermore, Rosenzweig held, the Church, which directs itself to the conversion of the pagans, "is always in danger of having the vanquished give laws to it" and of losing itself "in what is common to all men." Against this danger it is protected by the Synagogue, for

. . . whenever the Church forgets that it is a scandal and wishes to become reconciled with what is "common to all men" (something that would be highly welcome to the Greeks, who, like a certain emperor, would gladly build a statue to Christ also in the temple of their gods), the Church finds in the Synagogue the silent monitor, who, unseduced by what is common to all men, knows only of the scandal.

According to Rosenzweig, the Synagogue denies the world, while the Church affirms it.

But the Synagogue accepts the suffering of denying the world for the sake of the same final hope for which the Church accepts the suffering of affirming the world . . . Since the roots of this hope, the God of all *time*, here and beyond, spring from a common source, and the revelation of the Old Testament is common to both of us, the Church and the Synagogue depend on one another.[74]

In his wartime correspondence with Rosenstock, Rosenzweig developed further his understanding of the mission of Judaism (or the Synagogue) and its relation to the Christian Church. While denying that he was possessed of any *rabies theologica*, Rosenstock had fulminated in vehement language in one of his letters to Rosenzweig against the exclusiveness of Israel's claim to divine election and against the withdrawal of the Synagogue from activity in the world.

The Synagogue has been talking for two thousand years about what it has because it already has nothing, but it does not experience, and therefore will never experience what it is. It portrays the curse of self-assurance, of pride in nobility, and of thoughtless indifference toward the law of growth of the united cosmos, the "peace on earth to all men in whom he is well-pleased." Of that new humanity out of universal need and sin, of that ever newly born *corpus christianum* of all men of good will, of that "being called out from all the peoples," it knows nothing. It knows a causal union of blood, of the chosen people, but no final union of all the children of the Father. They (the Jews) have the saying that some day all the peoples will come to Jerusalem to pray, and they ever again crucify him who came to make the word true. In appearance they wait for the word of the Lord, but they have become so thoroughly without revelation that they do everything they can to hinder its reality. With all the power of their being they set themselves against their own promises. They are the copy on earth of Lucifer, the chief of the angels, chosen of God, who wanted to keep God's gift completely to himself as a power belonging to him by right, and fell. So Judea insists upon its own inalienable right. This naive way of believing that one has inalienable and perpetual rights against God, which "by nature" remain for posterity as properties inherited by bequest, is the blind antiquity in Judaism . . . You may well believe that you have your own ship. But you do not know the sea at all, or you would not talk that way. You do not know any shipwreck; you cannot go astray; you see God always with the same clarity, and so you need no mediator who looks at you when you, frustrated in failure, can no longer look out over the edge of the world. You do not know that the world is movement and change. The Christian says there are day and night. You are so moonstruck that you take the sight of night for the only sight there is, and take the minimum of light, the night, for the all-inclusive idea that embraces day *and* night! *Lasciavate ogni speranza; nondum viventes jam renuntiavistis.*[75]

Rosenzweig understood that, to an outsider, Judaism must, indeed, appear as Rosenstock saw it—sterile, stubborn, withdrawn, prideful in its unshakeable consciousness of being the faith of the people chosen by God, unconcerned with the salvation of men and with the sweep of universal life and history. And he also recognized that it was not possible for him to give his correspondent his own, very different, inside view of it.

I notice . . . that everything I now would have to write to you is something that I cannot express to you. For now I should have to show you Judaism from within, that is, in a hymnic way, just as you can show me, the outsider, Christianity; and for the same reason that you can do it, I can not. Christianity has its soul in its externals; Judaism has on the outside only its hard, protecting shell, and one can speak of its soul only from within . . .[76]

To the validity of his friend's comparison of Abraham's sacrifice and Christ's sacrifice, which Rosenstock had declared represented the contrasting "poles" of Judaism and Christianity, Rosenzweig, however, strenuously objected. Rosenstock had written: "Abraham sacrifices his son; in the New Testament he who brings the covenant with God sacrifices himself. That is the whole difference."[77] Rosenzweig replied:

You rightly grasp the difference in speaking of Moriah and Golgotha. But you have read Genesis 22 badly. You have confused Abraham and Agamemnon. The latter, indeed, sacrificed what he *had* for the sake of something else which he wanted, or, if you please, which he considered it his duty to want. Indeed, he did not himself perform the sacrifice; he only gave it up and stood near by with veiled head. But Abraham did not offer *something*, not *a* child, but his "only" son, and what is more the son of the promise, to sacrifice him to the God of this promise (the traditional Jewish commentary reads this paradox into the text), the meaning of which, according to human understanding, would become impossible through this sacrifice. Not for nothing does this story belong to our highest festivals; it is the prototype of the sacrifice not of one's own individuality (Golgotha), but of existence in one's people, of the "son" and of all future sons (for we *base our claim* before God on this sacrifice or, rather, on this readiness to sacrifice, and indeed on the sacrifice of the father, not of the son, as is so emphasized in the Biblical narrative). The son is given back; he is now only the son of the promise. Nothing else happens; no Ilium falls: only the promise remains firm; the father was ready to sacrifice not for the sake of some Ilium, but "groundlessly." Agamemnon sacrifices something "that he has"; Abraham all that he could be; Christ all that he is.

Yes, this is really, as you say, "the whole difference."
To the "naive" laying claim to an inalienable right
before God corresponds, you forget, the equally "naive"
taking up of a yoke of inalienable sufferings, of which
we—"naively?"—know that they are laid upon us (the
traditional commentary on Isaiah 53) "for the redemption of the world." (Lucifer? Please do not mix up the
symbols!) On the contrary, to the holy restlessness of
your work corresponds in us a holy dread that the
redemption might not come 'before the time.' . . .[78]

In another letter Rosenzweig replied to his friend's
charge that the Synagogue was prideful and exclusivist
and reiterated the idea that he had expressed to Rudolf
Ehrenberg several years earlier concerning the indis-
pensability of the Synagogue to the Church.

Your whole portrayal of the Synagogue since A.D. 70
forgets or refuses to admit that we consciously "take
upon ourselves the *yoke* of the Kingdom of Heaven,"
that we *pay a price* for the sin of pride, of walking
without a mediator in the light of God's countenance.
We pay subjectively, through suffering the awareness
of being shut out, of being alienated, and objectively, in
that we are to you the ever admonishing memorial of
your *not yet* (for you who live in an *ecclesia triumphans*
need a mute servant who cries, whenever you *believe*
yourself to have *partaken* of God in bread and wine,
"Master, remember the last things!").[79]

Rosenzweig no doubt had in mind here the story in
Herodotus of how the Persian emperor Xerxes had a
servant to stand behind him at table and cry, "Master,
remember the Athenians!"

To Rosenstock's accusation that Judaism was prideful
in its consciousness of divine election, Rosenzweig admitted that the "pride of the Jew" was, indeed a reality,
but that it was completely justified, insofar as Judaism had
long ago arrived at the goal toward which Christianity
was tending. The metaphysical reason for this pride,
according to Rosenzweig, is based on the following three
points:

(1) that we (Jews) have the truth; (2) that we have *reached* the goal; and (3) that at the bottom of his soul any Jew will consider the Christian's relationship to God, and therefore his religion, really a very poor, meager and roundabout affair. For to the Jew it is incomprehensible that one should need to learn from any one, whoever he may be, what is primary and self-evident to him, namely, to call God our Father.[80]

In *The Star of Redemption* Rosenzweig presented his final and most complete statement on the relationship of Judaism and Christianity. It is a development of the view he had expressed to Rudolf Ehrenberg in 1913. At that time, defending his decision to remain a Jew, he had declared that, while the Christian claim that no one can come to God the Father except through Christ and his Church is generally valid, it does not hold at all in the case of the people of Israel. Israel is already with the Father and has been so from its birth. This people, originally chosen by God, remains chosen until "that last, most distant point" when the Father, "the One and Only," will finally be "All in All." Until that time, Rosenzweig urged, "it is Israel's life-work to anticipate the eternal day in profession and deed, to exist as its living presage, to be a people of priests, to hallow God's name through its own holiness by means of the Law."[81] The Synagogue, he declared, must renounce work in the world and "concentrate all her power on maintaining herself in life and unsullied by life." Consequently, "she leaves the work of the world to the Church and recognizes in her the salvation of all heathens in all time."[82]

In *The Star of Redemption* this conception of the respective roles of the Church and the Synagogue (or Christianity and Judaism) and of their inter-relationship is expanded. Here Judaism is described as the "eternal fire" or "eternal life," while Christianity is the "eternal rays" or the "eternal way." The Jew is born a Jew.[83] He is not so much a believer as belief itself; it is not his faith that makes him Jew but he, as a Jew, creates the faith.[84] Having God within itself, Israel participates in God's eternity, and it assures its immortality by the procreation of successive generations.

"Blessed is He who has planted eternal life in our midst." The fire burns at the center of the star. The rays go forth only from the fire of the core and flow outward unresistedly. The fire of the core must burn ceaselessly. Its flame must forever feed upon itself. It requires no nourishment from without. Time must roll powerlessly over it. It must produce its own time. It must reproduce itself eternally. It must make its life eternal in the succession of generations, in which each produces the generation to come and bears witness to those gone by.[85]

For Rosenzweig, the Jewish people is and must continue to be a people beyond time and beyond history. The cathedral image of the Synagogue as blindfolded is apt insofar as the attention of the Jewish people is fixed on a single goal, the goal of redemption, the fulfillment of time and history. Such a people cannot participate in the struggles of the nations, which strive so relentlessly to preserve their possessions in space and time—their land, their language and their laws—precisely because they, unlike Israel, feel that these are ephemeral and perishable.

The peoples of the world foresee a time when their land with its mountains and rivers will lie beneath the sky as now but other men will dwell in it, when their language will be buried in books, and when their customs and laws will have lost their living power. We alone cannot imagine such a time, for we have long been robbed of all the things in which the peoples of the world anchor their lives. Land, language, custom and law have for us long been separated from the circle of the living and raised to the realm of holiness. But we still live, and live eternally. Our life is no longer interwoven with anything external. Rootless in the earth, we have struck roots in ourselves. Hence we are eternal wanderers, in our own body and blood. And this rootedness in ourselves and only in ourselves guarantees our eternity.[86]

Very different from the position of the Jew is that of the Christian. He is not born but becomes a Christian:

Christianus fit, non nascitur.[87] The Christian Church is not a "biological" entity, as is the Jewish people; it is a community of faith. One becomes a Christian not by birth into a Christian family but through personal faith, through being grasped by Christ, through religious feeling. As the individual is born a pagan and strives to become a Christian, so the Christian Church strives to overcome the paganism of the peoples and to Christianize them. This, indeed, is the God-appointed mission of Christianity or the Church. It is the "rays of the fire" which go forth from the burning core at the center of the Star of Redemption. The Synagogue or Judaism, which turns back on itself and lives in an isolated, transtemporal realm of holiness through observance of the Torah, would leave the world outside itself without knowledge of its God and, hence, without salvation. Therefore God required not only the covenant made at Moriah and renewed at Sinai but also the covenant of Golgotha, and sent Christianity into the world to conquer it and bring all men to the knowledge of Himself. Christianity must, by its nature, be a missionary religion.[88] While Israel "bears witness" to God by "bearing children," by perpetuating its biological existence, the Church bears witness to Him by its mission to the world and its numerical increase.

In Rosenzweig's view, as developed in *The Star of Redemption*, Judaism and Christianity are both authentic and valid expressions of one religious truth; both are paths that really lead to God, and the truth of God can be verified in each. Both have indispensable roles to play in the divine economy of salvation. Neither of them, however, is absolute. Both are human and, therefore, fallible and partial understandings of divine truth. God and God alone is Truth, and the full and absolute truth which is His will becomes manifest only at the end of time, when Redemption in the complete sense will take place. Then, when God will again be what He was in the beginning, All in All, all men will know and live His whole truth and the two paths that have led to Him will merge and become one.[89]

Rosenzweig's view of Christianity represents, despite his claim to the contrary, a radical departure from the classical tradition of Jewish theology. Traditional Jewish thought has tended to regard Christianity as, at best, an approximation to the truth of Judaism. Jehudah Halevi, for example, whom Rosenzweig quotes, held that Christianity was sent into the world to prepare the way for the Messiah, that is, the Messiah awaited by Judaism, not the Messianic Jesus.[90] Though Christianity is a tree overshadowing the earth, it has grown out of the seed of Judaism, and the fruit of the tree must contain the seed again. For Halevi, Christianity was clearly but an instrument to help spread the fuller truth of Judaism. So also Maimonides regarded Christianity (along with Islam) as an instrument in God's plan for the redemption of mankind and spoke of Jesus (and Mohammed) as preparing the way for the Messiah by bringing some knowledge of the Torah to the farthest coasts of the earth.[91] Rosenzweig's position, however, has been properly described as "the first attempt in Jewish theological thought to understand Judaism and Christianity as equally 'true' and valid views of reality."[92] Rosenzweig clearly hoped that this view would lead to an abandonment on the part of the Church of missionary activities directed toward the Jews, but this hope has not been realized.

NOTES

1. Symposium, "The Condition of Jewish Belief," *Commentary*, XLII, August 1966.
2. Steven S. Schwarzschild, *Franz Rosenzweig: Guide of Reversioners*, London, The Education Committee of the Hillel Foundation, 1960, p. 6.
3. See, e.g., Harold Stahmer, *"Speak That I May See Thee": The Religious Significance of Language*, New York, The Macmillan Company, 1968, pp. 149 ff.
4. Ernst Simon and Edith Rosenzweig, eds., *Franz Rosenzweig—Briefe*, Berlin, Schocken Verlag, 1935, p. 277. Rosenzweig's posthumously published letters are an immensely rich source both for his biography and his thought.
5. *Briefe*, p. 658.
6. Alexander Altmann suggests that Rosenzweig meant by this, if he could have split himself into two halves, a religious one and a worldly one. See his "Franz Rosenzweig and Eugen Rosenstock—Huessy: An Introduction to their 'Letters on Judaism and Christianity,'" *The Journal of Religion*, XXIV, 1944, p. 261.
7. *Briefe*, pp. 71–72.
8. *Ibid.*, p. 72.
9. *Ibid.*, p. 70.
10. *Ibid.*, p. 71.
11. *Almanach des Schocken Verlags auf das Jahr 5699*, 1938, p. 60. Quoted in Nahum N. Glatzer, ed., *Franz Rosenzweig—*

His Life and Thought, 2nd rev. ed., New York, Schocken Books, 1961, pp. xix–xx.

12. Rosenzweig, *Der Stern der Erlösung*, Vol. III, pp. 85–86. All references here are to the third edition, Heidelberg, Verlag Lambert Schneider, 1954. Hereafter referred to as *Stern* I, II, III. The translations of all the quotations from this work in the present essay are my own; occasionally they differ in minor respects from the translations of the same passages included in the Selections from Rosenzweig's Writings that follow.

13. The essay is to be found in Rosenzweig, *Kleinere Schriften*, Berlin, Schocken Verlag, 1937.

14. *Briefe*, p. 123.

15. The article was first published in Cohen's journal, *Neue Jüdische Monatsschrift*, at the end of 1917 and again in the spring of 1918.

16. *Briefe*, p. 195.

17. *Ibid.*, p. 319.

18. *Kleinere Schriften*, p. 398.

19. S. Noveck, ed., *Great Jewish Thinkers of the Twentieth Century*, Washington, D.C., B'nai B'rith Department of Adult Jewish Education, 1963, p. 166.

20. *Franz Rosenzweig: Eine Gedenkschrift*, 1930, pp. 35 f. Quoted in Nahum N. Glatzer, ed., *Franz Rosenzweig—His Life and Thought*, p. xxxiv.

21. The book was published by Noonday Press.

22. The work was published under the title *Sechzig Hymnen Und Gedichte des Jehuda Halevi*, Konstanz, 1924. In the second edition of 1927 it was expanded to ninety-two hymns and poems.

23. *Kleinere Schriften*, pp. 373–398.

24. Noveck, *op. cit.*, p. 170.

25. "Das neue Denken," in *Kleinere Schriften*, p. 377. The translations of all the quotations from this work in the present essay are my own; occasionally they differ in minor respects from the translations of the same passages included in the Selections from Rosenzweig's Writings that follow.

26. *Stern*, I, pp. 17 ff. In the third book of *Der Stern der Erlösung* Rosenzweig set forth the idea that the unification of the world and man with God is the final goal of history, but to be realized only at the end of time. Then the world and man will participate in God's absolute eternity.

27. *Stern*, I, p. 12.

28. *Ibid.*, 1, pp. 7–8.

29. *Briefe*, p. 597.

30. "Das neue Denken," *Kleinere Schriften*, p. 396.

31. *Ibid.*, pp. 395–396.

32. *Loc. cit.*

33. "Rosenzweig's 'Judaism of Personal Existence,'" *Commentary*, X, December 1950, p. 544.

34. "Das neue Denken," *Kleinere Schriften*, p. 396.

35. *Understanding the Sick and the Healthy* (English translation of Rosenzweig's *Das Büchlein vom gesunden und*

kranken Menschenverstand), New York, Noonday Press, 1954, p. 91.

36. *Stern*, II, p. 24.
37. *Ibid.*, II, p. 24; III, pp. 171 ff.
38. These lines are also quoted in "Das neue Denken," *Kleinere Schriften*, p. 384.
39. "Das neue Denken," p. 385.
40. *Loc. cit.*
41. *Ibid.*, p. 387.
42. *Ibid.*, p. 388.
43. In his "Principles of the Philosophy of the Future," in which he claimed that the foundation of truth is not the self-consciousness of the individual ego but the interrelationship of the I and Thou. Feuerbach's work was being rediscovered in Germany at the time Rosenzweig was writing.
44. "Das neue Denken," p. 388; cf. *Briefe*, p. 347.
45. "Das neue Denken," p. 388.
46. *Ibid.*, p. 389.
47. Though Heidegger probably did not know of Rosenzweig and *Der Stern der Erlösung* when he wrote his *Sein und Zeit* (first published in 1927), Rosenzweig was acquainted with Heidegger's work and noted the affinity between the latter's thought and that of Hermann Cohen, as well as his own. See his essay "Vertauschte Fronten" (Reversed Battlefronts) in *Kleinere Schriften*, pp. 354–356.
48. Heidegger, *Sein und Zeit*, Halle, Max Niemeyer Verlag, 1931, pp. 3, 38 ff.
49. *Kleinere Schriften*, pp. 363, 369.
50. *Ibid.*, p. 359.
51. Löwith, "M. Heidegger and F. Rosenzweig, or Temporality and Eternity," *Philosophy and Phenomenological Research*, II, 1942, p. 61.
52. *Stern*, II, pp. 112 ff. In this contention Rosenzweig follows Eugen Rosenstock's reformulation of the Cartesian *cogito, ergo sum* as "God called me, therefore I am." See Rosenstock, *Angewandte Seelenkunde*, Darmstadt, 1924, p. 36.
53. *Stern*, I, pp. 46 ff., 70 ff., 96 ff., 101 ff.
54. *Op. cit.*, II, pp. 41 ff.
55. *Ibid.*, II, pp. 32–41.
56. *Ibid.*, II, p. 46.
57. Guttmann, *Philosophies of Judaism*, Philadelphia, Jewish Publication Society, 1964, p. 385.
58. *Stern*, II, pp. 152 ff., 163 ff.
59. Quoted in Glatzer, *Franz Rosenzweig—His Life and Thought*, p. 285.
60. "The Builders" in Rosenzweig, *On Jewish Learning*, N. N. Glatzer, ed., New York, Schocken Books, 1955, p. 77.
61. Rosenzweig, *Briefe*, p. 518.
62. In a letter to Martin Buber, dated July 16, 1924. *Briefe*, p. 505.
63. "The Builders," *On Jewish Learning*, p. 85.
64. *Ibid.*, p. 86.
65. *Ibid.*, p. 91.

66. Rosenzweig, *Stern*, III, p. 156.
67. *Ibid.*, II, pp. 197–199.
68. *Ibid.*, II, p. 175.
69. *Ibid.*, II, pp. 220 ff.
70. *Ibid.*, II, pp. 194–195.
71. *Ibid.*, III, p. 159.
72. *Ibid.*, III, p. 160.
73. For an excellent discussion of Rosenzweig's views in this connection, see Alexander Altmann's essay, "Franz Rosenzweig on History" in *Between East and West: Essays Dedicated to the Memory of Bela Horowitz*, Altmann, ed., London, East and West Library, 1958, pp. 194 ff.
74. For the complete text of Rosenzweig's remarkable letter to Ehrenberg, see *Briefe*, pp. 71–76.
75. *Briefe*, pp. 681–682.
76. *Op. cit.*, p. 688.
77. *Ibid.*, p. 681.
78. *Ibid.*, pp. 688–689.
79. *Ibid.*, p. 690.
80. *Ibid.*, p. 671.
81. *Ibid.*, pp. 73–74.
82. *Ibid.*, p. 74.
83. *Stern*, III, p. 190.
84. *Op. cit.*, III, p. 105.
85. *Ibid.*, III, p. 48.
86. *Ibid.*, III, pp. 56–57.
87. *Ibid.*, III, p. 175.
88. *Ibid.*, III, p. 104.
89. *Ibid.*, III, pp. 200 ff.
90. Halevi, *Kuzari*, IV:23.
91. Maimonides, *Mishneh Torah, Melachim*, II:11.
92. Glatzer, *Franz Rosenzweig—His Life and Thought*, p. XXV.

Selections from Rosenzweig's Writings

····➤●◉●◀····

ON THE POSSIBILITY OF THE COGNITION OF THE ALL

"Against the philosophers!"

CONCERNING DEATH

ALL COGNITION of the All originates in death, in the fear of death. Philosophy takes it upon itself to throw off the fear of things earthly, to rob death of its poisonous sting, and Hades of its pestilential breath. All that is mortal lives in this fear of death; every new birth augments the fear by one new reason, for it augments what is mortal. Without ceasing, the womb of the indefatigable earth gives birth to what is new, each bound to die, each awaiting the day of its journey into darkness with fear and trembling. But philosophy denies these fears of the earth. It bears us over the grave which yawns at our feet with every step. It lets the body be a prey to the abyss, but the free soul flutters away over it. Why should philosophy be concerned if the fear of death knows nothing of such a dichotomy between body and soul, if it roars Me! Me! Me!, if it wants nothing to do with relegating fear onto a mere "body." Let man creep like a worm into the folds of the naked earth before the fast approaching volleys of a blind death from which there is no appeal; let him sense there, forcibly, inexorably, what he otherwise never senses: that his *I* would be but an *It* if it died; let him therefore cry his very *I* out with every cry that is still in his throat against Him from whom there is no appeal, from whom such unthinkable annihilation threatens—for all this dire necessity philosophy only has its vacuous smile. With index finger outstretched, it directs the creature, whose limbs are quivering with terror for its this-wordly existence, to a Beyond of which it doesn't care to know anything at all. For man does not really want to escape any kind of fetters; he wants to remain, he wants to—live. Philosophy, which commends death to him as its special protégé, as the magnificent opportunity to flee the straits of life, seems to him to be only mocking. In fact, man is only too well aware that he is condemned to death, but not to suicide. Yet this philosophical recommendation can truthfully recommend only suicide, not the fated death of all. Suicide is not the natural form of death but plainly the one counter to nature. The gruesome capacity for suicide distinguishes man from all beings known and unknown to us. It is the veritable index of this taking leave of all that is natural. It is presumably necessary for man to take his leave once in his life. Like Faust,* he must for once bring the precious vial down attentively; he must for once have felt himself in his fearful poverty, loneliness, and dissociation from all the world, have stood a whole night face to face with the Nought. But the earth claims him again. He may not drain the dark potion in that night. A way out of the bottleneck of the Nought has been determined for him, another way than this precipitate fall into the yawning abyss. Man is not to throw off the fear of the earthly; he is to remain in the fear of death—but he is to remain.

He is to remain. He shall be none other than what he already wills: to remain. The terror of the earthly is only to be taken from him with the earthly itself. As long as he lives on earth, he shall also remain in terror of the earthly. And philosophy deceives him about this "shall" by weaving the blue mist of its idea of the All about the earthly. For indeed, an All would not die and nothing would die in the All. Only the singular can die and everything mortal is solitary. Philosophy has to rid the world of what is singular, and this un-doing of the Aught is also the reason why it has to be Idealistic. For Idealism, with its denial of everything that distinguishes the singular from the All, is the tool of the philosopher's trade. With it, philosophy continues to work over the recalcitrant material until it finally offers no more resistance to the smokescreen of the one-and-all concept. If once all were woven into this mist, death would indeed be swallowed up, if not into the eternal triumph,** at least into the one and universal night of the Nought. And it is the ultimate conclusion of this doctrine that death is—

* Translator's addition.
** Isaiah 25:8 (Tr.).

Nought. But in truth this is no ultimate conclusion, but a first beginning, and truthfully death is not what it seems, not Nought, but a something from which there is no appeal, which is not to be done away with. Its hard summons sounds unbroken even out of the mist with which philosophy envelops it. Philosophy might well have swallowed it up into the night of the Nought, but it could not tear loose its poisonous sting. And man's terror as he trembles before this sting ever condemns the compassionate lie of philosophy as cruel lying.

THE PHILOSOPHY OF TOTALITY

By denying the sombre presupposition of all life, that is by not allowing death to count as Aught but turning it into Nought, philosophy creates for itself an apparent freedom from presuppositions. For now the premise of all cognition of the All is—nothing. Before the one and universal cognition of the All there now only counts the one and universal Nought. Philosophy plugs up its ears before the cry of terrorized humanity. Were it otherwise, it would have to start from the premise, the conscious premise, that the Nought of death is an Aught, that the Nought of every new death is a new Aught, ever newly fearsome, which neither talk nor silence can dispose of. It would have to have the courage to listen to the cry of mortal terror and not to shut its eyes to gruesome reality. Instead, it will grant precedence over the one and universal cognition only to the one and universal Nought which buries its head in the sand before that cry. The Nought is not Nothing, it is Aught. A thousand deaths stand in the sombre background of the world as its inexhaustible premise, a thousand Noughts that are Aught precisely because they are many, instead of the one Nought which really would be nothing. The multiplicity of the Nought which is premised by philosophy, the reality of death which will not be banished from the world and which announced itself in the inextinguishable cry of its victims—these give the lie to the basic idea of philosophy, the idea of the one and universal cognition of the All, even before it has been conceived. The millennial secret of philosophy which Schopenhauer spilled at its bier, namely that death was supposed to have been its Musaget, loses its power over us. We want no philosophy which joins death's retinue and deceives and diverts us about its enduring sovereignty by the one-and-all music of its dance. We want no deception at all. If death is something, then henceforth no philosophy is to divert our glance from it by the assertion that philosophy presupposes Nothing. Let us, however, look more closely at this assertion.

Was not philosophy itself already all full of presupposition, indeed all presupposition itself, through that presupposition that it presupposes nothing, its "sole" presupposition? Again and again one attached all else that was possibly worthy of inquiry to this question. Again and again one sought the answer to the question in reasoning. It is as if this presupposition of the intelligible All, so magnificent in itself, threw the whole circle of other possible inquiries into the shade. Materialism and Idealism, both—and not just the former—"as old as philosophy," have an equal share in this presupposition. One silenced or ignored whatever laid claim to independence in its face. One silenced the voice which claimed possession, in a revelation, of the source of divine knowledge originating beyond reason. Centuries of philosophical labors were devoted to this disputation between knowledge and belief; they reach their goal at the precise moment when the knowledge of the All reaches a conclusion in itself. For one will have to designate it as a conclusion when this knowledge completely encompasses no longer only its object, the All, but also itself, completely at least according to its own requirements and in its own peculiar manner. This happened when Hegel included the history of philosophy in the system. It seems that reason can go no further than to place itself visibly as the innermost fact known to itself, now as part of the system's structure, and of course as the concluding part. And at the precise moment when philosophy exhausts its furthest formal possibilities and reaches the boundary set by its own nature, the great question of the relationship of knowledge and belief which is pressed upon it by the course of world history seems now, as already noted, to be solved.

HEGEL

More than once, it already seemed as if peace were concluded between the two hostile powers, whether on the basis of a clean division of their respective claims, or on the basis of philosophy's supposing that it possessed in its arsenal the keys to unlock the secrets of revelation. In either case, therefore, philosophy allowed revelation to count as truth, inaccessible to it in the one case, confirmed by it in the other. But neither solution ever sufficed for long. The pride of philosophy very soon rose up against the first, unable to bear the thought of acknowledging a locked gate; belief, conversely, was bound to remonstrate against the second solution if it was not to be satisfied with being recognized, quite incidentally, as one truth among others by philosophy. What Hegelian philosophy promised to bring was, however, something entirely different. It asserted neither dichotomy nor mere congruity, but rather an innermost interconnection. The cognitive world becomes cognitive through the same law of reasoning which recurs as the supreme law of existence at the apex of the system. And this law, one and the same in thinking and being, was first annunciated, on the scale of world history, in revelation. Thus philosophy is in a sense no more than fulfilling what was promised in revelation. And again, philosophy carries out this function not merely occasionally or, say, only at the zenith of its orbit; in every moment, so to speak with every breath that it draws, it involuntarily confirms the truth of what revelation had declared. Thus the old quarrel seems settled, heaven and earth reconciled.

KIERKEGAARD

Yet the solution of the question of belief, as well as the self-fulfillment of knowledge was more apparent than real—most apparently apparent, it is true, for if that aforementioned presupposition holds and all knowledge pertains to the All, if it is all included in the All but at the same time omnipotent in it, then indeed that ap-

pearance was more than appearance, it was truth. Then
anyone still wanting to raise an objection had to feel an
Archimedean footing, a "place where to stand" outside
that cognitive All. A Kierkegaard, and not only he, con-
tested the Hegelian integration of revelation into the
All from such an Archimedean fulcrum. That fulcrum
was the peculiar consciousness of his own sin and his
own redemption on the part of Sören Kierkegaard himself or whatever might happen to be his first and last
names. This consciousness neither needed a blending
into the cosmos nor admitted of it, for even if everything
about it could be translated into universal terms, there
remained the being saddled with first and last name,
with what was his own in the strictest and narrowest
sense of the word. And this "own" was just what mat-
tered, as the bearers of such experiences asserted.

THE NEW PHILOSOPHY

At least this was a case of one assertion against another. Philosophy was accused of an incapacity, or more
exactly of an inadequacy, which it could not itself
admit since it could not recognize it. For if there was
here really an object beyond it, then philosophy itself,
especially in the conclusive form which it assumed under
Hegel, had locked this and every Beyond from its view.
The objection disputed its right to a sphere whose existence it had to deny; it did not attack its own sphere.
That had to happen in another manner. And it happened in the philosophical period that begins with
Schopenhauer, continues via Nietzsche, and whose end
has not yet arrived.

SCHOPENHAUER

Schopenhauer was the first of the great thinkers to inquire, not into the nature, but into the value of the
world. A most unscientific inquiry, if it was really meant
to inquire into its value for man, and not into its objective value, its value for some "something," the "sense"

or "purpose" of the world, which would after all have been only another way of saying an inquiry into its nature. Perhaps it was even meant to inquire into its value for the man Arthur Schopenhauer. And so it was in fact meant. Consciously, it is true, he only inquired into its value for man, and even this inquiry was deprived of its poisonous fangs by ultimately finding its solution after all in a system of the world. System of course already implies without more ado independent universal applicability. And so the inquiry of pre-systematic man found its answer in the saint of the concluding part produced by the system. Thus a human type and not a concept closed the arch of the system, really closed it as a keystone; it did not simply supplement it as an ethical decoration or curlicue. Even this was already something unheard of in philosophy. And above all, the enormous effect can only be explained by the fact that one sensed —and this really was the case—that here a man stood at the beginning of the system. This man no longer philosophized in the context of, and so to say as if commissioned by, the history of philosophy, nor as heir to whatever might be the current status of its problems, but "had taken it upon himself to reflect on life" because it— life—"is a precarious matter." This proud dictum of the youth in conversation with Goethe—it is already significant that he said "life" and not "world"—is complemented by the letter in which he offered the finished work to the publisher. There he declares the content of philosophy to be the idea with which an individual mind reacts to the impression which the world has made on him. "An individual mind"—it was then after all the man Arthur Schopenhauer who here assumed the place which, according to the prevailing conception of philosophizing, should have been assumed by the problem. Man, "life," had become the problem, and he had "taken it upon himself" to solve it in the form of a philosophy. Therefore the value of the world for man had now to be questioned—a most unscientific inquiry, as already indicated, but so much the more a human one. All philosophical interest had hitherto turned about the cognitive All; even man had been admitted as an object of philosophy only in his relationship to this All. Now something else, the living man, independently took its stand opposite this cognitive world, and opposite totality there stood the singular, the "unique and his own," mocking every All and universality. This novum was then thrust irretrievably into the riverbed of the development of conscious spirit, not in the book of this title, which in the last analysis was only that—a book—but in the tragedy of Nietzsche's life itself.

NIETZSCHE

For only here was it really something new. Poets had always dealt with life and their own souls. But not philosophers. And saints had always lived life and for their own soul. But again—not the philosophers. Here, however, was one man who knew his own life and his own soul like a poet, and obeyed their voice like a holy man, and who was for all that a philosopher. What he philosophized has today already become almost a matter of indifference. Dionysiac and Superman, Blond Beast and Eternal Return—where are they now? But none of those who now feel the urge to philosophize can any longer by-pass the man himself, who transformed himself in the transformation of his mental images, him whose soul feared no height, who clambered after mind, that daredevil climber, up to the steep pinnacle of dementedness, where there was no more Onward. The fearsome and challenging image of the unconditional vassalage of soul to mind could henceforth not be eradicated. For the great thinkers of the past, the soul had been allowed to play the role of, say, wet nurse, or at any rate of tutor of Mind. But one day the pupil had grown up and went his own way, enjoying his freedom and unlimited prospects. He recalled the four narrow walls in which he had grown up only with horror. Thus spirit enjoyed precisely its being free of the soulful dullness in which non-mind spends its days. For the philosopher, philosophy was the cool height to which he had escaped from the mists of the plain. For Nietzsche this dichotomy between height and plain did not exist in his own self: he was of a piece, soul and mind a unity, man and thinker a unity to the last.

MAN

Thus man became a power over philosophy—not man in general over philosophy in general, but one man, one very specific man over his own philosophy. The philosopher ceased to be a negligible quantity for his philosophy. Philosophy had promised to give him compensation in the form of mind in return for selling it his soul, and he no longer took this compensation seriously. Man as philosophizer had become master of philosophy—not as translated into spiritual terms, but as endowed with a soul, whose mind only seemed to him the frozen breath of his living soul. Philosophy had to acknowledge him, acknowledge him as something which it could not comprehend but which, because powerful over against it, it could not deny. Man in the utter singularity of his individuality, in his prosopographically determined being, stepped out of the world which knew of itself as the conceivable one, out of the All of philosophy.

METAETHICS

Philosophy had intended to grasp man, even man as a "personality," in ethics. But that was an impossible endeavor. For if and as it grasped him, he was bound to dissolve in its grasp. In principle ethics might assign to action a special status vis-à-vis all being; no matter: in practice it drew action, of necessity as it were, back into the orbit of the cognitive All. Every ethics ultimately flowed together again with a doctrine of the community as a unit of being. Merely to distinguish the special nature of action vis-à-vis being offered, apparently, insufficient guarantee against this confluence. One should have taken one more step backwards and anchored action in the foundation of a "character" which, for all it partook of being, was nevertheless separated from all being. Only thus could one have secured action as a world to itself vis-à-vis the world. But that never happened apart from the one Kant. And by formulating moral law as the universally valid act, the concept of totality again carried off the victory over the unicum of man just with Kant. With a certain logical consequence, the "miracle in the phenomenal world"—as he happily designated the concept of freedom—sank back into the miracle of the phenomenal world with the post-Kantians. Kant himself serves as godfather to Hegel's concept of universal history, not only with his political philosophy and his philosophy of history, but even with his ethical fundamentals. And while Schopenhauer incorporated Kant's doctrine of intelligible character into his doctrine of the will, he debased the value of the former doctrine, and that in the opposite direction from the great Idealists. He made will the essence of the world and thereby let the world dissolve in will, if not will in the world. Thus he annihilated the distinction so alive in himself, between the being of man and the being of the world.

The new world which Nietzsche unlocked to reason thus had to lie beyond the orbit described by ethics. One must acknowledge the otherworldliness of the new inquiry vis-à-vis everything which the concept of ethics hitherto solely meant and solely was meant to mean, the more so if one wants the spiritual achievement of the past to count for everything which it accomplished rather than to destroy it in a riot of blind destructiveness. A way of looking at life (*Lebensanschauung*) confronts a way of looking at the world (*Weltanschauung*). Ethics is and remains a part of the *Weltanschauung*. Its special relationship with a life-focussed point of view is only that of a particularly intimate contradiction, just because both seem to touch each other, indeed repeatedly lay claim mutually to solve the problems of the other together with their own. It remains to be shown in what sense this is actually the case. But the contrast of the life-centered and the world-centered points of view comes down so sharply to a contrast with the ethical portion of the world-centered view, that one is inclined to designate questions of the life view as veritably metaethical.

THE WORLD

Personal life, personality, individuality—all these are concepts loaded with the uses to which the philosophy of the world-centered point of view has put them and thus concepts which we cannot employ without more ado. What is, however, more or less clearly so labelled, in other words the "metaethical" questions, cannot thus step out of the realm of the knowledge of the world without having some traces in the latter itself. With this establishment of an—as it were—indigestible actuality outside of the great spiritually mastered factual wealth of the cognitive world, a basic concept, nay the basic concept, of this world is dethroned. It claimed to be the All; "all" is the subject of the first sentence spoken at its birth. Now a self-contained unity rebelled against this totality which encloses the All as a unity, and extorted its withdrawal as a singularity, as the singular life of the singular person. The All can thus no longer claim to be all: it has forfeited its uniqueness.

On what, then, does this totality rest? Why, then, was not the world interpreted, say, as a multiplicity? Why just as a totality? Apparently we have here again a presupposition, and again that aforementioned one: the conceivableness of the world. It is the unity of reasoning which here insists on its right over against the multiplicity of knowledge by asserting the totality of the world. The unity of the logos establishes the unity of the world-as-totality. And the former unity proves in its turn the extent of its truthfulness by establishing this totality. Thus a successful uprising against the totality of the world implies at the same time a denial of the unity of reasoning. In "All is water," that first sentence of philosophy, there already lurks the presupposition of the possibility of conceiving the world, even if Parmenides first pronounced the identity of being and reasoning. For it is not self-evident that one can ask "what is All?" with the prospect of an unambiguous answer. One cannot ask "what is much?" and expect an unambiguous answer. But the subject All is assured in advance of an unambiguous predicate. He who denies the totality of being, as we do, thus denies the unity of reasoning. He throws down the gauntlet to the whole honorable company of philosophers from Ionia to Jena.

This our times have done. True, one has always realized the "contingency of the world," its state of "that's the way it is." But the point is that this contingency had to be mastered. In fact this was precisely the function of philosophy. In the process of being thought about, the "incidental" became something essential. This rational tendency attained its final conclusion in German Idealism, and again it was only thereafter that an opposite tendency emerged with Schopenhauer and the later philosophy of Schelling. "Will," "freedom," "unconscious" were able to hold sway over a world of coincidence as intellect had not been able to. Thus certain medieval tendencies, which asserted the *contingentia mundi* in order to secure the irresponsible caprice of the Creator seemed to be reviving again. But precisely this historical memory leads us to question this conception. It fails to explain just that which calls for explanation: how the world can be coincidental when it is supposed to be conceived as essential. There is, to put it very crudely, a non-identity of being and reasoning which has to show itself in being and reasoning themselves. It cannot be harmonized by a third party, will, stepping in as a *deus ex machina* which is neither being nor reasoning. And if the basis for the unity of being and reasoning is sought in reasoning, then the basis for their non-identity should in the first instance be uncovered in reasoning.

(From *Der Stern der Erlösung*, Vol. I, pp. 7–19; translated by William Hallo.)

THE ETERNAL PEOPLE

THE PROMISE OF ETERNITY

"Blessed art Thou . . . who has planted eternal life in our midst." The fire burns at the core of the star. The rays go forth only from this fire; and flow unresisted to the outside. The fire of the core must burn incessantly. Its flame must eternally feed upon itself. It requires no fuel from without. Time has no power over it and must roll past. It must produce its own time and reproduce itself forever. It must make its life everlasting in the succession of generations, each producing the genera-

tion to come, and bearing witness to those gone by.
Bearing witness takes place in bearing—two meanings
but one act, in which eternal life is realized. Elsewhere,
past and future are divorced, the one sinking back, the
other coming on; here they grow into one. The bearing
of the future is a direct bearing witness to the past. The
son is born so that he may bear witness to his father's
father. The grandson renews the name of the forebear.
The patriarchs of old call upon their last descendant by
his name—which is theirs. Above the darkness of the
future burns the star-strewn heaven of the promise: "So
shall thy seed be."

THE ETERNAL PEOPLE: JEWISH FATE— BLOOD AND SPIRIT

There is only one community in which such a linked
sequence of everlasting life goes from grandfather to
grandson, only one which cannot utter the "we" of its
unity without hearing deep within a voice that adds:
"are eternal." It must be a blood-community, because
only blood gives present warrant to the hope for a future.
If some other community, one that does not propagate
itself from its own blood, desires to claim eternity for its
"we," the only way open to it is to secure a place in the
future. All eternity not based on blood must be based on
the will and on hope. Only a community based on common blood feels the warrant of eternity warm in its veins
even now. For such a community only, time is not a foe
that must be tamed, a foe it may or may not defeat—
though it hopes it may!—but its child and the child of its
child. It alone regards as the present what, for other
communities, is the future, or, at any rate, something
outside the present. For it alone the future is not something alien but something of its own, something it carries in its womb and which might be born any day.
While every other community that lays claim to eternity
must take measures to pass the torch of the present on
to the future, the blood-community does not have to resort to such measures. It does not have to hire the services of the spirit; the natural propagation of the body
guarantees it eternity.

Franz Rosenzweig

THE PEOPLES AND THEIR NATIVE SOIL

What holds generally for peoples as groups united through blood relationship over against communities of the spirit, holds for our people in particular. Among the peoples of the earth, the Jewish people is "the one people," as it calls itself on the high rung of its life, which it ascends Sabbath after Sabbath. The peoples of the world are not content with the bonds of blood. They sink their roots into the night of earth, lifeless in itself but the spender of life, and from the lastingness of earth they conclude that they themselves will last. Their will to eternity clings to the soil and to the reign over the soil, to the land. The earth of their homeland is watered by the blood of their sons, for they do not trust in the life of a community of blood, in a community that can dispense with anchorage in solid earth. We were the only ones who trusted in blood and abandoned the land; and so we preserved the priceless sap of life which pledged us that it would be eternal. Among the peoples of the world, we were the only ones who separated what lived within us from all community with what is dead. For while the earth nourishes, it also binds. Whenever a people loves the soil of its native land more than its own life, it is in danger—as all the peoples of the world are—that, though nine times out of ten this love will save the native soil from the foe and, along with it, the life of the people, in the end the soil will persist as that which was loved more strongly, and the people will leave their lifeblood upon it. In the final analysis, the people belong to him who conquers the land. It cannot be otherwise, because people cling to the soil more than to their life as a people. Thus the earth betrays a people that entrusted its permanence to earth. The soil endures, the peoples who live on it pass.

THE HOLY LAND

And so, in contrast to the history of other peoples, the earliest legends about the tribe of the eternal people are not based on indigenousness. Only the father of mankind sprang from the earth itself, and even he only in a physical sense. But the father of Israel came from the outside. His story, as it is told in the holy books, begins with God's command to leave the land of his birth and go to a land God will point out to him. Thus in the dawn of its earliest beginnings, as well as later in the bright light of history, this people is a people in exile, in the Egyptian exile and subsequently in that of Babylonia. To the eternal people, home never is home in the sense of land, as it is to the peoples of the world who plough the land and live and thrive on it, until they have all but forgotten that being a people means something besides being rooted in a land. The eternal people has not been permitted to while away time in any home. It never loses the untrammeled freedom of a wanderer who is more faithful a knight to his country when he roams abroad, craving adventure and yearning for the land he has left behind, than when he lives in that land. In the most profound sense possible, this people has a land of its own only in that it has a land it yearns for—a holy land. And so even when it has a home, this people, in recurrent contrast to all other peoples on earth, is not allowed full possession of that home. It is only "a stranger and a sojourner." God tells it: "The land is mine." The holiness of the land removed it from the people's spontaneous reach while it could still reach out for it. This holiness increases the longing for what is lost, to infinity, and so the people can never be entirely at home in any other land. This longing compels it to concentrate the full force of its will on a thing which, for other peoples, is only one among others yet which to it is essential and vital: the community of blood. In doing this, the will to be a people dares not cling to any mechanical means; the will can realize its end only through the people itself.

THE PEOPLES AND THEIR LANGUAGES

But is a native land the only thing aside from blood on which a people's community can rest? Does not a people have a living sign of solidarity, no matter where its children may go? Has not every people its own language? It would seem that the language of the peoples of the world is not bound to something lifeless, something external. It lives together with man, with the whole of man, with the unity of his bodily and spiritual life, which cannot be broken as long as he lives. So language is not bound to anything external. But is it really less transitory because of this? If it is closely bound up with the life of the people, what happens to it when that life dies? The same that happens to it so long as that life lives: the language participates in the ultimate experience of this life: it also dies. Down to the most subtle detail, the languages of the peoples follow the live changes in their destinies, but this very dependence forces them to share the fate of all things alive: the fate of dying. Language is alive because it too can die. Eternity would be an unwelcome gift to it. Only because it is not eternal, only because it is a faithful reflection of the destiny of a people among other peoples, of a people passing through the various phases of its life, does it deserve to be called the most vital possession of a people, yes, its very life. And so every people of the world is doubtless right in fighting for its own language. But the peoples should know that it is not their eternity they are fighting for, that whatever is gained in the struggle is something quite other than eternity; it is time.

THE HOLY LANGUAGE

That is why the eternal people has lost its own language and, all over the world, speaks a language dictated by external destiny, the language of the nation whose guest it happens to be. And if it is not claiming hospitality but living in a settlement of its own, it speaks the language of the people from whose country it emigrated, of the people that gave it the strength to found a new settlement. In foreign lands it never draws this strength from itself alone, from its own community of blood, but always from something that was added elsewhere; the "Spaniol" in the Balkan countries, the Yiddish in Eastern Europe, are the best-known instances of this. While every other people is one with its own language,

while that language withers in its mouth the moment it
ceases to be a people, the Jewish people never quite
grows one with the languages it speaks. Even when it
speaks the language of its host, a special vocabulary, or,
at least, a special selection from the general vocabulary,
a special word order, its own feeling for what is beautiful or ugly in the language, betray that it is not its
own.

Since time immemorial, the Jewish people's own language has ceased to be the language of daily life and yet
—as its constant influence on the language of daily life
shows—it is anything but a dead language. It is not dead
but, as the people themselves call it, a holy language.
The holiness of the people's own language has an effect
similar to that of the holiness of its own land: it does not
allow all their feeling to be lavished on everyday life.
It prevents the eternal people from ever being quite in
harmony with the times. By encompassing prayer, the
ultimate, loftiest region of life, with a holy region of
that language, it even prevents this people from ever
living in complete freedom and spontaneity. For the
freedom and spontaneity of life rest on the fact that man
can express in words all he thinks, and that he feels he
can do this. When he loses this ability, when he thinks he
must be silent in his anguish because it is given only
to the "poet to say what he suffers," not alone is the
strength of a people's language broken, but its spontaneity too is hopelessly destroyed.

Precisely this ultimate and most fundamental spontaneity is denied the Jew because he addresses God in
a language different from the one he uses to speak to
his brother. As a result he cannot speak to his brother at
all. He communicates with him by a glance rather than
in words, and nothing is more essentially Jewish in the
deepest sense than a profound distrust of the power of
the word and a fervent belief in the power of silence.
The holiness of the holy language which the Jew employs only for prayer does not permit his life to put out
roots into the soil of a language of its own. So far as his
language is concerned, the Jew feels always he is in a
foreign land, and knows that the home of his language
is in the region of the holy language, a region everyday
speech can never invade. The proof of this lies in the

peculiar circumstance that, at least in the silent symbols of writing, the language of everyday tries to maintain contact with the old holy language which everyday speech lost long ago. This is altogether different from the situation of the peoples of the world; for with them, the case is that the spoken language survives a written language that is lost, rather than that the written language survives a language no longer spoken on everyday occasions. In his very silence, and in the silent symbols of speech, the Jew feels a connection between his everyday language and the holy language of his holiday.

THE PEOPLES AND THEIR LAW

For the peoples of the world, language is the carrier and messenger of time-bound, flowing, changing, and, therefore, transitory life. But the language of the eternal people drives it back to its own life which is beyond external life, which courses through the veins of its living body and is, therefore, eternal. And if the Jew is thus barred from his own soil and his own language, how much more is he deprived of the outwardly visible life the nations live in accordance with their own customs and laws. For a people lives out its day in these two: in custom and law, in what has been handed down from yesterday through force of habit, and in what has been laid down for the morrow. Every day stands between a yesterday and a tomorrow, and all that lives proves it is alive by not standing still one certain day but making of that day a yesterday, and setting in its place a tomorrow. Peoples, too, stay alive by constantly transforming their today into new customs, into new eternal yesterdays, while at the same time they lay down new laws structured out of their today, for the service of their tomorrow. Thus, in the life of the nations, today is a moment which passes fleet as an arrow. And so long as this arrow is in flight, so long as new custom is added to the old, new law outstrips the old, the river of a people's life is in flux, alive. For so long do peoples live within time; for so long is time their heritage and their acre. In addition to their own soil and their own language, the increase in custom and the renewal of law give them the final and strongest guarantee of their own life: a time of their own. So long as a people computes a time of its own—and it computes this time according to its still living store of customs and memories, and the continuous renewal of its lawgiving powers, its leaders and kings—just so long has it power over time, just so long is it not dead.

THE HOLY LAW

And here again the eternal people buys its eternity at the cost of its temporal life. Time is not its time, nor its acre and heritage. For this people, the moment petrifies and stands between unincreased past and immovable future, and so the moment is not fleeting. Custom and law, past and future, become two changeless masses; in this process they too are transmuted into a changeless present. Custom and law, not to be increased or changed, flow into the common basin of what is valid now and forever. A single form of life welding custom and law into one fills the moment and renders it eternal. But because of this, the moment is lifted out of the flux of time; and life, sanctified, no longer has the quality of temporal life. While the myth of peoples changes incessantly —parts of the past are continually being forgotten while others are remembered as myth—here the myth becomes eternal and is not subject to change. And while the peoples of the world live in a cycle of revolutions in which their law sheds its old skin over and over, here the Law is supreme, a law that can be forsaken but never changed.

The holy teaching of the Law—for the name Torah designates both teaching and law as one—raises the people from the temporality and historicity of life, and deprives it of the power over time. The Jewish people do not count years according to a system of its own. For it, neither the memory of its history nor the years of office of its lawgivers can become a measure of time. That is because the memory of its history does not form a point fixed in the past, a point which, year after year, becomes increasingly past. It is a memory which is really not past at all, but eternally present. Every single mem-

ber of this community is bound to regard the exodus
from Egypt as if he himself had been one of those to go.
Here there are no lawgivers who renew the law according to the living flux of time. Even what might, for all
practical purposes, be considered an innovation must
be presented as if it were part of the everlasting Law
and had been revealed in the revelation of that Law.
And so the chronology of this people cannot be a reckoning of its own. It must count years according to the
years the world exists. And so again, and for the third
time, we see here, in the relation to its own history,
what we saw before in its relation to language and land,
that this people is denied a life in time for the sake of
life in eternity. It cannot experience the history of the
nations creatively, and fully. Its position is always somewhere between the temporal and the holy, always separated from the one by the other. And so, in the final
analysis, it is not alive in the sense the nations are alive:
in a national life manifest on this earth, in a national territory, solidly based and staked out on the soil. It is alive
only in that which guarantees it will endure beyond
time, in that which pledges it everlastingness, in drawing its own eternity from the sources of the blood.

FATE AND ETERNITY

But just because this people trusts only in the eternity
it creates and in nothing else in the world, it really believes in its eternity, while all the peoples of the world
believe in common with individual man that death, even
although it be at a very distant juncture, must come
eventually. The love they bear their own group is grave
and sweet with this premonition of death. Love is wholly
sweet only when it is love for what is mortal. The secret
of ultimate sweetness is bound up with the bitterness of
death. The peoples of the world, then, foresee a time
when their land with its mountains and rivers will lie
beneath the sky even as now, but be inhabited by others,
a time when their language will be buried in books and
their customs and laws stripped of living force. We
alone cannot imagine such a time. For we have long ago
been robbed of all the things in which the peoples of

the world are rooted. For us, land and language, custom
and law, have long left the circle of the living and have
been raised to the rung of holiness. But we are still
living, and live in eternity. Our life is no longer meshed
with anything outside ourselves. We have struck root in
ourselves. We do not root in earth and so we are eternal
wanderers, but deeply rooted in our own body and
blood. And it is this rooting in ourselves, and in nothing
but ourselves, that vouchsafes eternity.

THE ONE PEOPLE: JEWISH ESSENCE— INDIVIDUALITY AND UNIVERSALITY

What does this mean: to root in one's self? What does
it mean that here one individual people does not seek
the warrant of its existence in the external, and reaches
out for eternity in its very lack of relations with the outside world? It means no more and no less than that one
people, though it is only one people, claims to contain
the All. For whatever is individual is not eternal because the All is outside it. It can maintain its individuality only by becoming somehow a part of that All. An
individual entity which, in spite of its individuality,
strove for eternity, would have to take the All into itself.
With reference to the Jewish people this means that it
would have to collect within itself the elements of God,
world, and man, of which the All consists. God, man, and
world of a people are the God, man, and world of that
people only because they are just as different and differentiated from other gods, men, and worlds as the people itself from other peoples. The very difference of
an individual people from other peoples establishes its
connection with them. There are two sides to every
boundary. By setting separating borders for ourselves,
we border on something else. By being an individual
people, a nation becomes a people among others. To
close oneself off is to come close to another. But this does
not hold when a people refuses to be merely an individual people and wants to be "the one people." Under
these circumstances it must not close itself off within
borders, but includes within itself such borders as would,
through their double function, tend to make it one indi-

vidual people among others. And the same is true of its God, man, and world. These three must likewise not be distinguished from those of others; their distinction must be included within its own borders. Since this people wants to be the one people, the God, man, and world must contain the distinguishing characteristics that make them God, man, and world of the one people. In order that each be something very definite and particular, one God, one man, one world, and yet at the same time the All: God, man, and world, they must contain opposite poles within themselves.

POLARITY

God within himself separates into the God who creates and the God who reveals, the God of omnipotent justice, and the God of love and mercy. Man within himself separates into the soul beloved by God and the lover who loves his neighbor. The world separates into the existence of the creature that longs for God's creation, and life that grows toward and into the kingdom of God. Up to now, we regarded all these separations not as separations but as a sequence of voices taking up the theme in the great fugue of God's day. Up to now, we regarded as essential not separation but union, the union into one harmony. Now, for the first time, now that we are preparing to see eternity as something present at every hour instead of as the twelfth stroke of the world clock, these synthesizing voices appear as antitheses. For in the sheer present which renews itself hour by hour, it is no longer possible for them to pass one another, to interweave in contrapuntal motion; they oppose one another with inflexible rigidity.

THE JEWISH GOD

To his people, God the Lord is simultaneously the God of retribution and the God of love. In the same breath, they call on him as "our God" and as "King of the universe," or—to indicate the same contrast in a more intimate sphere—as "our Father" and "our King." He wants to be served with "trembling" and yet rejoices when his children overcome their fear at his wondrous signs. Whenever the Scriptures mention his majesty the next verses are sure to speak of his meekness. He demands the visible signs of offering and prayer brought to his name, and of "the affliction of our soul" in his sight. And almost in the same breath he scorns both and wants to be honored only with the secret fervor of the heart, in the love of one's neighbor, and in anonymous works of justice which no one may recognize as having been done for the sake of his name. He has elected his people, but elected it to visit upon them all their iniquities. He wants every knee to bend to him and yet he is enthroned above Israel's songs of praise. Israel intercedes with him in behalf of the sinning peoples of the world and he afflicts Israel with disease so that those other peoples may be healed. Both stand before God: Israel, his servant, and the kings of the peoples; and the strands of suffering and guilt, of love and judgment, of sin and atonement, are so inextricably twined that human hands cannot untangle them.

THE JEWISH MAN

And man, who is created in the image of God, Jewish man as he faces his God, is a veritable repository of contradictions. As the beloved of God, as Israel, he knows that God has elected him and may well forget that he is not alone with God, that God knows others whom he himself may or may not know, that to Egypt and Assyria too, God says: "my people." He knows he is loved— so why concern himself with the world! In his blissful togetherness—alone with God, he may consider himself man, and man alone, and look up in surprise when the world tries to remind him that not every man harbors the same certainty of being God's child as he himself. Yet no one knows better than he that being dear to God is only a beginning, and that man remains unredeemed so long as nothing but this beginning has been realized. Over against Israel, eternally loved by God and faithful and perfect in eternity, stands he who is eternally to come, he who waits, and wanders, and grows eternally—

the Messiah. Over against the man of earliest beginnings, against Adam the son of man, stands the man of endings, the son of David the king. Over against him who was created from the stuff of earth and the breath of the mouth of God, is the descendant from the stem of anointed kings; over against the patriarch, the latest offspring; over against the first, who draws about him the mantle of divine love, the last, from whom salvation issues forth to the ends of the earth; over against the first miracles, the last, which—so it is said—will be greater than the first.

THE JEWISH WORLD

Finally, the Jewish world: it has been dematerialized and permeated with spirit through the power of blessings which are said over everything and branch everywhere. But this world, also, is twofold and teeming with contradictions in every single thing. Everything that happens in it is ambivalent since it is related both to this and the coming world. The fact that the two worlds, this world and the coming, stand side by side, is all-important. Even the object that receives a soul by a benediction spoken over it has a twofold function: in "this" world it serves everyday purposes, almost as though it had never been blessed, but at the same time it has been rendered one of the stones of which the "coming" world will be built. Benediction splits this world in order to make it whole and one again for what is to come, but for the present all that is visible is the split. As the contrast between holy and profane, Sabbath and workaday, "Torah and the way of earth," spiritual life and the earning of a livelihood, this split goes through all of life. As it divides the life of Israel into holy and profane, so it divides the whole earth into Israel and the peoples. But the division is not simple in the sense that the holy shuts out the profane. The contrast penetrates to the innermost core, and just as the benediction touches everything that is profane and makes it holy, so, quite suddenly, the devout and the wise among all the peoples will participate in the eternal life of the coming world, which but a short time ago seemed reserved for Israel alone. Those who were blessed will themselves become a blessing.

(From *Der Stern der Erlösung*, Vol. III, pp. 48–61; translated by William Hallo.)

THE STAR OF REDEMPTION

RECAPITULATION: THE FACE OF THE FIGURE

The Eternal had become figure in the truth. And the truth is none other than the countenance of this figure. Truth alone is its countenance. And be very careful for the sake of your souls: you have seen no figure, only heard speech—as it is said in the revealed world around-and-about. But in the redeemed world above-and-beyond, brought about forcibly by the more powerful blessing recited at the right place, there the word falls silent. Of this world, consummate and pacified, it is said: "May he make his countenance to shine upon you."

GOD'S COUNTENANCE

The truth is this shining of the divine visage alone. It is not a figure of its own, hovering freely, but solely the countenance of God, shining forth. But for him whom he lets his visage shine upon, to him he also turns his visage. As he turns his visage to us, so may we recognize him. And this cognition does not recognize figuratively. Rather it recognizes the truth as it is, that is, as it is in God: as his countenance and part. By no means does it become a figurative truth because this countenance is turned toward us, God's portion is imparted to us; for even as literal and most literal truth it would be none other than—portion and countenance. In the Star of Redemption, then, in which we saw divine truth become figure, there shines forth none other than the countenance which God turned shiningly toward us. Yea, we now recognize the Star of Redemption itself, as it has at last emerged as figure for us, in the divine visage. And only in this recognition is its cognition consummated.

THE DAY OF GOD

For as long as we only knew its course, without as yet seeing its configuration, just so long the order of the original elements remained unfixed. True, the unrestrained to-and-fro fluttering of the Perhaps had long since sunk away powerlessly; God, world and man had structured themselves in a definite mutual order which came to them on the course; the sequence of the three hours of the day of God had ordained an unalterable relationship among themselves to the elements of the All so that the course was recognized as the course of the constellation to which these elements of the course belonged. But though the Star was thus sighted, it still seemed able to rotate about itself, so that world and man seemed nonetheless still to experience their own day within the already fixed sequence of the three periods of the day of God, with which this day of their own did not simply coincide. Only for God was redemption really the Ultimate. For man, however, his creation in the image of God already implied being redeemed for every conceivable consummation, for the world likewise the descent of God in revelation. Thus it seemed as though the three hours were only hours of the day of God, while the day of man and the day of the world would be another (day).

The whole object of the third volume, which dealt with the Eternal of the redeemed hyper-cosmos, was to prove the contrary. That apparent interchangeability was here itself rooted to the spot in configurations which were assigned their fixed position in the eternal truth of the day of God. In eternal life, admittedly, redemption was already anticipated for the world in revelation which, after all, contains everything; eternal life was planted in the revelation to the one people, so that it itself no longer alters; this eternal life will one day return in the fruit of redemption as it was once planted.

So too a piece of redemption is here already really placed into the world, the visible world, and it becomes true that, seen from the world, revelation would actually already be redemption. And on the eternal way, for its part, one really does again begin with man's innate image-of-God character. Here redemption takes place through the new Adam, free of sin, not fallen, and with him it already exists. The miraculous birth of the second Adam renews this creation in the image of God, and man, endowed with soul, here makes it his own and thus becomes heir to redemption, to a redeemedness which is his own from of yore, from creation on and only waits to be claimed by him. Thus it becomes true that, from man's point of view, creation would actually already be redemption.

GOD'S TIME

Thus the relationships of time here find their precise place. For man was created as man in revelation, and in redemption he was permitted and required to reveal himself. This simple and natural temporal relationship, in which being created preceded revealing oneself, now establishes the entire sequence of the eternal way through the world, its own chronology, the consciousness which is found in every present between past and future and on the way from past to future. On the other hand the peculiar inversion of chronological sequence for the world, which we have noticed several times already, now receives its graphic confirmation. For to the world, the experience of awakening to its own manifest consciousness of itself, namely, the consciousness of the creature, occurs at its creation, and only in redemption is it first properly created; only there does it acquire its firm durability, that constant life in place of the ever-new existence born of the moment. Thus awaking precedes being for the world, and this inversion of chronological sequence establishes the life of the eternal people. For its eternal life constantly anticipates the end and thus turns it into beginning. In this inversion, it denies time as decisively as possible and places itself outside of time. To live in time means to live between be-

ginning and end. He who would live an eternal life, and
not the temporal in time, must live outside of time, and
he who would do this must deny that "between." But
such a denial would have to be active if it is to result,
not just in a not-living-in-time but in a positive living-
eternally. And the active denial would occur only in
the inversion. To invert a Between means to make its
After a Before, its Before an After, the end a beginning,
the beginning an end. And that is what the eternal people does. It already lives its own life as if it were all the
world and the world were finished. In its Sabbaths it
celebrates the sabbatical completion of the world and
makes it the foundation and starting-point of its existence. But that which, temporally speaking, would be
but starting-point, the law, that it sets up as its goal.
Thus it experiences no Between for all that it naturally,
really naturally, lives within it. Rather it experiences the
inversion of the Between. Thus it denies the onmipotence
of the Between and disavows time, the very time which is
experienced on the eternal way.

THE ETERNAL GODS

Under the signs of the eternal life and the eternal
way, the two "views" thus harden from the "viewpoint"
of world or man into figures visible in their own right,
and enter under the one sign of the eternal truth. And
with that the question as to which order of the three
hours is required for the eternal truth itself is simplified.
For having recognized eternal truth as that truth which
will be at the end and which originates with God at the
beginning, it follows that only that order does justice to
the ultimate truth which presents itself as from God and
in which redemption is really the Last. And precisely in
this order-from-God, even the orders from the world or
from man, which apparently are still at least possible by
its side, find their domicile. There they can reside in
safety and recite their Truly as essential and visible
configurations under the dominion of the eternal truth.
Paganism will live on to the eternal end in its eternal
gods, the state and art, the former the idol of the real-
ists, the latter that of the individualists; but these gods

are there put in chains by the true God. Let the state claim the supreme place in the All for the world, and art, for man; let the state dam up the current of time at the epochs of world history, and art try to divert it into the endless irrigation-system of experiences—just let them! He who thrones in heaven mocks them. He confronts their bustling activity, which already is at cross purposes, with the quiet effectiveness of created nature in whose truth the deified world is defined and configured for eternal life, where deified man is bent and dispatched on the eternal way and thus both, world and man, are jointly subordinated to God's dominion. In the struggle for time, state and art must destroy each other, since the state wishes to stop the flow of time, while art would drift in it. But even this struggle is settled in divinely-ruled nature. World and man find room side by side in the eternity of life and the eternity of the way; there they are deified without being idolized.

THE GOD OF GODS

Thus it is only before the truth that the frenzy of all paganism collapses. Its blind and drunken desire to see itself and only itself, climaxing in the eternal struggle of art and the state, is confronted by the quiet superior power of the divine truth which, because everything lies at its feet as one single great nature, can assign to each its portion and thus order the All. As long as art and the state, each for itself, may both regard themselves as omnipotent, just so long each claims all of nature for itself, and rightly so. Both know nature only as their "material." Only when the truth limited both, the state by means of eternal life, art by means of the eternal way, could it free nature from this double slavery and restore its unity; in this state and art may claim their portion, but no more. As for the truth—whence should it draw its power of carrying the All of nature like a pillar if not from the God who gives himself figure in it and only in it. In the sight of the truth not only does the Perhaps lose its validity—for that had long since disappeared—but in the final analysis every Possibly too. The Star of Redemption, in which the truth achieves configuration, is not in orbit. That which is above, is above and stays above. Viewpoints, *Weltanschauungen*, philosophies of life, isms of every sort—all this no longer dares to show itself to this last simple view of the truth. The points of view are submerged before the one constant sight. Views of the world and of life are absorbed into the one view of God. The isms' retreat before the rising constellation of redemption which, irrespective of whether one believes in it or not, is at any rate meant as a fact and not an ism. Thus there is an Above and a Below, inexchangeable and irreversible. Even the cognizant one may not say If. He too is governed by the Thus, the Thus-and-not-otherwise. And just because there is an Above and a Below in the truth, therefore we may, nay we must call it God's countenance. We speak in images. But the images are not arbitrary. There are essential images and coincidental ones. The irreversibility of the truth can only be enunciated in the image of a living being. For in the living being, an Above and a Below are already designated by nature prior to all theory or regulation. And of living beings in turn there, where self-consciousness is awake to this designation: in man. Man has an above and a below in his own corporeality. And just as the truth, which gave itself configuration in the Star, is in turn assigned within the Star to God as whole truth, and not to man or the world, so too the Star must once more mirror itself in that which, within the corporeality, is again the Upper: the countenance. Thus it is not human illusion if Scripture speaks of God's countenance and even of his separate bodily parts. There is no other way to express the Truth. Only when we see the Star as countenance do we transcend every possible possibility and simply see.

THE FACE OF MAN

Just as the Star mirrors its elements and the combination of the elements into one route in its two superimposed triangles, so too the organs of the countenance divide into two levels. For the life-points of the countenance are, after all, those points where the countenance comes into contact with the world about, be it in passive or active contact. The basic level is ordered according to the receptive organs; they are the building blocks, as it were, which together compose the face, the mask, namely, forehead and cheeks, to which belong respectively nose and ears. Nose and ears are the organs of pure receptivity. The nose belongs to the forehead; in the sacred tongue (Hebrew) it veritably stands for the face as a whole. The scent of offerings turns to it as the motion of the lips to the ears. This first triangle is thus formed by the midpoint of the forehead, as the dominant point of the entire face, and the midpoints of the cheeks. Over it is now imposed a second triangle, composed of the organs whose activity quickens the rigid mask of the first: eyes and mouth. Not that the eyes are mutually equivalent in a mimic sense, for while the left one views more receptively and evenly, the right one fixes its glance sharply on one point. Only the right one "flashes"—a division of labor which frequently leaves its mark deep in the soft neighborhood of the eye-sockets of a hoary head; this asymmetric facial formation, which otherwise is generally conspicuous only in the familiar difference between the two profiles, then becomes perceptible also en face. Just as the structure of the face is dominated by the forehead, so its life, all that surrounds the eyes and shines forth from the eyes, is gathered in the mouth. The mouth is consummator and fulfiller of all expression of which the countenance is capable, both in speech as, at last, in the silence behind which speech retreats: in the kiss. It is in the eyes that the eternal countenance shines for man; it is the mouth by whose words man lives. But for our teacher Moses, who in his lifetime was only privileged to see the land of his desire, not to enter it, God sealed this completed life with a kiss of his mouth. Thus does God seal and so too does man.

PROSPECT: THE EVERYDAY OF LIFE

The Last

In the innermost sanctum of the divine truth, where man might expect all the world and himself to dwindle into likeness of that which he is to catch sight of there, he thus catches sight of none other than a countenance like his own. The Star of Redemption is become countenance which glances at me and out of which I glance. Not God became my mirror, but God's truth. God, who is the last and the first—he unlocked to me doors of the sanctuary which is built in the innermost middle. He allowed himself to be seen. He led me to that border of life where seeing is vouchsafed. For "no man shall see him and live." Thus that sanctuary where he granted me to see him had to be a segment of the hyper-cosmos in the world itself, a life beyond life. But what he gave me to see in this Beyond of life is—none other than what I was already privileged to perceive in the midst of life; the difference is only that I see it and no longer merely hear it. For the view on the height of the redeemed hyper-cosmos shows me nothing but what the word of revelation already enjoined in the midst of life. And to walk in the light of the divine countenance is granted only to him who follows the words of the divine mouth. For—"he has told thee, oh man, what is good, and what does the Lord thy God require of thee but to do justice and to love mercy and to walk humbly with thy God."

THE FIRST

And this Last is not Last, but an ever Nigh, the Nighest; not the Last, in short, but the First. How difficult is such a First! How difficult is every beginning. To do justice and to love mercy—that still looks like a goal. Before any goal, the will can claim to need a little respite first. But to walk humbly with thy God—that is no longer goal. That is so unconditional, so free of every condition, of every But-first and Tomorrow, so wholly Today and thus wholly eternal as life and the way. And therefore it partakes of the eternal truth as directly as do life and the way. To walk humbly with thy God— nothing more is demanded there than a wholly present trust. But trust is a big word. It is the seed whence grow faith, hope and love, and the fruit which ripens out of them. It is the very simplest and just for that the most difficult. It dares

at every moment to say Truly to the
truth. To walk humbly with thy
God—the words are written
over the gate, the gate which
leads out of the mysterious-
miraculous light of the divine sanctuary in which
no man can remain
alive. Whither, then,
do the wings of the
gate open? Thou
knowest it not?
INTO LIFE.

(From *Der Stern der Erlösung*, Vol. III,
pp. 203–211; translated by William Hallo.)

THE NEW THINKING

Philosophy has always inquired into the "essence" of
things. This is the concern that marks it off from the
unphilosophical thinking of sound common sense, which
never bothers to ask what a thing "actually" is. Common
sense is content to know that a chair is a chair, and is unconcerned with the possibility that it may, actually, be
something quite different. It is just this possibility that
philosophy pursues in its inquiry into the essence of
things. Philosophy refuses to accept the world as world,
God as God, man as man! All these must "actually" be
quite different from what they seem, for if they were
not, if they were really only what they are, then philosophy—God forbid!—would be utterly superfluous. At
least, the species of philosophy that insists on discovering something "entirely different." . . .

In its effort to "reduce" the essence of one thing back
to the essence of another, philosophy continues, tirelessly, to work out all possible permutations. From a general point of view, this effort has characterized the three
epochs of European philosophy: cosmological antiquity,
the theological Middle Ages, and our anthropological
modern era—with special emphasis on the pet idea of

this modern era: the idea of reducing everything back to *the self*. The method of basing the experience of the world and of God on the experiencing self is still so much a commonplace of the contemporary philosopher that anyone who rejects this method and prefers instead to trace his experience of the world back to the world, and his experience of God to God, is simply dismissed. This philosophy regards the reductive method as so self-evident that when it takes the trouble to sentence a heretic it is only because he has been guilty of the wrong variety of reduction. He is burned at the stake, either as a "rank materialist" who claimed that everything is world, or as an "ecstatic mystic" who claimed that everything is God. This philosophy never admits that perhaps someone might not want to say that everything "is" something else. However, precisely the "what is?" question applied to "everything" is responsible for all the wrong answers. If it is worth expressing, then a clause with "is" as its main verb must contain something new after the "is"—something that has not been said before. And so, if such "is" questions are put concerning God and the world, we must not be surprised when they evoke the "I" as answer. What else remains? For has not everything else, the world and God, already been disposed of before the "is"? And this is true also when the pantheist and his associate the mystic discover that the world and man are of divine "essence," or when the other firm of Messrs. Materialist and Atheist establishes that man is only a sport of "Nature," and God nothing but a reflection of it.

The truth of the matter is that these three first and last subjects of all philosophizing are like onions, and—pare them down to the ultimate shred—you will find nothing but layer on layer, and never anything "entirely different." It is only thinking that is driven into a labyrinth through the alienating power of the little word "is," which replaces one thing by another. But experience, no matter how deeply it probes, will find only the human in man, the worldly in the world, and the godly in God. And it will find the godly only in God, the worldly only in the world, and the human only in man. Is this, then, the *finis philosophiae*? If it were, so much the worse for philosophy! I do not think it is so bad as

that. More likely, this very point, where traditional philosophy comes to the end of its way of thinking, is the
beginning of philosophy based on experience [*erfah-
rende Philosophie*]. . . .

The question as to the essence of things can produce
nothing but tautological answers. Burrow down and still
further down, and God will still be only godly, man
only human, and the world only worldly. And this holds
equally for all three terms. The concept of God is by no
means an exception. God as a *concept* is no more remote
than the concepts of man and of the world. On the other
hand, the essence of man and the essence of the world
are no easier to understand than the essence of God. We
know equally much—or equally little—about each of
them; we know everything and nothing. If we take each
separately, we have exact knowledge, the immediate
knowledge of experience, of what God, man, and the
world are. If we did not know, how could we talk about
it, and—above all—how could we reduce two of these
three substances to the third, or deny the possibility of
the other two reductions? And we certainly do not know
through any knowledge gained from that thinking which
maliciously replaces one thing by another, what else
may be the nature of God, the world, and man. For if we
did so know, how then could immediate knowledge still
persist strong enough to impel us to raise this question
over and over, and to repeat our attempts at reduction!
Ghosts vanish at the cockcrow of knowledge. These
ghosts never vanish. Our assumption that one of these
essences could be closer, the other remoter from us,
rests on a confusion between the *essence* and the *reality*
of God, world, and man—a confusion closely related to
the misapplication of the meaningless words "immanent"
and "transcendent." Between God, world, and man there
can indeed be nearness and distance, approach and
withdrawal, but these do not take shape as permanent
qualities in the sense that God, for instance, must be a
transcendent being. So far as their essence is concerned,
God, the world, and man are all equally transcendent in
regard to each other, and as to their reality, we cannot
say what they "are," only—but this belongs to a later
chapter.

What do we know of them beyond and in between

this "everything" and "nothing"? We do at any rate know something, the something we mean by the words godly, human, and worldly. For in using these we mean definite things, one of which cannot be mistaken for the other. Just what do we mean? Where shall we find the three essences as unreal and at the same time as immediate as these three adjectives which keep them thoroughly apart seem to imply?

Where are such forms [*Gestalten*] that have essence yet lack truth, life, or reality, to be found? Where is there a God who is not the true one, and not real, a world not living and not true, and human beings neither real nor alive; forms, each of which does not know and does not want to know anything about the other two? In other words, forms that do not occupy the same space with what we call our reality, our truth, our life, and yet hover over everything that goes on within that space? If the reader will recall his Spengler, he can give his own answer. Spengler's Apollonian culture is concerned with just those gods, worlds, and men that we are speaking of. Spengler's concept of the Euclidean accurately designates the separation in essence, the "transcendence" with relation to one another, which we have here described. Only that Spengler, as always, interprets falsely what he sees correctly.

The mythical Olympus, the plastic cosmos, and the hero of tragedy are not done away with just because they are have-beens. In the strict sense of the word they never "have been" at all. For when the man of ancient Greece prayed, his prayers were certainly not heard by Zeus or Apollo, but obviously by God. Nor did the Greek live in the cosmos. He lived in the created world, whose sun is our sun and shone for Homer as it does for us. And this Greek was, moreover, no hero of Attic tragedy; he was a poor human being, even as you and I. Yet in spite of the fact that these three forms never were real, they are the premise of our reality. God is as much alive as the gods of mythology. The created world is as real, and as little mere appearance, as the plastic, finite pales which the Greek thought he was inhabiting, or which as a political being he wished to inhabit, and in his capacity of artist had created around himself. The man to whom God speaks is just as much the true man, just as far from being a mere husk filled with ideals as is the tragic hero stubbornly defying fate. The spiritual forms which, in world history, were isolated only here, only in Spengler's "Apollonian culture," so becoming visible, are present in all life as its secret and invisible premises, regardless of whether it has entered visibly into history, or remained unlimned. That is the character of classical antiquity. . . .

Paganism is not, indeed, the mere bugbear that philosophers of religion make use of to terrorize adults, a role in which the orthodoxy of former centuries cast it. Paganism is no more, no less than truth itself, but truth reduced to its elements, invisible and unrevealed truth. So that whenever paganism sets out to represent the whole instead of an element, the form instead of the invisible, revelation instead of the unrevealed, it becomes a lie. But as an element and the unrevealed contained in the whole, the visible, the revealed, it is everlasting. Just as everlasting as the great objects, the "substances" of thought, in real, unobjective, and unsubstantial experience.

For experience knows nothing of objects. It remembers, it senses, it hopes, and it fears. One might perhaps understand the content of memory by taking it as an object; this would be then a matter of understanding, and no longer the content of memory itself. For I do not remember the content as *my* object. It is only a prejudice of the past three centuries that the "I" must play a part in all consciousness: that a tree cannot be seen by me unless my self sees it. As a matter of fact, that ego of mine comes to the fore only—when it *comes* to the fore, when, for example, I must emphasize that I for one see the tree because someone else does not see it. In that case, my knowledge shows the tree certainly associated with me, but in any other case, I know only about the tree, and about nothing else. Philosophy's claim that the self is omnipresent in all knowledge distorts the content of this consciousness. . . .

What the new philosophy, the new thinking, actually does is to employ the method of sound common sense as a method of scientific thinking. How is this sound common sense distinguished from the unsound that gets its teeth into something and will not let go until it has gulped the something in its entirety, in the same way as the old philosophy? Common sense waits, goes on living; it has no fixed idea; it knows: all in due time! This is the secret that constitutes the wisdom of the new philosophy, which instructs us to think what Goethe had in mind when he wrote his lines on "understanding in time":

> Why is the truth so woefully
> Removed? To depths of secret banned?
> None understands in time! If we
> But understood betimes, how bland
> The truth would be, how fair to see!
> How near and ready to our hand!

The New Thinking, like the age-old thinking of sound common sense, knows that it cannot have cognition independent of time—though heretofore one of philosophy's boasts has been that it is able to do this very thing. One cannot begin a conversation with the end, or a war with a peace treaty (as the pacifists would like), or life with death. Willy-nilly, actively or passively, one must await the given time; one cannot skip a single moment. At every moment, cognition is bound to that very moment and cannot make its past not passed, or its future not coming. This holds for everyday matters, and everyone grants it. Everyone knows that the physician, for instance, must consider his treatment bound up with the present, the beginning of his patient's illness with the past, and the death certificate with the future, and that it would be absurd of him to cling so stubbornly to the theory of timeless cognition as to exclude knowledge and experience in making his diagnosis, boldness and individuality in determining his therapy, and fear and hope in giving his prognosis. To cite another example: no one who is making a purchase seriously believes that what he sees, colored by his desire to buy, will look the same to him later when he regrets having bought it. Yet, this is equally true of great, ultimate matters that we think we behold only as something timeless. What God has done, what he does, what he will do; what has happened to the world and what will happen to it; what has happened to man and what he will do—all this cannot be disengaged from its connection with time. One cannot, for instance, perceive the coming kingdom of God as one perceives the created world, and one must not look upon creation as one looks upon the kingdom of the future; no more than one should allow the flash of present experience to char to a past, or wait for the future to bring it; for this lightning flash is always only in the present and to wait for it is the surest way to prevent it from striking. Similarly, a deed is a deed only while it is still in the offing. Once done, it is merely something that has happened, quite indistinguishable from anything else that has happened.

Thus the tenses of reality cannot be interchanged. Just like every single happening, so reality as a whole has its present, its past, and its future, without which it cannot be, or—at any rate—cannot be *properly* known. Reality too has its past and its future, an everlasting past and an eternal future. To have cognition of God, the world, and man, is to know what they do or what is done to them in these tenses of reality, and to know what they do to one another or what is done to them by one another. And here we presuppose that these three have separate existence, for if they were not separate, they could not act upon one another. If in the "deepest core" the other were identical with myself, as Schopenhauer asserts, I could not love him, for I should be merely loving myself. If God were "within me," or if he were "only my loftier self" then this would be no more than an unnecessarily obscure formulation of an otherwise clear relationship. Above all, this God would hardly have anything to tell me since I know anyhow what my loftier self wishes to tell me. And if there were such a thing as a "godly" man, a theory proclaimed by some German professor fresh from the impact of Rabindranath Tagore's robe, this man would find himself barred from the path to God that is open to every truly human man. Such is the importance of the premise of separate existence, though I shall say no more about it now. For, within reality, and that is all we can experience, the separation is spanned, and what we experience is the experience of the spanning. God veils himself when we try to grasp him; man, our self, withdraws, and the world becomes a visible enigma. God, man, and the world reveal themselves only in their relations to one another, that is, in creation, revelation, and redemption. . . .

In the New Thinking, the method of speech replaces the method of thinking maintained in all earlier philosophies. Thinking is timeless and wants to be timeless. With one stroke it would establish thousands of connections. It regards the last, the goal, as the first. Speech is bound to time and nourished by time, and it neither can nor wants to abandon this element. It does not know in advance just where it will end. It takes its cues from others. In fact, it lives by virtue of another's life, whether that other is the one who listens to a story, answers in the course of a dialogue, or joins in a chorus; while thinking is always a solitary business, even when it is done in common by several who philosophize together. For even then, the other is only raising the objections I should raise myself, and this is the reason why the great majority of philosophic dialogues—including most of Plato's—are so tedious. In actual conversation, something happens.

I do not know in advance what the other person will say to me, because I do not even know what I myself am going to say. I do not even know whether I am going to say anything at all. Perhaps the other person will say the first word, for in a true conversation this is usually the case; a glance at the Gospels and the Socratic dialogues will show the contrast. Usually it is Socrates who sets the conversation going—going in the direction of philosophical discussion. For the thinker knows his thoughts in advance, and his expounding them is merely a concession to what he regards as the defectiveness of our means of communication. This defectiveness is not due to our need of speech but to our need of time. To require time means that we cannot anticipate, that we must wait for everything, that what is ours depends on what is another's. All this is quite beyond the comprehension of the thinking thinker, while it is valid for the "speaking thinker."

I use the term "speaking thinker" for the New Thinking. Speaking thought is, of course, still a form of thinking, just as the old thinking that depended solely on thinking could not go on without inner speech. The difference between the old and the new, the "logical" and the "grammatical" thinking, does not lie in the fact that one is silent while the other is audible, but in the fact that the latter needs another person, and takes time seriously—actually, these two things are identical. In the old philosophy, "thinking" means thinking for no one else and speaking to no one else (and here, if you prefer, you may substitute "everyone" or the well-known "all the world" for "no one"). But "speaking" means speaking to some one and thinking for some one. And this some one is always a quite definite some one, and he has not merely ears, like "all the world," but also a mouth.

Whatever the Star of Redemption can do to renew our ways of thinking is concentrated in this method. Ludwig Feuerbach was the first to discover it. Hermann Cohen's posthumous work reintroduced it to philosophy, though the author himself was not aware of its iconoclastic power. When I wrote the Star of Redemption, I was already familiar with the pertinent passages in Cohen's book, but their influence was not decisive for the genesis of my own work. The main influence was Eugen Rosenstock; a full year and a half before I began to write I had seen the rough draft of his now published *Angewandte Seelenkunde*. Since then, the new philosophy has been expounded in another work, besides the Star, in the first volume of Hans Ehrenberg's *Fichte*, a study of Idealism written in the new form of the true, time-requiring dialogue. Victor von Weizsäcker's *Philosophie des Arztes* will appear shortly. Rudolf Ehrenberg's *Theoretische Biologie* is the first work to subordinate the doctrine of organic nature to the law of real, irreversible time. Martin Buber in his *I and Thou*, and Ferdinand Ebner in *Das Wort und die geistigen Realitäten*, written at exactly the same time as my book, approached the heart of the New Thinking (I dealt with that in the middle section of the Star) independently of the aforementioned books, and of each other. The notes to my Judah ha-Levi give instructive examples of the practical application of the New Thinking. The epochal, largely unpublished works of Florens Christian Rang are founded on a precise and profound knowledge of all this.

With all these men, theological concerns have assisted the New Thinking in coming to the fore. But this does not mean that the New Thinking itself is theological, at least not in the sense in which the term has been used up to now, either with respect to the end or the means. The New Thinking does not center on the so-called "religious problems," which it treats side by side with, or rather together with, the problems of logic, ethics, and aesthetics; nor has it anything in common with the attitude characteristic of thinking along theological lines, an attitude made up of attack and defense, and never quietly concentrated on the matter in hand. If this is theology, it is, at any rate, no less new as theology than as philosophy. . . . Theology must not debase philosophy to play the part of a handmaid, yet the role of charwoman which philosophy has recently assigned to theology is just as humiliating. The true relationship of these two regenerated sciences is a sisterly one, and this must necessarily lead to the personal union of those who deal with them. Theological problems must be translated into human terms, and human problems brought into the pale of theology. The problem of the name of God, for example, is only part of the problem of the logic of names in general, and an aesthetics that is not concerned with whether artists may attain salvation is an agreeable but incomplete form of scholarly investigation.

God did not, after all, create religion; he created the world. And when he reveals himself, that world not only persists all around us but is more created than ever. For revelation does not at all destroy true paganism, the paganism of creation; it only accords it the miracle of return and renewal. Revelation is always present, and if it occurred in the past, then it was in that past which is the beginning of the history of mankind: it is the revelation granted to Adam. . . .

We have not yet touched on the two distinct historical manifestations of revelation, on Judaism and its antipodal offspring, Christianity. The New Thinking is Jewish or Christian thinking only because and to the extent that these renew the "revelation granted to Adam." On the other hand, because and to the extent that paganism in its historic forms has forgotten or denied this revelation to Adam (who was no more pagan than he was Jewish or Christian), to this extent historic paganism, hardened as it is into a form of its own, is not in the least perennial. Its very independence and rigid form debar it from true reality. It is quite justified that the temples of the gods have crumbled, and their images stand in museums. The part of their service which was governed by prescribed rites may have been nothing but stupendous error, yet the prayers that rose to the gods from a heart in torment, the tears in the eyes of the Carthaginian father offering his son up to Molech—these cannot have remained unheard and unseen. Did God wait for Mount Sinai or, perhaps, Golgotha? No paths that lead from Sinai and Golgotha are guaranteed to lead to him, but neither can he possibly have failed to come to one who sought him on the trails skirting Olympus. There is no temple built so close to him as to give man reassurance in its closeness, and none is so far from him as to make it too difficult for man's hand to reach. There is no direction from which it would not be possible for him to come, and none from which he must come; no block of wood in which he may not once take up his dwelling, and no psalm of David that will always reach his ear.

Judaism and Christianity have a peculiar position in common: even after having become a religion, they find in themselves the impulse to overcome the fixity of a religious institution, and to return to the open field of reality. All historical religions are "founded." Only Judaism and Christianity are not founded religions. Originally they were something quite "unreligious," the one a fact, the other an event. They were surrounded by all kinds of religion, but they themselves would have been dumbfounded to be taken for religions. It is their parody Islam that is a religion from its very start, and never aims to be anything else; it is a deliberately founded religion. . . .

Judaism and Christianity are the two eternal dials for the week- and year-hand of time, time that is constantly being renewed. In them, in their year, the course of world-time, which cannot be imaged forth but only experienced and told, takes shape as an image. In their God, their world and their man, the secret of God, of the world and of man, which can only be experienced but not expressed in the course of life, can be expressed. We do not know what God "is," what the world or what man "is." We only know what they do or what is done to them. But we do know quite accurately what the Jewish or Christian God, the Jewish or Christian world, the Jewish or Christian man, look like. In place of existing substances [*seiende Substanzen*] which are everlasting only in that they are the secret premises of ever renewed reality, we have forms [*Gestalten*] that eternally reflect a reality eternally renewed.

In the Star of Redemption the picture of Judaism and Christianity is determined above all by the quest for an eternity that *exists*, hence by the task of fighting the danger of interpreting the New Thinking in the sense (or rather non-sense) of tendencies directed toward a "philosophy of life" or other irrational goals. In our day and age, all those who are clever enough to avoid the jaws of the Scylla of Idealism seem to be drawn into the dark whirlpool of this Charybdis. In both cases, Judaism and Christianity, the picture is not beholden to the ways in which they interpret themselves; in Judaism it does not proceed from the Law, in Christianity it does not proceed from Faith: but in both, from the external, visible forms by whose means they wrest their eternity from time; in Judaism from the fact of the Jewish people, in Christianity from the event on which the Christian community is founded, and only through these do Law and Faith become visible. And so here Judaism and Christianity are set both side by side and in contrast, on a sociological basis. This gives rise to a picture not quite fair to either of them, but which (taking this sacrifice into account) goes beyond the usual apologetics and polemics in the field—probably for the first time. . . .

There still exists the belief that all philosophy should begin with considerations that are part and parcel of a theory of knowledge. Actually, it may end with them. Kant, the originator of the epistemological bias, is— through his criticism—himself such an end, the end of the epoch in history which began with the natural science of the seventeenth century. His criticism is directly applicable only to the philosophy of that epoch. Copernicus pronounced man a mote of dust in the vast universe. Kant's own "Copernican turn of thought," which—

to restore the equilibrium—sets man on the throne of that same universe, corresponds to the mote-of-dust idea much more precisely than he himself realized. But his excessive correction of the terrible humiliation Copernicus inflicted on man and his humanity has also been made at the cost of the human quality in man. All criticism follows upon performance. The drama critic will have little to say *before* it, no matter how clever he may be, for his criticism is not supposed to testify to what cleverness he had prior to the performance but to that which the performance evoked in him. Similarly, a theory of knowledge that precedes knowledge has no meaning. For all knowing—whenever anything is really known—is a unique act, and has its own method. Methodological speculation on history in general cannot replace an investigation based on the work of an individual historian any more than the opinion of a professor of literature on some drama will replace the newspaper criticism formulated under the immediate impression of the stage performance. In fact, methodological thought replaces such an investigation to an even slighter degree; for in the case of drama and performance, both are, at least, a matter of the same book, while—fortunately!—there is no "history in general." Now philosophy is governed by the same laws as every piece of scholarly work. Such work must approach its material with methods and instruments never before used in order to discover the secret of just this material, and it is only the student who allows the professor—instead of the material itself—to prescribe the method of approach. . . .

If something is to come out of knowledge, it means that—exactly as in the case of a cake—something has to be put into it. What was put into the Star of Redemption was, first of all, the experience of factuality that precedes all facts of real experience, factuality that forces thinking to employ (instead of its favorite term "actually") the little word "and," the basic word of all experience, the word the philosopher's tongue is not used to. God *and* the world *and* man! This "and" was the beginning of experience and so it must recur in the ultimate aspect of truth. For there must be an "and" within truth itself, within ultimate truth that can only be *one*. Unlike the truth of the philosophers, which is not allowed to know anything but itself, this truth must be truth for some one. If it is to be the one truth, it can be one only for the One, God. And that is why our truth must of necessity become manifold, and why "the" truth must be converted into "our" truth. Thus truth ceases to be what "is" true and becomes a verity that wants to be verified, realized in active life. This becomes the fundamental concept of this new theory of knowledge. This theory replaces the old theories of non-contradiction and objects, and introduces a dynamic for the old static concept of objectivity. Regarded from this new plane, hopelessly static truths like those of mathematics, which the old theory of knowledge took as its point of departure without really ever getting beyond that point, are on the limits (the inferior limits), just as rest is a limit case of motion. The higher and the highest truths can be conceived as truths only via the New Thinking, which does not necessitate their being altered to fiction, postulates, or human desiderata. From those most unimportant truths, such as "two times two are four," on which people are apt to agree without making more than a minimum use of their brains (a little less for the multiplication table through ten, a little more for the theory of relativity), the way leads over those truths for which man is willing to pay, on to those that he cannot verify save at the cost of his life, and finally to those that cannot be verified until generations upon generations have given up their lives to that end.

But this messianic theory of knowledge that values truths according to what it has cost to verify them, and according to the bond they create among men, cannot lead beyond the two eternally irreconcilable hopes for the Messiah: the hope for one to come and the hope for one to return; it cannot lead beyond the "and" of these final efforts in behalf of truth. Beyond this, only God can verify the truth, and for him only is there only one truth. Earthly truth still continues to be split, as split as extra-divine factuality, as the original facts: world and man, which—along with the "and"— return in the ultimate facts of Judaism and Christianity, as the world of Law and the Faith of man, as the Law of the world and the man of Faith. . . .

The reader has been denied what he asks and what, after all, he has a right to ask: a slogan under which to bury whatever he has learned about the New Thinking in the cemetery of his general education. It was not from ill will that I failed to give him that slogan, but because I really don't know any. It is true that the work in which I have tried to expound the New Thinking attacks certain slogans with an animus that goes far beyond any general animus of mine against *isms* of all sorts. But must I, therefore, allow the book to be tagged with the usual opposites of those *isms*? How can I? The designation I would soonest accept would be that of absolute empiricism; this at least covers the attitude of the New Thinking in all three areas: the primordial world of the idea, the world of reality, and the transcendental world of truth; the attitude that claims to know nothing more of the divine than what it has experienced—but to know this really, in the teeth of philosophy, which may brand this knowledge as "beyond" the "possible" experience; and nothing more of terrestrial matters than it has experienced—but nothing, although philosophy may laud it as a knowledge "anterior" to all "possible" experience. Such faith in experience might constitute the formulable element in the New Thinking, if the aforementioned slogan didn't constitute in itself one of those formulations which, precisely because they come from the author, strike the reader as on the one hand not only simple but too simple, and on the other, more difficult than the book itself. Both are inevitable. The greatest of the Jewish poets [Judah ha-Levi] knew the former when he made the sage answer the heathen king [the Kuzari] thus: "My words are too difficult for you, and that is why they seem too simple to you." And the greatest of the German poets knew the latter when he made Mephistopheles answer Faust's eager words, "There many riddles will be solved," with, "But many riddles will also be propounded."

(From *Franz Rosenzweig: His Life and Thought*, pp. 190–208.)

WORLD—MAN—GOD

THE WORLD

Nowadays a *Weltanschauung* is a valuable asset, and it would appear quite natural and obvious that the world should be "viewed." However, the truth of the matter is that man becomes acquainted merely with certain fragments of the world, at best coming in contact with only a limited number of things and people and events. If such a loose agglomeration of accidentally encountered fragments is considered the world, no harm need result from having a *Weltanschauung*. The word *Weltanschauung* is, however, sometimes associated with a much less modest claim. Here the word signifies more than a mere river bed passively permitting the stream of things and people and events to flow by; it is understood as a bowl which the observer dips into the stream and fills—not always to the brim—and which he then gazes at in undisturbed wonder. He gazes at the bowl and not at the river. The river cannot be dammed. It pays no heed to the attempts to dam it; it rushes on. The bowl, however, can be dipped into the stream and brought up at will.

It can be brought up and considered by itself. Once something is isolated from the flow of real objects—in our case the world—the question "What is it? What is it in essence?" is inevitably raised. And so once again the question is repeated. The answer to this question is always the same: Whatever it is, it is not what it appears to be. And what does it appear to be? Well, the world. This, then, is mere appearance, an illusion [*Schein*]. But what is it in truth—"essentially"?

Several answers suggest themselves; and each of these answers represents the phenomenon seen from a certain point of view. First and foremost, it may be considered mere appearance, an illusion. Here we refrain from expressing its "essence" further, and catch hold of this single statement. Nevertheless we delve beneath the surface. A glance is sufficient to clear up the "mystery of es-

sence" for us; we come to the conclusion that beneath
the surface there is nothing. The essence of the world
then is, Nothing. A number of world views and even religions have happily attained to this ultimate wisdom.

It is also possible to begin with the assumption that
appearance conceals "something" which is not mere appearance. The world, then, is not what it appears to be,
but is something entirely different. It is unfortunate that
so little is left in the world which can be entirely different. That all-inclusive term "world" includes so much.
Two words, however, do escape by the skin of their
teeth. The first of these words is "I," and there can be
no doubt that it has had great popularity with the philosophers. After all, who is it that encounters the world?
I do. Confronted by the world, my "ego" remained. I
think, therefore I am. My "ego" is the only certainty.
The world is appearance, illusion. However, it does appear to me; this is more than mere illusion. This is
"essence," and it is concluded that the "ego" is the essence of the world. All the wisdom of philosophy can
be summed up in this sentence. Of course there are distinctions and "schools of thought," and I am told that
these distinctions are weighty and important.

And yet all the efforts, no matter how sublime or subtle, to bolster these distinctions are to no avail. There is
no reason to assign to the "ego" a certainty which it cannot maintain. My own "ego" can certainly not lay claim
to such a privileged position. Inasmuch as it is mine it is
a part of the world and hence not distinguished from any
other "ego" which it encounters. Any claim to the contrary must be based upon that which is suprapersonal in
my "ego"—that is, its ability to become aware of its distinctive individuality. Strictly speaking, it is only my
consciousness of self that I cannot encounter beyond the
realm of myself. And yet, when taken as a datum, such
consciousness is encountered outside my self. I am forced
to accept, for better or worse, the statement of others
that they also possess consciousness of self, although in
their case it is a consciousness of their selves, not mine.
It would seem to follow that the world possess as many
"essences" as there are "egos" with separate conscious-
nesses. To avoid this absurd conclusion we are forced to
revert to some abstract consciousness-in-itself. Of this "con-

sciousness-in-itself," however, we know nothing. And furthermore the definition of pure suprapersonal consciousness excludes the possibility of knowledge. And so the "ego" is thwarted in its attempt to become the essence of the world; it turns out to be nothing. It is neither "subject" nor "object"—nothing. To justify its claims it must be nothing. The result: the essence of the world is "nothing"; nothing is at the core of the "world of appearance." It seems we have been overcharged for this delicious bit of information.

At this point we are informed that the fault rests with us. We have undertaken a fallacious enterprise—philosophy. This much philosophy understood correctly—the world must be something other than it appears to be. But this something cannot be identified with the Self. The "ego" also dwells in the world and is perhaps the most problematic of all "appearances." That which exists behind and beneath appearance has to be something wholly other. The world appears to the Self, but conversely the Self also appears to the world. The witness is witnessed while witnessing. The astonishing fact about the world's appearance is not that there is someone to whom it appears. That a lucent eye catches sight of a sunbeam does not explain the luminary. It is the sunlight which illuminates the eye, dispels its darkness and acts upon the iris which mirrors its rays. The brilliance of light informs us of an illuminating source. No blaze without a fire. Light may shine without an eye to see, but not without a source. It is not man to whom light appears, but He who kindles the light, the illuminator, not the illuminated, who is concealed behind appearance. God, not man, exists behind the world.

God? Who is He? We have just detected the emptiness of the argument which posits the "ego" as world-essence. Is this another attempt to deceive us by a second empty word? We know that inevitably we will be given the answer of the mystics. But does mysticism make out a better case than philosophy? What can one comprehend of Him except that He is "wholly other" than the world and therefore its essence? Can one dare to call anything, anything at all, in this world of appearances, divine? This would be sufficient to divest God of His one significant function: to be wholly other than the world. The world, it was claimed, is appearance, and nothing but appearance: would any manifestation of God within the world then be a mere reflection of appearance? Everything in the world which bears the name of God—the burning faith deep in the heart of men as well as the flame dedicated to Him at the altar— must be considered merely shimmer and appearance. Such a God can have nothing in common with the God who acts as trustee of the world as it "appears," and of all "appearance." There is a remarkable resemblance between this God, the trustee of appearance, and the Self, in which appearance reappears. A God who deviates even by a hair's breadth from sheer, absolute nothing cannot be accepted as transcending appearance. To be essence He must be nothing. Again we have attempted to pierce the veil of appearance, and again all we have to show for our pains is nothing. Truly, once again, we have been overcharged.

Is *nothing* truly the "order" which is the essence behind appearance—pure, unadulterated appearance as well as the appearance of something, to somebody, about something? Is there no other way out? Is it not possible that appearance is everything and everything is only appearance? Is it not possible that there is nothing beyond appearance, not even something "wholly other"? And, if this is granted, can we not say that the world is everything [*Alles*]? Thus man, himself appearance, reflects a segment of the mirage, or, indeed, (why not?) the complete mirage. And God is merely the shadow cast by the frame of the mirror, or possibly the reflection of the mirror's glass.

This *is* undoubtedly the world with which we are so well acquainted. It is a world unaware of an Outside, of Before and After, of Hither and Yon, of Foremost and Hindmost, a world which refuses to acknowledge anything but itself. And even this acknowledgment is negated by its view that its very own self is mere appearance, illuminated by nothing and illuminating nothing. It is a world which has no reality beyond appearance, which is made up of multilateral refractions of appearance, appearance irradiated by appearance and the source itself of more appearance, reflecting nothing but appearance. There are no limits to this universal interaction of appearances. It is futile therefore to consider it as a whole; a whole would have boundaries and their shape would be a reality and not merely the reflection of an appearance.

Yes, indeed, we know this world. It belongs to "science" which at the present time constitutes a power next to "philosophy" and "mysticism." It presents unlimited claims and yet is easily satisfied. The discovery of a new beam of experience makes it happy; it would be contented if it could obtain another ray by rearrangement of the points of irradiation; such contentment is gained daily. The ultimate in satisfaction would be reached if science could chart the infinite possibilities of the reflections and deflections of appearance. This is a satisfaction that can never be had.

The essence of the world is appearance, boundless and undetermined. The undetermined character of appearance is thus, nothingness. It is nothingness which must be reaffirmed incessantly. In this respect it is unlike that nothingness which is commonly accepted as self-evident by those who regard the world as sheer appearance from the very first. It is rather a nothingness which only becomes aware of its true character when it arrives at the conclusion that it will never reach its goal. It becomes aware of itself as nothingness if it does not deceive itself by the paradoxical concept of approximating the infinite—a paradox obvious to any student of mathematics, although it seems to frustrate our scholars. The sum of all appearances does not create Being; this could only happen if appearance ceased to be appearance. And that the world *is* appearance is the very foundation of this particular world-view. Being must be a stable something, not an appearance, in brief not an "essence"; it must *be*.

Is this perhaps the answer? All other answers to our question concerning the essence of the world of appearances have proved fruitless. We found that the answers, "Nothing," "I," "God," "Everything," were all reducible to the first answer, namely "Nothing." Does this last possible answer survive the test of such a reduction? Are we justified in saying that the world is—something?

"Something" is a simple word. Is it too trivial in its simplicity? Can such a word serve as a proper answer?

Is it not lightly used by exasperated parents to allay the curiosity of their children? And furthermore, even if we take this answer seriously, even if we say "the world is something," is this not an example of the "it is truly" type of answer, the acceptance of which cannot be expected from simple common sense? Yes, we have here an "it is" answer, but why? Since the question inquired about "essence," the answer that it elicited had to be in a corresponding form. Our answer is, however, characterized by a lack of presumption, quite unlike those answers which insisted on plumbing the "deeper regions" in order to demonstrate "essence." The latter pretended to ultimate profundity, while ours does not desire to be profound but prefers to keep to the surface. It does not wish to speak of an ultimate issue but of primary ones. It does not wish a person to remain with it. It must be just a beginning. It does not claim to be truth —it does, however, aspire to *become* true. Thus it is merely a diving board.

To dive from this board is neither impossible nor difficult. A man destroys any possibility of acquiring knowledge of the world unless he begins with the commonplace that the world is something rather than nothing, something—not I, not God, not everything. It does not matter whether this course is taken consciously as a thinking person might take it, or unconsciously in the process of living. Man takes his first step towards an answer as part of the continuing process of life and of thought. Having served its initiation purpose, it turns out that there is nothing final about the answer, that it is as inadequate and incorrect as the question which brought it into existence.

The world is something. That is to say, it is not nothing; neither is it everything. There are other entities. This preliminary knowledge presupposes that the other entities, namely God and I, are at every moment accessible to the world, reach the world. Mention of the world requires the very next instant mention of man and God. The world is something only because it enters the stream to which it and everything else belongs. It is drawn into the stream by something which is not a part of the world, yet does not claim to be its "essence." The world clings to this something in a purely external manner, indicating thereby that there is something which may be considered outside of the world. God and man are truly external to the world, not its interior, nor "essence." By saying that the world is something, we merely express the fact that it is neither man nor God, that neither constitute its "essence." Thus at last we discover something which is the companion of everything, including every event which takes place in the world, and yet is external to them all: the Word. Language is not the world, nor does it make such claims. What actually is it? Unlike "thought," language cannot presume to be the "essence" of the world. If the world is something which permits the existence of other things exterior to the world but not its essence, there is only one thing that language can be; it must be a bridge between the world and these other things. And that is precisely what it is.

What spans the gap between my Self and the world? Moreover, since I am a part of the world, its citizen, how can I make a distinction between my Self and the world? Am I not merely a part among parts, a citizen among other citizens? The argument that I think the world, that I mirror it in thought and observation turns out to be invalid since the world, in return, mirrors my Self even as it thinks and observes. Therefore my thought cannot be the world's essence; and indeed the contrary assumption forced us to reduce thought to the nothing that it is. Language makes no such claims. It neither can, nor does it want to be, the world's essence. It only names the things of the world. Adam gives names; words find their way to things. To utter a word is to affix a seal as a witness of man's presence. The word is not part of the world; it is the seal of man.

Is it exclusively this? Then sick reason's characteristic distrust of words is justified. After all, at some point man must have *begun* to name. Even today it is frequently possible to determine when a thing was assigned a name, when it was discovered in its seclusion. In addition, human language is equivocal; a thing is besieged by a multitude of words, and scarcely two of them have precisely the same meaning. People speaking the same language may not even understand each other. What bearing, then, does the word have upon the thing to which it belongs? Obviously the words of humans are in themselves insufficient. In addition, there must be the certainty that what the individual has begun by his act of naming will be continued until the ultimate goal of common language is reached. Each word, as soon as it comes into existence, requires the strength of continuation and the capacity to traverse the river of time so that it may finally become the ultimate word. The word of man, an initial word whenever it is uttered by man, joins that which was ultimate from the first, the word of God. The intention of language to form composite designations and double names, its capacity to create such designations, is shown by the way things obtain a name whenever someone confronts them. To name is the primal right of all men, a right which they are forever exercising. The one condition required is that the creator of the name actually confront the thing. At this stage the name is only a cognomen. And then also the person, or persons, to whom the originator of the name exhibits the thing, must be present. Thus Adam performed the act of naming, and so also do his offspring.

In addition to these names, a thing has names which it does not receive. It already possesses them. They also may have been "cognomens," at some moment uttered for the first time. However, as soon as they are spoken, they adhere to the thing. From then on the thing goes by that name. The thing possesses equally the right to keep the name it has, and to receive new names. Whoever gave the old name may be absent or even dead; in spite of this the name he gave still clings to the thing. And furthermore each new name must come to terms with the old ones. The thing gathers names, and indeed its capacity to do this is inexhaustible. It is man's privilege to give new names. It is his duty to use the old ones, a duty which he must perform, though unwillingly. His obligation to pass on the old names, to appropriate them and translate them into names he himself designates— this creates the continuity of mankind. Mankind is always absent. Present is a man, this fellow or that one. The thing, however, is tied to all of mankind by language and by its inherent law of transmission and translation. These linguistic laws require that each new word confront the old.

And where does the presence of mankind manifest

itself? Not in the word of man, of course, but in that of God. It is not entirely by accident that the Bible is the most widely translated of all books. (It is probably the first book of consequence to have been translated.) The word of God implies the certainty that it will become the word of all. We say there is a certainty, not merely a probability. There is no one for whom the word of God is not meant, whose presence is not implied by it; the word of man implies the presence of the speaker and someone to whom his speech is addressed—and so also with the word of God. If it were not necessary that the word of God become the word of all, we should consider the existence of such a possibility just one of the aspects of "civilization," or something of the sort. But it is not enough to rely upon the good intentions of man to integrate his own newly formed names into the context of all names which have been designated and are yet to be designated. Man is under the obligation to exact such an integration. He is in need of those names which are absent. He needs all of them without exception. Although they should remain forever absent, he must nevertheless take them into account. Being absent, they do not force themselves upon man's attention; but He, for whom both he and they are present, forces man to pay attention. And thus things insist on their privilege of being named and going by a name.

There is no thing which does not share in the language of man and God through its name, through the innumerable words spoken in its vicinity. Language stamps the sign of God and man upon all the things of this world. That a thing is considered something by the world gives it its continuity. The thing is not an appearance, an illusion; it is something. The thing does not gain in definition by being isolated and made stagnant; certainty of being "something" is not achieved by plumbing the depths of such an entity, but rather by opening the floodgates and permitting the stream of which it is part to inundate it. Our patient found himself incapable of purchasing a slab of butter because he could no longer avail himself of his God-given right, his privilege as a man, of conferring names. He had lost faith in the continuity of names and of other things; he had renounced his human privilege. And it was because he did not

believe in the divine quality of language that he became uncertain of the names which he and others assigned to things. This necessarily followed from his insistence that the word "be" the thing, that his word be
the word of others. We have learned that this is something that must be foregone. The thing is and as such
immediately acquires a name. Its name bears it into the
flow of things, and hence the question concerning the
essence of things becomes meaningless. Even the world
turns out to be only a segment of the whole, not an
"essence," a part to which, like to other parts, something
may occur [*geschehen*].

Three forces, thus, act upon even the smallest thing.
Any thing is part of the world, and receives its name
through man. God pronounces the judgment of fate
upon this carrier of many names. New "things" are happening at every stage in this process, and they become
events. This course of events, originating in things, never
comes to an end. Since the world of things is itself only
a segment of the whole, it suffers—as any something
must, even as the whole does—the process of history and
it is through this process that it is realized. The world is
real only insofar as it enters into this process, a process
which brings all of it within the context of the human
word and God's sentence. The world as such does not
exist. To speak of the world is to speak of a world which
is ours and God's. It becomes the world as it becomes
man's and God's world. Every word spoken within its
confines furthers this end.

This is the ultimate secret of the world. Or rather, this
would be its ultimate secret, if there were anything
secret. But common sense blurts out this secret every
day. As for common sense, it regards each day as final,
"ultimate." We face the world each day innocently and
fearlessly, considering it as the ultimate that it is; we confront all of its reality, willing to submit to each name.
We are certain that our names are the names of things
and that the name we bestow will be confirmed by God.

And thus each day we solve the ultimate question,
frankly confronting each thing as we encounter it; we
look for nothing beyond, do not try to walk suspiciously
around the object; nor do we peer into its depths, but
accept it rather as it is, as it hastens towards us. And

then we leave it behind and wait for whatever is to come tomorrow.

MAN

Life is not the most precious of all things; nevertheless it is beautiful. And what is life? This obviously is not the same question we asked before—our question concerning the world. Man has a view of life—*Lebensanschauung*—and this is a different matter from having an opinion about the world—*Weltanschauung*. We do not acquire a view of life; we are born with it. At any rate one day we notice that we possess one. Somehow or other it is a part of being human. What is life? And what is man? These are one and the same question asked in different terms.

What is man? What am I? Again the question is an ultimate one involving essence, a "what is it" question. This time, however, the inquiry is not about the "It" of the world but rather about the "ego" of man. Again an easy answer is on hand. Whatever this "ego" may be, it is certainly not what appears to me. It cannot be simply my "ego," that "ego" which constantly shows up in all experience and even beyond experience constantly ready to encounter life once more. This is certainly delusion, perhaps self-delusion. Though it confounds both deceiver and deceived, yet it remains deception.

But why must we accept this answer? Is it not because of the way the question has been posed? The nature of such an answer, beginning with "It is," requires that the predicate give additional knowledge. The predicate must add to our wisdom; it must have more of essence about it, be closer to the truth, if by only a hair, than the subject—as for instance four is as regards two times two. If I extract my "ego" from the environment in which it exists, if I observe it in isolation, then it immediately dissolves into hundreds of experiences scarcely distinguishable from each other. It will be difficult to discover a relationship between the "being" I was yesterday and the "being" I am today, or rather, with my present experience; equally difficult to discover will be the relationship between the "being" I will be tomorrow and tomorrow's experiences. The "ego" cannot be saved.

Is this actually so? A voice gives us contradictory advice; the "ego" must be saved. We must cling to it desperately, reflect on it, penetrate to its depths. Its surface, of course, is nothing but self-delusion but in its interior its essence will be revealed to us, that hiding place which the "ego" seeks and must then find. Beware of him who despairs and agrees to doubt with you. Beware of that straying mind whose "ego" has dissipated into thin air. Do not believe his loud assertion that the "ego" is nothing. The poor misguided fellow does not know that, if we are to enjoy life, we ourselves must give it significance. And even if he wishes to dispute that life has value, he first must live. Whether one doubts or believes, one cannot dispense with the "ego," with ourselves.

This indispensable Self is by no means identical with that Self which we found it impossible to save. Abandon that which is beyond recovery, let it fragment into its elements of personal experience; this is not that Self which is indispensable. To doubt or to believe, for yea or for nay, one requires that other Self which dwells beneath self-deception in the hidden house of essence. You lose your "ego" only insofar as you insist that it remain personal. Raise it; it lives beyond the narrow confines of your being in which it seemed to be imprisoned. Invest it with the authority for which it was ordained, and not only your own Self, but the whole world with its idols and gods, will be subject to you. There is nothing but you, if you will it so. If you liberate your will from petty stubbornness, it becomes omnipotent volition—God; within you, it is God who wills; you are merely His tool, His voice. True, then, your Self is only a deception, a self-deception. But have the courage to be God. There is no God if you are willing to take upon yourself His office. Should you refuse to do this and deprive your Self of being God, how can such a Self endure God's existence?

Madness! another voice shouts. What absurdity! First you believe that your Self, as a reflection of the "ego" within you, is self-delusion, and then you inflate the Self until it is too large to pass for deception; you regard it as not deception, if it is God's self-delusion. You are a fool and you know it, and that is all you know. Who, then, is the deceiver? An "ego," even the hugest "ego," would only deceive itself, if it believed that beyond its needs and desires, its knowledge and requirements, another "ego" was hidden which also needed and desired and knew.

The magician who dwells in the cave below the Self cannot be another "ego"; this which releases the effervescence of your petty self as well as the giant bubble of divine consciousness must be an altogether different entity. You dare not name that from which the divine and human "egos" emerge, which, relinquishing them, allows them to brighten the short spans of their existence with dreams of power and feeling. You dare not name such an entity because you lack the courage to live without deceit. Your wretched little wisp of life must be in the center of the universe, and should you sneeze, you expect the stars to come tumbling down.

Pretending to the throne of the world, you are expelled from your own home; it is what you deserve; your pretensions made you despise your rightful place and you acted as though you headed a government of the world in exile instead of taking care of your house. The world can safely leave you to your pretensions; you are incapable of making a single move on its chessboard. And even were you to attain to the authority you claim, you would be incapable of doing more than confirm the statutes already in existence. Through the eyes of your giant, self-inflated ego, absolute nothing grins—absolute nothing which neither knows nor feels nor wants.

I fortunately have recognized my proper place from which nothing can budge me. The law of the world is my law; to obey it willingly, my duty and privilege. There is only one world and it is ruled by a single law. This world and this law determine even that ignorant self-delusion which believes itself independent of such law. Your Self is of the world, a part of it—nothing more. It has become detached according to the principles of eternal law, just as the bough sprouts from the tree, the sprig from the branch, and finally the leaves and blossoms from the sprig. Each believes itself to be more than it is; sprig believes itself to be branch, leaf, sprig, blossom, leaf—each a complete Self, and yet they are Selves only through that law which brings forth the sprout from the tree and permits it to feed upon it, age with it, die and disappear. The blossom may believe that its will determined the number of its leaves and the form of its seed, that it created the laws which ruled the tree—it may believe this, but soon it withers away and as it drops from the tree it wakes from its delusive dream. But the law of the tree remains unaltered. And so also the world remains unaltered while the dance of the Self, the witches' dance of human "egos" and deified "egos" continues, forever creating new steps and yet repeating the same pattern.

But let us pause a moment and have a closer look at this world which you have erected as a foundation underlying my "ego." You speak of its law in much the same way as your adversary spoke of the will of God. You attacked his position maintaining that whatever he said of God's will, I could say of mine as well. You argued that he could know nothing about God's will, since such a will could not properly serve as the essence of mine. God was allowed to will, think, know, only as I will and think and know. His own will, thought, and knowledge had to be completely vacant of personality, if my dream of being a Self was not to be destroyed. It was necessary that his will be nothing, or else it became impossible for me to deceive myself into the belief that *I* was something.

In precisely the same way, you now empty your law of all the qualities one might expect a world law to have. The tree which you describe has no bark of its own, no roots. It consists entirely of sprigs and leaves and blossoms. Where then is the law of the tree appointing you to the post in which you have established yourself? You are not, as you wish us to believe, the bearer of the world's law. You have appointed your own kind as law of the world; all turns into a black nothingness unless you color the world—yours are the tinges that illuminate it. Your antagonist received his authority from pale nothing, and you would like to derive your dignity from a nothing that is black. Unless you stand on your own, unless you live independently, neither God nor the world can help you. No matter whether you deceive in the guise of master or knave, whether you prefer to deceive by your deceit or be deceived by it, your acts and transactions are fraudulent. Be yourself. Be what you are, a human being, or else renounce yourself.

Very well then, let us adopt the other possibility. Let us not seek for anything beyond ourselves. Let us be ourselves and nothing more. Such a moment of existence may be nothing but delusion; we shall, however, choose to remain within the moment, deceived by it and deceiving it, rather than live in deception above or below the moment. Let our personal experience, even though it change from instant to instant, be reality. Let man become the bearer of these shifting images. It is preferable that he change masks a hundred times a day (at least they do belong to him) rather than wear continually the mask of the divine ruler of the world (gained by thievery) or that of the world's bondservant (forced upon him). The hundred masks will serve in lieu of one countenance. Whenever I encounter man, I shall steep my countenance in his until it reflects his every feature. Even should I confront only the shadow of a face, buried deep in the mute and accusing eyes of an animal or in the silent gaze of ancient ritual stones, I shall submerge myself in them until I have absorbed their countenances and thus come in contact with everything that ever existed. Thus, traveling about the earth, I shall come face to face with my own Self. The innumerable masks of the innumerable instants, yours and mine, they are my countenance.

My face? Would I then find myself? Do I find myself, finding the world, deciphering everything that ever wore human features? The human eye may well have drunk in the dying murmurs of the sea and witnessed the waning stars of the nocturnal sky. Thus it is possible that I have participated in every spark of life, whether animal, man or God, which ever glowed within the expanse of sea or sky—but where has my own life gone, where shall it find a dwelling-place? What fate awaits the traveler who voyages to every shore? He is estranged from his own hearth, and yet he seeks his image there, unaware that his Self watches him through the ancient flames burning on the stationary hearthstones. Did our traveler forget that he is only a shadow of himself, a nothing, deluding himself and others by the innumerable masks he wears? Indeed he has shared in all lives but his own.

So it turns out that no matter what we do the life of man dissolves into nothing. We heeded him who promised salvation by divinizing human life, and it was to no avail. His God we discovered was nothing. We went the way prescribed by him who said we should be saved if we submitted to the law of the world—but in vain. His world was also nothing. And finally we attempted to live life, without dependence, with complete self-reliance, all of life—and our own life becomes nothing. Nothing, always nothing. We seek a life which is something—not everything, only something, but a something which truly is.

Again we must deal carefully with that ever-recurring question, "What actually is it?"; again we must remember that when we reply to that question, "something," this is in reality not an answer but only a point of departure, a starting point. What is revealed is that he who seeks to find out everything through life and through life alone discovers nothing. Just as we caught hold of a world existing in the realm of God and man, we must daringly seize upon a life which is content to be an in-between state, merely a transition from one thing to another. Let us reject the ever-present answer, "Life is," "Man is—" and let us become part of the onward-moving life of man. Here life "is" not, it simply occurs [*geschieht*].

Once again it is language which erects the visible bridge from man to that which is not man, to the "other." A person's name, his first name, is so external [*äusserlich*] to him, that it is sufficient witness to the fact that there is something exterior to man, a "without" [*Aussen*] surrounding him. Man, however, attempts to invalidate this testimony by use of the little word "merely," merely a name. This "merely" implies that he might have a different name (how true this is). He received his name from his parents (what a profound observation!) and he could if he wished change it legally (an argument of incontrovertible validity). To sum up: a name is an intrinsically human affair; but this does not mean that it does not differ from other intrinsically human matters. The very acute observations which we have seen advanced as objections form the basis of this difference: a name is external to a person. When, then, is a name required, and what happens to a man when his name is spoken?

Here, again, the answer is simple. It can be seen most clearly in the case of a somnambulist or a person only half alive. He is forced into the presence of mind, to the internal, to himself. And where was he before? He dwelt in the past, in the "external," completely dominated by it. He was a particle in the world, ruled by its laws—laws which are always the laws of the past and which always act from without. His name liberated him from these laws. It recalls him from the world in which he was imprisoned, and returns him to his Self which, once his name is uttered, is free of the past, devoid of the external. Suddenly, hearing his name spoken, man knows that he is himself. He recognizes that he has the ability to begin again. But what, we wonder, enables him to be himself, to start all over? What gives him this spiritual power, this capacity to discover himself as present? His name represents permanence; it is the only tangible thing giving continuity to man's existence. Is it possible, then, that that which is permanent endows man with power over the moment?—for to discover oneself as present occurs in the instant. Is this the permanent essence of man—to be present to himself? Essence again? In spite of everything?

No, this is definitely not essence. How can a moment constitute "essence"—the moment which is forever disappearing, forever being devoured by the past? If the moment were essence, human freedom would suffer irreparable damage. It would be eternally swallowed up in the concatenation of cause and effect which is the law of the world. If freedom is to be the essence of man, it will pay dearly for such pretensions. The moment cannot be "essence." The moment cannot be at all. And even if it could exist, it is already gone, it has turned into the past. It cannot struggle, not even for an instant, against the pull of the past. And so the moment must be lost, and with it the present, and with it man's being present to himself.

To escape the power of the past, to transcend the law which constitutes causation, the moment must, at each instant, be reborn. This continuous renewal and resumption of the present is a contribution of the future. The future is the inexhaustible well from which moments are drawn; every instant new-born moments rise and replace the moments disappearing into the past. At each moment the future presents to man the gift of being present to himself. And so man may use his moments freely and then deposit them in the vast receptacle of the past. In the enduring process of receiving and using his moments he is man, master of the present, of his present—for it is truly his, if it is present. It is indeed born anew each instant, and each instant it dies.

Even his proper name bears witness that man has a twofold nature, that he is a child of the world and a child of God. Man has two names: a family name—or at least the name of his father—and a proper name. Through his surname, man belongs to the past; all that coerces him is contained in that name. Fate has a hold on him, and his surname is the gate by which fate enters—the gate cannot be entirely closed—enters and bears down on him. His other name is his proper name. His parents chose it, and in choosing it drew a line of demarcation beyond which fate cannot trespass. A man's proper name serves as a declaration that this is to be a new human being; it lays claim to the present by confronting man with a future. It always bears with it dreams and desires. And this is true, perhaps even more so, when a new-born child is "named" after someone. Such an act of naming expresses that the child be like "him" for whom he is named.

However, just as a surname does not compel a man to enter upon his inheritance, so giving him a proper name does not generate magical powers. His name neither coerces man nor gives him freedom; it merely indicates, it is only a sign post. And indeed it is a sign. His name refers man to something beyond himself; through it comes the compelling word of memory and the liberating word of hope. Because of it, he cannot even hope to remain in isolation. His double name reminds him that he can only be a child of man if he does not refuse to be a child of the world and God as well. These latter powers exert their reality by speaking through the mouth of his environment. Can they, addressing him by his family name, coerce him? No, he both wants and does not want to be coerced by them. The ever-passing world speaks through his mouth. And does the man who calls him by his proper name wish to free him? Scarcely ever; perhaps he even attempts to make his life conform to a certain attitude; and yet he does liberate him, though not intending to; he summons him to live his particular and unique present. The future, alive with dreams and desires, speaks through his mouth. Through the voice of many callers, a single voice calls. Each call summons to the future. Who is the caller?

This again is the ultimate secret, and again it is no secret at all. It was never hidden to the healthy. For have not men always understood when they were in full possession of their senses, when they did not fall prey to that madness which robs a man of his capacity to know himself and the present? Did they not always act in accordance with this secret when their trust in themselves was not undermined, and they refused to be enslaved by the laws of yesterday? Was this not no secret at all when they cast from themselves the burden and responsibilities of the ever-dissolving present and had access to that source which forever renews the present? And you, have you not always had the courage to live when you simply proceeded on your way, with the past at your heels and the light of a dawning tomorrow already touching your brow?

GOD

God—who is God? It is beyond the capacity of man to fathom God, it is said. Even if this be true, we have discovered that the same can be said of man and the world. We could discover no answer, or at best fallacious answers, to our questions, What "is" man? What "is" the world? So we are scarcely surprised to hear this statement about God. Statements about the essence of God are given more timidly perhaps than about the essence of man and the world. And yet they are certainly given. They are given even more frequently. The philosophic coterie, and mankind in general, as soon as it begins to philosophize, has a special liking for them. In spite of the modern predilection for *Weltanschauung* and *Lebensanschauung*, God still remains the favorite subject of philosophy. Metaphysics began as the science of God and it has never changed. If one investigates the views of the great philosophers, one makes the following odd discovery: none of them, up to Schopenhauer, would admit to being an atheist. Indeed, just shortly before Schopenhauer's time, one of the "greats" fought the view that his teachings were atheistic, as though his personal honor were at stake. Schopenhauer, however, openly declared that he was not concerned with God. He made atheism respectable. Even if this was his only merit, he would deserve to be commended.

This is, as a matter of fact, one of the answers that can be given concerning the essence of God. As in the case of man and the world, this question again presupposes that whatever knowledge we have is held precariously. Our knowledge of our various "gods and idols" seems at first to consist of nothing but fanciful imagery. But, it is maintained, these creations of ours may stand for something real. On the other hand, they may have no foundation in reality whatsoever. They may have been created by fear, lust, a creative instinct, a desire to explain, etc. It is necessary to entertain openly that they are possibly nothing, unreal. Moreover, the man who takes such a point of view should not be accused of ignorance nor threatened with ignominy. As posed, the question requires this answer, among other answers, as does every question which asks about the essence of a particular phenomenon or appearance.

Anyone who seeks another answer finds once again that he is faced with two alternatives. Both of these alternatives rest on the assumption that "something" exists behind appearance which is "altogether different" from what appears. They neither assume that there is a fantast concealed behind our phantasmagoria who indulges in fantasies "within ourselves," very much like raving children in certain types of delirium appear to be possessed by an *alter ego* which seems to be their nature and yet is not their true self. Or they conceive of a phantom-reality existing behind the images we see, in much the same way as a frightened child transforms a white sheet into a ghost, or the design on the wallpaper into a gorgon's head. Mother's common sense will not hesitate to disabuse the child. The resourceful woman will not tell him that this delirious second self, these ghosts and contorted faces, are real. She will attempt to awaken the child, will teach him to distinguish the sheet and the wall-paper design from ghosts and apparitions, his self from that which is alien. Philosophy, however, takes a different attitude and finds itself in an alliance with sick reason; for either it attempts to construct a god from the *alter ego* which possesses the patient, or else from those objects which turned into phantoms.

Nature is God. So enthusiastic adolescents, snobbish striplings, and unthinking adults, from university lecturers on, repeat the message of the Dutch Jew. These phantoms within us which we associate with God are explained by the white sheet that produced them. But the sheet is not the sheet, and God forbid that the world should be the world. The sheet and the ghost are "essentially" one; the world is God (in essence). Mother, having embroidered and hemmed the sheet, is quite well aware of the fact that her sheet is really a sheet. One would think that mankind, busily developing the technical possibilities of nature, would know better than to doubt that its world is *the world*. But no! it must be "God"—God, of all things! Such prattlers pretend to believe in nature and do not have the faintest notion of the injustice they do to it by depriving it of its reality and labelling it a phantom. What sort of faith is it which must rename the object of faith so it may believe in it? Ordinarily, to have something means to accept it just as it is. This is the way I have faith in an act of friendship or an item of information. If I seek for the "true attitude" behind the friendly act, for the "true facts" upon which the item is based, I merely demonstrate that I lack faith in them. This is, however, how these people believe in the world. They believe in it—or rather pretend to believe in it—only if they are permitted to give it another name—the name of God.

To be God, the world must be shelled and husked, deprived of its reality. Heaven forbid that the world should be an ordinary, natural world. It has to be viewed in ecstasy. Mother must not say that the sheet was bought and hemmed by herself, that it is merely a piece of linen, because in this way she would deprive her child of its nightmare. Baruch Spinoza was no Spinozist. The spirit of Spinoza's concept of nature was rarefied by Goethe and Herder. It was this deified "nature" robbed of all natural qualities, not Spinoza's *deus sive natura,* which became the God of the enthusiasts. Only a voided and annihilated world, a world turned into nothing was approved of as the nature of God. The statement "God is the world" can be made only if the world is nothing.

I hear a voice cheering. "Go ahead," the voice says, "give a good beating to those who would transform God into nature and make him all-embracing matter. However, you must exempt from your attacks that god who is Mind." My reply is that I shall never say anything against him which has not already been said by those who profess faith in this God with every word they utter. The beginning of all their wisdom is that to fear God is an insane fancy. To discover the truth, they say, we need not consider him whom these phantoms signify, that is the feared Lord. Oh no! He is utterly inaccessible, completely unknowable, like all which is "deep" under the "surface." We need not even consider the occasion which induces the phantasm. We must consider, however, the fantast, that is, man in fear of God. Man and man's prostrate mind is to be the essence of God. Thus the mind of man has won a promotion. It is unfortunate but inevitable that it should lose the very quality which earned it its promotion, that is, that quality which permitted it to comprehend its limitations, namely, the fear of something higher than man. In its exalted condition it has no use for such a quality. It is impossible to assert, God is venerating mind. We must keep to the statement, God is Mind.

Consequently, mind, the human mind, becomes God's essence. And so man's fantasies of gods and spirits become fantasies of the one and only mind, which is now divine. We have already pointed out that elevating the human mind to the position of being God's essence deprived it of its intrinsic relationship to God, a relationship present in man's fantasies; in these fantasies God was feared and venerated, and also present in these fantasies was the longing for love and creativity and the thirst for knowledge. Now it becomes clear that man is perfectly capable of referring these feelings and qualities to himself. Man's mind is capable of loving, creating, and exploring itself. This is made possible by the fact that generation follows upon generation; the inherent possibilities of this situation are summed up in the words "development," "evolution." Thus to say that there is divine mind means that God Himself is mind, evolving and unfolding. And consequently it is through evolution that the human mind's claim to be God's essence is validated. But what follows from this?

It follows from this that God is not. What does evolution or development mean when we speak of the human mind? When do I make much of the fact that I am still developing? Is it not when I am apologizing for a shortcoming, for not having accomplished something which was expected of me? Mind which requires further evolution is simply not yet Mind. A citizen of the future may be a wonderful person, but he is nevertheless not a citizen of the present. A man who adores the world of his children may be esteemed by all, but he is no lover of his own world. A jack-of-all-trades is a dabbler in his own profession.

Man is privileged to have everything that he needs to be man. He is in possession of the moment. And as for the rest, God and the world assist him here. He is in possession of the moment and so he has everything. Thus he is enabled to fulfill the commandment given to him because the command is for the moment and always only for the moment. The person whom he confronts represents the whole world and the very next instant may represent eternity. But the notion of development deprives him of the privilege of being human—a privilege which is also a duty. Evolution takes the place of man. That human mind, which was proclaimed to be the essence of God, is consequently not the true mind.

It is rather a mind deprived of its human privileges, a mind annihilated. Nothingness replaces the living human being and this nothingness is proclaimed to be the essence of God.

All that remains, then, is as we have seen twice before, the attempt to take this phantasm seriously. Let us seek for the essence in the heart of appearance, not somewhere behind it; let us look for it not in a single phenomenon but in the abundant whole. God is thus not something wholly other, essentially mind or world, but everything. He is everything which at any time bore the name of God; all the gods and idols of man assemble and in their transient manifestations and transformations make up that which we call God. God is the sum of all of his manifestations transient though they be. That is all. But if these manifestations are truly "everything," then all things, both human and of the world, must be contained in them. Each and every one of the gods is a giant grave containing in it all of the men who professed faith in this god, as well as the world in which their creativity enclosed him. Are these sepulchral vaults anything but giant, empty halls, graves of graves? Forgotten are the dead, covered by their tombstones; nothing remains but the stones, and these empty sepulchres of the departed gods—or rather of the god who dies in all gods. May he rest in peace!

We do not wish to disturb his slumber, and if we did we would find no corpses. All we would find is nothingness. If God is to be *something*, He can be neither mind nor nature; nor can He be everything. All such attempts lead to nothing. To be something He must be Something. World must be a Something, man a Something, God a Something.

Our reluctance to accept the notion of God being "Something" is incomparably stronger than our previous tendency to reject the idea of man and the world as "Something." In the latter case it was merely the trivial manner of expression which repelled us; but a touch of impropriety—indeed a suggestion of blasphemy—is added when we speak so of God. God—"Something"? Do others exist besides Him? So the philosopher, and the man infected by philosophy (and after all who is not?) will express his doubts. And he will come to the conclusion

that such a degradation of God must inevitably revolt
the *homo religiosus*, a species which is a favorite topic
with our philosopher; he certainly knows everything
worth knowing. But his conclusion in this instance is
by no means correct. Common sense knows as a matter
of course—and common sense may even be encountered
in this territory, covered though it is with philosophic
mouse-traps—that I and God are not identical, nor is He
identical with the tree I see in blossom before me, nor
for that matter with any "ideal" ego I may possess, or
any "final" ego I may aspire to. Common sense, on the
contrary, will tend to think of such a confusion of God
with other things and ideas as "pagan," and will attack it
accordingly. However, how can common sense reconcile
the two statements that God is "Something" and that
man and the world are also "Something," inasmuch as
it must admit that "to be Something" has a different
meaning when it refers to God?

Of course, it does admit such a difference. This ad-
mission, however, grants merely—as in the case of man
and the world—that the word "something" cannot adequately describe an essence. Common sense neither describes nor designates this essence; it makes no attempt
to grasp it; no sooner has the thought "God is Something" occurred to common sense than the thought is left
behind. Common sense expresses this thought and, as it
does so, learns that God cannot be spoken of unless, at
the very same moment, a bridge is constructed to man
and the world.

What forces us, when we speak of God, to build such
bridges? What quality of God is beyond the reach of all
of our ideas and fantasies? How does it happen that so
many of our ideas of Him, in fact all of them, agree that
He is One, unite in Him as One. What is there sufficiently
external to God, yet despite its externality so inseparable from Him that it belongs to Him—what is there
sufficiently "extrinsic" to reach across to that which is
without?

It is His name. To utter God's name is entirely different from uttering the name of a man or a thing. True,
they have something in common; the name of God, His
proper name, and a term of designation are not identical with the bearers of these names. But except for this

they differ widely. Man has a name so that he may be called by it. To be called by his name is for him an ultimate distinction. God does not have a name so that He may be called by it. To Him it is irrelevant whether His name is called or not; He heeds him who calls Him by His name as well as those who call Him by other names or those who speak to Him in name-less silence. He bears a name for our sake, so that we may call Him. It is for our sake that He permits Himself to be named and called by that name, since it is only by jointly calling upon Him that we become a "We."

And thus the name of man remains a proper name and clings to him; he keeps the name bestowed on him. God's name, however, is subject to change although, at any particular instant, it is conceived of as a proper name. Indeed the encounter with God is established and transmitted from place to place, from thing to thing, from man to man, from people to people, from order to order, by this very alteration of names.

In this respect the name of God resembles that of a thing. A noun does not remain at the place where it was first spoken. It may have originated as a proper name; when it becomes a noun not only does it reach many people—that happens to a proper name as well—but it also reaches many things. At this point a noun grows in size and intertwines with other words; thus words lose their meaning as proper names, meanings which made them adhere, as it were, to individual things. Thus words intertwine and the unity of language is established. Here is a world in which many things are merged and resolved. The language of the individual, so far merely a personal world, begins to blend into the language of a people, and in turn the language of a people blends into that of mankind. And things are drawn along in the wake of this movement, proceeding from the single object designated in the Here and Now toward a more highly integrated world-order, toward the ultimate order.

The name of God proceeds on its way above these two movements, the movement of proper names towards the ultimate community and the movement of words denoting things towards the ultimate order—it proceeds on its way both as a name and as a term of designation,

and it participates in both of the movements. Invoked
by men as a name, it spreads itself above the congregations of men, the congregations with their originally
divergent names; as a noun it consecrates things, and
things are dedicated to it; thus it acts as a force gathering
things and giving them order.

This dual task undertaken by the name of God—dual
since in one aspect it concerns man, and in the other
the world is reflected in its tendency to split and become a two-fold name. Man invokes God by His name;
the world speaks to Him through His word. On the one
hand He embraces sinners; on the other, He proclaims
law for the world. The root of all of man's various
heresies is to confound the two parts of His name with
one another; God's love encroaches upon His justice,
His justice upon His love. It is indeed God's task both
to maintain the two-fold character of His name as well as
reconcile them. So long as there is reason for such a
division, so long as God is not the God-in-Himself [*Gott
an sich*] whom philosophers drivel about; if He remains
God of man and the world, then it is He, who by means
of His two-fold name transforms—and we use the word
in its technical sense—human energies into the energies
of the world.

Man and the world go their separate ways; and this
cannot be, nor should it be, changed. Man should remain human; he should not be converted into a thing,
a part of the world, prey to its organization. And the
world's law and order should be neither rescinded nor
sentimentalized. Man ought to be able to abide by the
world's constitution, judge by its laws, measure according to its standards, and yet remain human. He
should feel no necessity to withdraw from the world's
order because of his humanity. He should not despair
and leave unfilled his obligation to judge, to designate,
to name those things which the world parades before
him. Yet how could he act, were he not sure that his
actions and the world-process, his sentiments and its
orders, interrelate and agree?

This certainty belongs to him and he is justified in
keeping it. There is, in addition to the world and himself, He who turns His face towards both. He it is who
summons man by name and bids him take his place

in the congregation which calls upon Him. He it is who orders things so that they may form a kingdom bearing His name. Thus man may act unconcerned with the outcome; he may act according to the requirements of the world as it is today. That day, the day when action is required, lets him understand what he must perform. The realm of time is the proper arena for his action. He does not need to wait until truth has risen from the depths. Truth waits for him; it stands before his eyes, it is "in thy heart and in thy mouth," within grasping distance; "that thou mayst do it." In the same way as he has achieved certainty concerning the reality of the world and has found the courage to live his life, he must also have faith in Him who brought him into existence. It is at this very point that Hamlet, finding himself in the world, gives way to shame and despair. But even Hamlet persists in his despair only as long as he remains in soliloquy. As soon as the requirements of the moment take hold of him, once the solitude of his soliloquy is destroyed, he does the correct thing unhesitatingly and makes his disjointed world whole. When man is in need he depends on common sense; he has no time to waste on such a luxury as sick reason. The proper time then is the present—today. To avail himself of today, man must, for better or worse, put his trust in God.

Is this not the way things are with you? When need forces you into the present, do you still insist on asking about yesterday and tomorrow? Do you still require eternity to give you proof of the Here and Now? No, there is no time for such things. For the proper time has come, and thus God assists you.

(From *Understanding the Sick and the Healthy*, pp. 53–81.)

Martin Buber
1878-1965

I

It is generally agreed that Martin Buber must be reck-
oned one of the foremost religious thinkers of the twentieth century. Emil Brunner in Switzerland has said
that Buber's discovery and analysis of the *I-Thou* and
I-It relationships constituted "a 'Copernician revolution'
in the thinking not only of Europe but of the whole of
mankind." Reinhold Niebuhr in America has described
him as "the greatest Jewish philosopher of our time" and
called the appearance of his little book *I and Thou* "a
great event in the religious life of the West." Of the same
volume J. H. Oldham in England has written, "I question whether any book has been published in the present
century the message of which, if it were understood,
would have such far-reaching consequences for the life
of our time." Statements such as these from non-Jewish
authorities, and they could be multiplied tenfold, testify
to the tremendous impact of Martin Buber not only on
Jewish but also on Christian thinking. Besides being one
of the most creative voices in contemporary religious
thought, his was also a prophetic voice that called men
to moral responsibility and maturity. For this reason
his name was often coupled with those of Albert
Schweitzer and Mahatma Ghandi as men who represented the conscience of the age. In addition, Buber's
work, particularly his philosophy of dialogue, has exercised a profound influence on such diverse fields as
education, psychology, social work, medicine, sociology
and political science.

Buber was born on February 8, 1878, in Vienna.
When he was three years old his parents were divorced,
and he was sent to live in the Galician home of his
paternal grandfather, Solomon Buber. The latter was a
prosperous merchant as well as a fine Hebraic scholar
who devoted much of his time to editing and interpreting ancient rabbinic texts. In his grandfather's home,
where classic Hebrew was spoken, the boy was exposed

to the influence of deep, yet enlightened Jewish piety and received the rudiments of a traditional Jewish education. Of his grandfather he later wrote: "The spiritual passion which manifested itself in his incessant work was combined with the untouchable, unperturbable childlikeness of a pure, human nature and an elementary Jewish being . . . He did not trouble himself about Judaism, but it dwelled in him."[1]

As a child Buber was occasionally taken by his father, on whose estate he spent several summers, to visit the Hasidic community of the village of Sadagora. He was repelled by the conspicuous splendor of the court of the *rebbe*, as well as by the prayer house of the Hasidim. "But," he later admitted, "when I saw the *rebbe* striding through the rows of the waiting, I felt, 'leader,' and when I saw the Hasidim dance with the Torah, I felt, 'community.' At that time there rose in me a presentiment of the fact that common reverence and common joy of soul are the foundations of genuine human community."[2]

Shortly after celebrating his *bar mitzvah* the thirteen-year-old Buber ceased putting on *tefillin* and gave up most of the other religious practices that he had been observing. A year later he left his grandfather's home to go and live with his father in Lemberg. There he entered a Polish gymnasium, from which he was graduated in 1896. He then matriculated at the University of Vienna, later also attending the universities of Berlin, Leipzig and Zurich. After eight years of study of philosophy, religion and art history he received his doctorate at Vienna in 1904 for a dissertation on German mysticism from Meister Eckhart to Angelus Silesius.

Among the teachers who influenced Buber in his university days were the philosopher and psychologist Wilhelm Dilthey (1833–1911), who developed a profound philosophy of culture in which he insisted on the need for applying to the study of man and human institutions a methodology different from that employed in the natural sciences. Another teacher who affected Buber was the sociological theorist Georg Simmel (1858–1918), whose philosophy was characterized by a strong vitalist strain. The social thought of Gustave Landauer (1869–1919), who, though ten years older than Buber, became his close friend, also exerted a major influence on his intellectual development. Landauer not only introduced his younger colleague to his own religiously based socialist theory, which stressed the need for genuine community among men, but also led Buber to his youthful concern with the realm of mystical thought in which Landauer himself had become deeply interested long before.

Aside from the Bible and Hasidic literature, in which he immersed himself only later, perhaps the chief spiritual influence on the young Buber, as well as on many of his contemporaries (including Lev Shestov and, to a lesser extent, Franz Rosenzweig), was the work of three great nineteenth century figures who have come to be recognized as the founders of modern existentialism— the German philosopher Friedrich Nietzsche (1844–1900), the Danish religious thinker Sören Kierkegaard (1813–1855), and the Russian novelist Feodor Dostoevsky (1821–1881). From Nietzsche Buber learned to value the concrete and immediate over against the abstract and the ideal, as well as the necessity for affirming life and its elemental powers in the face of the traditional values and ideals which tended to choke them. From Kierkegaard he derived several elements that are basic in his own religious thought—the immediacy of the divine-human relation, the fearfulness and insecurity of man as he is called to exercise responsible freedom before the demands of any particular situation, and the requirement that man achieve authentic existence by becoming a "single one," a unique person. And in Dostoevsky Buber found, as Nietzsche had before him, one of the greatest of psychologists, who laid bare the deepest springs of man's inner being. There was much in these three mentors that Buber came in time to reject and attack, but that they decisively molded his outlook can hardly be questioned.

Though engrossed in the study of mystical literature, Buber in his university days was not without a practical concern for the welfare of his people. He was strongly attracted to the newly emerging Zionist movement created by Theodor Herzl, and in 1901 became the editor of Herzl's journal *Die Welt*. Buber, however, soon found himself out of sympathy with the purely political program of the dominant group in the Zionist movement; he was drawn, instead, to that minority faction which stressed the idea that Zionism must be based on a great Jewish cultural renaissance and direct its efforts to achieving a larger measure of spiritual health and integrity among Jews everywhere in the world. For some years Buber gave up active participation in the Zionist cause, but he returned to it in 1916 when he established the journal *Der Jude*. This magazine, which Buber edited from its inception until 1924, soon became the leading voice of German-speaking Jewry in Europe. In its pages Buber and his colleagues gave repeated and eloquent expression to the higher aspirations of the Zionist movement and influenced the thinking of many of their contemporaries. When, later in life, Buber settled in Palestine, he developed further his vision of the building of Zion as an unfinished task whose completion has been imposed upon the Jewish people by God himself. This vision, though not shared by the masses of his fellow Jews and often attacked by those who insisted on the necessity of maintaining an attitude of hardheaded *Real-politik* in the struggle to establish a state, was not without its effect on the life of the Jewish community in the years both before and after the founding of the State of Israel.

In his late teens and early twenties Buber found himself in a condition of spiritual confusion without any center or substance to his existence, living, as he later put it, "in versatile fulness of spirit, but without Judaism, without humanity, and without the presence of the divine."[3] An entrance to Judaism and humanity he found in his Zionist work, but the discovery of the presence of the divine was to come only with his exploration of the world of Hasidism. Having resolved to become genuinely acquainted with Judaism, he returned to the study of the Hebrew that he had learned and spoken as a child in his grandfather's house and to the Hasidic world of which he had had a glimpse in Sadagora. He began reading Hasidic texts which, he confessed, at first repelled him with their formlessness and strangeness. One day in 1904 he chanced to pick up a little book called *Zevaat Ribesh*, the testament of Rabbi Israel Baal Shem Tov, the founder of Hasidism; at that moment, he later wrote,

. . . the words flashed toward me, "He takes unto himself the quality of fervor. He arises from sleep with fervor, for he is hallowed and become another man and is worthy to create and is become like the Holy One, blessed by He, when He created His world." It was then, that, overpowered in an instant, I experienced the Hasidic soul. The primally Jewish opened to me, flowering to newly conscious expression in the darkness of exile: man's being created in the image of God I grasped as deed, as becoming, as task. And this primally Jewish reality was a primal human reality, the content of human religiousness. Judaism as religiousness, as "piety," as *Hasidut*, opened to me there. The image out of my childhood, the memory of the *zaddik* and his community, rose upward and illuminated me: I recognized the idea of the perfected man. At the same time I became aware of the summons to proclaim it to the world.[4]

Following this experience, Buber decided to withdraw from practical activity for a time and spent five years in a secluded and intensive study of Hasidic texts. The result of this study, as of his continued, lifelong immersion in Hasidism and Hasidic literature, was a stream of books setting forth the teachings and ideals of this mystical, pietistic movement which swept through the Jewish communities of Eastern Europe beginning in the middle of the eighteenth century. In a very real sense, it was Buber who, almost singlehandedly, brought to the West a knowledge of this movement which he once described as "the most powerful and unique phenomenon which the Diaspora has produced." Some of his books on Hasidism have been widely acclaimed as religious and literary gems. Herman Hesse, in nominating Buber for a Nobel Prize in Literature in 1949, declared, "He has enriched world-literature with a genuine treasure as has no other living author—the *Tales of the Hasidim*." Of the same work, Walter Kaufmann has written, "He has given us one of the great religious books of all time, a work that invites comparison with the great Scriptures of mankind." Buber's version of the sayings and stories of the Hasidim, Kaufmann added, "will surely be remembered widely when the theologians of our time have gone the way of Harnack and Schleiermacher, not to mention lesser names that have long been forgotten by all but specialists."5

Though Buber at first tended to compare rabbinic Judaism quite unfavorably with Hasidism, he later came to believe that Hasidism was "merely a concentrated movement, the concentration of all those elements which are to be found in a less condensed form everywhere in Judaism, even in 'rabbinic' Judaism."6 What impressed Buber about Hasidism was not only the simple and deep wisdom of its teachers, its emphasis on the mutuality and directness of the relationship between the individual and God, and its unremitting concern with "hallowing the everyday," but also the fact, as he saw it, that it made the most serious effort at the establishment of genuine community undertaken in Jewish quarters from the time of the Hebrew prophets to the pioneering settlements in Palestine in modern times. "Hasidism," he wrote, "was the one great attempt in the history of the Diaspora to make a reality of the original choice and to found a true and just community based on religious principles."7 Among the reasons that this attempt failed, according to Buber, was the fact that "it did not aim for the independence, for the self-determination of the people; or, to state it differently, because its connections with Palestine were only sporadic and not influenced by the desire for national liberation."8 Buber himself could not become a practicing Hasid because he was not able to accept the authority of the traditional Halakhah in its entirety as divinely revealed. But it is abundantly clear that the spirit of Hasidism, its fundamental ethos, as he discovered it and rendered it so masterfully in his books, made a decisive contribution not only to the development of his dialogical philosophy but also to his social thought and his view of the nature and destiny of Judaism.

In his early years of preoccupation with Hasidism Buber tended to concentrate on the mystical side of Hasidic teaching, its emphasis on ecstatic prayer as the means whereby the individual may at rare moments attain unity with God. As time went on, however, he came to value more highly the practical aspect of Hasidism, its

endeavor to "hallow the everyday." Indeed, Buber ultimately came to the conclusion, as a result of certain
personal experiences, one of which he movingly describes,[9] that mysticism is illegitimate, insofar as its
concern with extraordinary moments of "religious enthusiasm" tears religion out of the fabric of man's everyday existence and introduces a harmful division into his
life. The mystical claim to union with the divine, he
also came to believe, must be regarded as illusory, since
the separated self persists.

By the time (1922) he finished writing *Ich und Du*
(*I and Thou*), Buber had completely given up individualistic mysticism and arrived at his mature philosophy
of dialogue, with its emphasis on the *I-Thou* relationship,
the relationship of total presentness and responsibility,
in both inter-human encounters and the encounter between man and God. Buber later recognized that out of
the "Vesuvian hour" of the First World War a number
of thinkers "of different kinds and traditions" had been
impelled to devote themselves "to the search for the
buried treasure," i.e., the dialogical understanding of
human existence, and he mentioned some who, largely
independently of each other, were working along similar lines. Among those cited by Buber as contributing
significantly to the development of "the dialogical principle" are Hermann Cohen, Franz Rosenzweig, Friedrich Ebner, Eugen Rosenstock, Friedrich Gogarten, Karl
Heim, Gabriel Marcel, Karl Löwith and Karl Jaspers.[10]
But it was, of course, Buber's own *I and Thou* and his
elaboration and application of its fundamental principles
in a spate of later books and articles that were to have
the largest influence on contemporary thought.

In 1923 Buber was appointed to the newly established
Chair of Jewish Religious Thought, the first at a German
university, at Frankfurt. The chair was to have been
occupied by Franz Rosenzweig, but the latter, already
afflicted with paralysis, persuaded his friend to accept it.
Buber taught at the University of Frankfurt for a decade,
until he was dismissed from his post by the Nazis. In
addition, he was significantly involved for a number of
years in the work of Rosenzweig's *Freie Jüdische Lehrhaus*
in Frankfurt. During this period, from 1926 to 1930, he
also edited, along with the Catholic theologian Joseph

Wittig and the Protestant physician and psychotherapist Viktor von Weisäcker, the journal *Die Kreatur*, which was devoted to social and educational problems common to the various religions.

The major fruit of the friendship between Buber and Rosenzweig in the 1920's was their collaboration on a new translation of the Hebrew Bible into German. In this epoch-making work the two men attempted to create a text in which the "holy" tone and stilted language of previous versions would be avoided and which would reflect as accurately and responsibly as possible the precise meaning, structure and poetic power of the original Hebrew. That the attempt was a brilliant success has been widely recognized.

Buber's profound concern with the Bible led him, in the course of his translating work, to write a number of books and monographs on Biblical history and theology, which have established for him a reputation, in Jewish as well as in Christian circles, as one of the foremost contemporary interpreters of the Bible. Of Buber as Biblical commentator James Muilenberg has written,

> He, more than any other Jew in our time, tells the Christian what is to be heard in the Old Testament, what the Old Testament is really saying and what it certainly is not saying, what the direction is in which the words are moving on their way through history. He, more than any other Jewish writer, tells the Christian what he ought to see, what the road on which he walks is like, whence the journey begins and whither it leads.[11]

But Buber was more than an outstanding Biblical historian and commentator. His view of the nature of the Hebrew Bible as a whole and of its central themes constitutes, as we shall suggest below, one of his enduring contributions to the religious thought of our age. And his own philosophy is, as he repeatedly pointed out, thoroughly grounded in his understanding of Biblical faith.

Following the rise of the Nazis to power in 1933 and during the subsequent persecution of the Jews, Buber served as director of the Central Office for Jewish Adult

Education in Germany. Besides organizing the training of teachers for the new schools set up for Jewish students, who had been barred by the Nazis from all German schools, Buber lectured on Judaism and set up adult discussion groups for Jews all over Germany. Carrying on what he called "a spiritual war against Nazism," he worked tirelessly to maintain the spirit and build up the inner resources of the beleaguered German-Jewish community in the years before its tragic end.

In 1938, when the continuation of his work in Germany became impossible and he was convinced that he could no longer be of any real service to his fellow Jews there, Buber sorrowfully left Germany for Palestine to accept the post of professor of social philosophy at the Hebrew University. He continued to teach at the university until his retirement in 1951, and during these years wrote some of his most important works. In 1949, shortly after the establishment of the State of Israel when thousands of immigrants were streaming into the country every month, Buber founded an Institute for Adult Education, which had for its mission the training of teachers who would work in the new settlements and seek to integrate the immigrants into their new environment.

In the years before the proclamation of Israel as an independent state Buber took a leading role, along with Judah Leon Magnes, Henrietta Szold and several others, in the *Ihud* (Union) Association which advocated greater co-operation between the Jewish and Arab communities of Palestine and the ultimate establishment of a bi-national Jewish-Arab state. This was a distinctly unpopular position in the charged atmosphere of the time and in view of the immovable opposition of the Arabs to further immigration of Jews into the country, and Buber and his associates often found themselves derided and attacked. Nevertheless, Buber's deep sincerity and moral passion were respected by many. Ten years after the establishment of the state, when the great philosopher reached his eightieth birthday, the occasion was marked by a week-long, nationwide celebration, and Prime Minister David Ben Gurion himself came to the Hebrew University to pay homage to him.

Martin Buber died in Jerusalem, full of years and honors, on June 13, 1965.

II

There is little question but that the single contribution for which Buber will be remembered best and longest is his anthropology. To an age which no longer had any central or controlling image of man he presented one that compelled widespread assent. His image is both descriptive and normative, portraying man as he is and as he ought to be: as he all too often is—self-centered, fragmentized, lonely, alienated from self, from nature, from fellowman and from God, and as he ought to be— turned toward others, integral, involved in a genuine dialogical relationship with his fellow creatures and God.

The categories in which Buber expressed his under- standing of the human situation, *I-Thou* and *I-It*, have, of course, by now become commonplaces of contem- porary intellectual discourse. But when Buber first enun- ciated them almost half a century ago in the richly tex- tured, deeply evocative and poetic pages of *I and Thou*, they inaugurated a fresh and luminous way of ap- proaching man not only in religious anthropology and ethics but in virtually all of the pure and applied sci- ences that deal with man.

In an era of massive depersonalization and dehuman- ization, when genuine relations between individuals have been largely obliterated, Buber proclaimed that man can achieve authentic human existence only by turning, at least at times, to his fellowman as a whole being in the posture of *I-Thou*, in which the other is made really present in his concrete wholeness and uniqueness and where there is a genuine response to the irreducible claim of the encounter itself.

"All real living is meeting"[12]—this insight is at the heart and center of Buber's vision of man. Man becomes what he essentially is and should be—what Kierkegaard called a Single One—only in the sphere of *das Zwischenmensch- liche*, "the between man and man." If he withholds him- self entirely from the sphere of *I-Thou* relationships with other human beings—a perilous and burning sphere, since it demands of one radical responsibility, decision, direction and trust—and concentrates upon his own self-development, or seeks in mystic fashion to plunge his individuality into the infinite abyss of God, or confines himself entirely to the world of *I-It*, wherein the other becomes merely the object of his knowledge, experience, use, enjoyment or control, he may gain comfort and security but he will not know what it is to be genuinely human.

Buber himself did not, to be sure, restrict the possibility of an *I-Thou* encounter to the life between man and man. He held that the world of relation may be entered not only through our life with other human beings but also through our life with nature and with "spiritual beings." By the latter term he meant, as he once explained,[13] "spirit in phenomenal forms," i.e., works of art, literature, philosophy—in general, any spiritual creation of man. But the main entrance to the world of relation which, he insisted, is the world of authentic human existence, was, for him, through interpersonal relationships. This is so because plants and animals and artistic creations, while they do, in a sense, "speak" to us, cannot become our partners in a fully reciprocal dialogical encounter, as other human beings can. And yet what is ultimately important is not the gateway by which man enters the world of relation or real life but that world or that life itself. "Form's silent asking, man's loving speech, the mute proclamation of the creature, are all gates leading into the presence of the Word. But when the full and complete meeting is to take place, the gates are united in one gateway of real life, and you no longer know through which you have entered."[14]

Buber, let it be noted, did not at all condemn the *I-It* attitude of objectification and detachment in approaching persons and things as an unmitigated evil. He fully recognized its legitimacy and necessary place in human life. Through scientific knowledge, acquired by means of dispassionate, objective observation and experiment, man obtains an ordered, reliable world whose behavior he can predict and often control. Of the world perceived by science and technical knowledge Buber said, "You cannot hold on to life without it; its reliability sustains you."[15] What he insisted on, however, is that this

world is not enough, for "you cannot meet others in it . . .
should you die in it, your grave would be in nothingness."[16] Unless a man, at least at times, leaves the world
of knowledge, experience, use and control and steps
into the world of relation, the deeper levels of existence
will remain forever closed to him and he will not attain
authentic selfhood. "Without *It* man cannot live, but he
who lives with *It* alone is not a man."[17]

Dialogic life, existence in the *I-Thou* relation, Buber
further recognized, is not something that can be sustained permanently or even very long. It is "the exalted
melancholy of our fate that every *Thou* in our world
must become an *It*."[18] But the situation is reversible; the
person or thing that has become an *It* may again become a *Thou*. While man can only live in an interchange
of actual and potential dialogical relationship, it is his
entry over and over again into the reality of the relationship, Buber suggested, that brings him to that *Thou*
who can never become an *It*, the Eternal Thou or God.
"Though the graciousness of its comings and the solemn
sadness of its goings it [the *I-Thou* relationship] leads
you away to the *Thou* in which the parallel lines of relation meet."[19]

The life of dialogue, Buber insisted, is not an exalted
activity to be indulged in by choice spirits at rare moments. It is "no privilege of intellectual activity like dialectic. It does not begin in the upper story of humanity . . . There are no gifted and ungifted here, only
those who give themselves and those who withhold
themselves."[20] It can be practiced not only in the relationship between two persons directly encountering each
other but even by the head of a large factory or business
enterprise in his attitude to the thousands of employees
who work in it.

He practises it when he experiences it [the business
he leads], instead of as a structure of mechanical
centers of force and their organic servants . . . as an
association of persons with faces and names and biographies, bound together by a work that is represented
by, but does not consist of, the achievements of a
complicated mechanism. He practises it when he is
inwardly aware, with a latent and disciplined fantasy,

of the multitude of these persons, whom naturally he cannot separately know and remember as such; so that now, when one of them for one reason or other steps really as an individual into the circle of his vision and the realm of his decision, he is aware of him without strain not as a number with a human mask but as a person.[21]

Buber saw man in the twentieth century coming increasingly under the sway of a "pantechnical mania." The unchecked growth of the *I-It* attitude, it seemed to him, would in the end completely dehumanize man. Hence, he was not content calmly to diagnose the situation but felt called passionately to urge the application of the remedy. Only a renewal of dialogical existence, he was convinced, could save man's humanity from progressive atrophy and ultimate disappearance.

Buber's central teaching that human beings are ordained to find fulfillment and authentic selfhood by living with each other in a relationship in which they mutually confirm one another as unique persons and turn to one another in the presentness and openness of love— and love, it must be emphasized, was understood by Buber in a thoroughly non-sentimental and non-romantic way as *the responsibility* of an I for a Thou[22]—has been, in an important sense, implicit in the Jewish view of man ever since the Bible first proclaimed, "You shall love your neighbor as yourself." It was Buber's merit to restate the Biblical truth for our time in a new and compelling way and to remind us that through *teshuvah*, that total reorientation of life involved in turning in his relations with others from the attitude of objectification and manipulation to the dialogical attitude, "man is, as man, redeemable."

III

Another major contribution of Buber's is his opening of the way to the possibility of moving to a view of the Bible that transcends the sterile opposition of traditionalist literalism ("every word of the Bible is, as the infallible revelation of God, factually true") and modernist relativism ("the Bible is merely the surviving folk literature of ancient Israel"). For Buber, who regarded his whole philosophy of dialogical encounter as rooted in Biblical faith, the Hebrew Bible is properly to be understood as neither of these, but rather as the record of the actual meetings between Israel and God. It is the witness to a thousand-year-long dialogue between "the 'I' of the speaking God and the 'Thou' of the hearing Israel."[23] Buber insisted that, despite the apparent diversity of its materials, the Bible "is really one book, for one basic theme unites all the stories and songs, sayings and prophecies contained within it. The theme of the Bible is the encounter between a group of people and the Lord of the world in the course of history, the sequence of events occurring on earth."[24] As a report of divine-human encounters, it is, essentially and throughout, both human and divine.

In enunciating its basic themes of Creation, Revelation and Redemption—the themes on which the structure of Jewish faith is reared—the Bible, according to Buber, declares that the world has an origin, midpoint and goal and confronts every generation "with the claim that it must be recognized as a document of the true history of the world."[25] Buber was poignantly aware of the difficulties encountered by the modern Jew and modern man in general in accepting the truth-claim of the Bible. "Could we believe it? Can we do more than believe that people once did believe as this book reports and claims?"[26] The answer, he insisted, may be Yes—provided one approaches the Bible without "religious" or "scientific" preconceptions but with deep seriousness, yielding to it totally, withholding nothing of his entire being from it, letting whatever will occur between himself and it occur, keeping himself open to the possibility of faith. If he does this, that is, if he approaches the Bible with the attitude of *I-Thou*, then even the modern man who has "lost the reality of creation in his concept of 'evolution,' that of revelation in the theory of the 'unconscious,' and that of redemption in the setting up of social or national goals"[27] may regain a conviction of these actualities which the Bible proclaims in a "legitimately stammering account" as it utters in the language of men that which is essentially unutterable. And Buber explained how, on the basis of our own experience, we may obtain some gateway into understanding what Creation, Revelation and Redemption mean.

Something of the reality of the Biblical proclamation that the world and man are the creation of God may be appropriated by one who comes to recognize existentially that he himself is irreducibly unique and individual. "Suppose," Buber wrote,

> it were possible for a man to make a psychophysical inventory of his own person, to break down his character into a sum of qualities; and now suppose it were possible for him to trace each separate quality, and the concurrence of all, back to the most primitive living creatures, and in this way make an uninterrupted genetic analysis of his individuality by determining its derivation and reference—then his form, his face, unprecedented, comparable to none, unique, his voice never heard before, his gestures never seen before, his body informed with spirit, would still exist as the untouched residue, underived and underivable, an entity which is simply present and nothing more. If after all this futile effort, such a man had the strength to repeat the question "whence," he would, in the final analysis, discover himself simply as something that was created. Because every man is unique, another first man enters the world whenever a child is born. By being alive, everyone groping like a child back to the origin of his own self, we may experience the fact that there is an origin, that there is creation.[28]

As for revelation, there are again, Buber maintained, personal experiences related to those recorded as the great revelations of the Bible and capable of opening for us the way to apprehending them. When we suddenly and unexpectedly become aware of a certain apperception now present within ourselves but lacking just a moment ago whose origin we cannot discover, we realize that what happened to us is "otherness." We know that something has been given us, we experience it as bestowed upon us from a source outside ourselves, not something produced from our own unconscious and that was always latent in the depths of our soul. But when we recognize the gift as gift we have discovered that revelation exists. We have "set foot on the path which will reveal our life and the life of the world as a sign communication."[29]

According to Buber, what man receives in religious revelation is not a specific "content" but rather "a Presence, a Presence as power." Revelation is simply the experience by the individual of the living presence of God. In this experience three things are included in an undivided way, though they may be described separately. When addressed by the Eternal Thou in revelation, man is first of all "raised and bound up in relation." He is no longer isolated or alienated from other beings; an overarching framework that he cannot explain but that makes his life "heavy with meaning" has been created for him. Secondly, there is in the experience of revelation "the inexpressible confirmation of meaning" in life. This meaning cannot be exhibited or defined in conceptual terms by the individual but its certainty is for him greater even than that of his sense perceptions. "What does the revealed and concealed meaning purpose with us, desire from us? It does not wish to be explained (nor are we able to do that) but only to be done by us." Thirdly, this meaning does not refer to some transcendent life and world but to *this* life and *this* world. It is to be done and confirmed in the here and now. "The assurance I have of it does not wish to be sealed within me, but it wishes to be born by me into the world."[30]

Revelation, Buber insisted, cannot be a system of dogmas. Such a system is not the reflection of the actual presence of God in the revelatory encounter but a set of statements formulated about Him in His absence. Nor is revelation a system of laws. The confirmation of that meaning to be done which is given in the experience of revelation cannot, he wrote "be transmitted as a valid Ought; it is not prescribed, it is not specified on any tablet, to be raised above all men's heads. The meaning that has been received can be proved true by each man only in the singleness of his being and the singleness of his life."[31] For Buber there could be no set of moral prescriptions of eternal and universal validity. The ethical demand is absolute, but since it always arises out of a unique situation, its fulfillment requires unique responsiveness to that situation. Because every living situation, despite certain similarities to others, is essentially something "that has never been before and will never come again," an authentic response to it demands "a reaction which cannot be prepared beforehand. It demands nothing of what is past. It demands presence, responsibility; it demands you."[32] Norms have their usefulness, and no responsible person will ignore them. "But the command inherent in a genuine norm never becomes a maxim, and the fulfillment of it never a habit . . . What it (the command) has to tell him is revealed whenever a situation arises which demands of him a solution of which till then he had perhaps no idea."[33]

In the Bible itself the supreme revelatory event is, of course, the encounter of God and Israel at Sinai. But Buber, who held that the Biblical themes of Creation, Revelation and Redemption are the proclamation that the world has an origin, midpoint and goal, refused to identify the midpoint with the event at Sinai.

> . . . the Jewish Bible does not set a past event as a midpoint between origin and goal. It interposes a movable, circling midpoint which cannot be pinned to any set time, for it is the moment when I, the reader, the hearer, the man, catch through the words of the Bible the voice which from earliest beginnings has been speaking in the direction of the goal. The midpoint is this mortal and yet immortal moment of mine. Creation is the origin, redemption the goal. But revelation is not a fixed, dated point poised between the two. The revelation at Sinai is not this midpoint itself, but the perceiving of it, and such perception is possible at any time.[34]

It was no doubt this unjustified refusal to recognize the centrality of the Sinai event in Israel's history, to which the Bible itself bears repeated witness throughout its entire course, along with his individualistic, situational view of the ethical demand, that led Buber to his weak and finally unsatisfactory (at least from the perspective of fidelity to Jewish tradition it must be so regarded) view of Torah and Halakhah.

As for Redemption, the Biblical promise that "in the end of days" the contradictions and ambiguities of history will be resolved and the world—this world—perfectly redeemed is, according to Buber, again, like the Biblical story of creation, a "legitimate stammering account." Here, too, there is a possibility of apprehending what the Bible proclaims through the individual's personal experience. When a man, Buber said, recalls his own dark and silent hours, "those hours in the lowest depths when our soul hovers over the frail trap door which, at the very next instant, may send us down into destruction, madness and 'suicide' at our own verdict," and suddenly at that instant felt the touch as of a hand, reaching down to him, wishing to be grasped, and found in himself the incredible courage required to take hold of it and let it draw him up out of the darkness (that courage which Paul Tillich called "the courage to be"), then he has experienced the reality of what the Bible means by redemption. Then he can say, with Job, "I know that my redeemer liveth."[35]

The redemption which the Bible and Jewish tradition proclaim as the goal of the historical process, Buber held, involves the whole man, body and soul. "The redemption must take place in the whole corporeal life. God the Creator wills to consummate nothing less than the whole of his creation; God the Revealer wills to actualize nothing less than the whole of his revelation; God the Redeemer wills to draw into his arms nothing less than the all in need of redemption."[36] The prophetic vision of the end of time, which Buber sharply distinguished from the apocalyptic, promises "the consummation of creation" rather than its "abrogation and supersession by another world, completely different in nature." According to the prophetic conception, "the evil" will find the direction that leads toward God and enter into the good, the earth will ultimately be hallowed, and God's creative original will is destined finally to be completely fulfilled. It was the early Talmudic teachers, Buber noted, who helped this "prophetic messianism to triumph over the apocalyptic conception, and in doing so saved Judaism."[37]

In Buber's view God's redeeming power is constantly and universally at work but there is no time and no place where a complete state of redemption actually exists. The Jew, he held, knows existentially that the world lacks redemption. "He feels this lack of redemption against his skin, he tastes it on his tongue, the burden of the unredeemed world lies on him."[38] With such a knowledge, the Jew finds it impossible to admit the Christian claim that redemption has already taken place.

> It is true that he can discover prefigurations of redemption in past history, but he always discovers only that mysterious intimacy of light out of darkness which is at work everywhere and at all times; no redemption which is different in kind, none which by its nature would be unique, which would be conclusive for future ages, and which had but to be consummated.[39]

Like Rosenzweig, Buber saw the heart of Biblical and later Jewish faith as well in the triad of Creation-Revelation-Redemption. His interpretation of these central Biblical teachings and of the nature of the Bible as a whole, while arguable at various points, has unquestionably made the Bible, for many who formerly had no serious or vital relationship to it, once again a living book and the source of a meaningful personal faith.

IV

In Buber's teaching about God—the way to find Him and the way to lose Him—we find perhaps his most important contribution to the religious life and thought of our age. For Buber's God is the living, personal God of the Hebrew Bible—the God, in Pascal's terms, "of Abraham, of Isaac and of Jacob, and not of the philosophers"; and he showed a generation living in a time when this God has been eclipsed and even, for many, died, a way, perhaps the only possible way, of regaining a sense of His living reality.

How is God, the God whom Buber called the *Eternal Thou*, to be found or met? Buber taught that He may be partially glimpsed and is, in fact, addressed through every particular *Thou*, for He is present in all true dialogical encounters, underlying them, making them possible, gathering them up, fulfilling them.[40] God, or the *Eternal Thou*, is met by us only through our existence as persons, only in our encounter with others. Outside this encounter we can know nothing of Him, and the philosopher who grasps this "must renounce the attempt to include God in his system in any conceptual form" and be content to "point toward God, without actually dealing with Him."[41] How is God as the power making dialogical encounters possible to be understood? Malcolm Diamond has offered an analogy from the realm of Platonic thought to explain Buber's meaning. "As the sun is the most luminous of objects and the source of luminosity in all other objects, so the *Eternal Thou* is the consummate instance of a Thou and the source of the dialogic power of relation in all beings."[42]

As far as prescribing what a person must do to have the supreme meeting, the absolute encounter, with the *Eternal Thou*, Buber admitted that no general rules, formulas or *exercitia spiritualia* are possible. On God's side, whether He reveals or conceals Himself—and Buber knew, as does the Bible,[43] that God is at times an *El mistatter*, a God Who hides Himself—is a matter of divine grace. As far as man is concerned, what he can and must do is nothing more than open himself totally to other beings, surrender his "false self-asserting instinct" toward objectification and detachment and enter, with the whole of his being, the world of relation with all things. In short, he must overcome the barrier of separation that prevails in the *I-It* attitude.

This, Buber declared, does not mean a surrender of selfhood or a mystical withdrawal from this world to another, super-sensible realm. It does not require, contrary to what Kierkegaard believed and taught, renunciation of ordinary life, the beings and things of this world, so that one can concentrate exclusively on relationship with God, but encountering them in all presentness and with one's total personality as *Thous* who are included in the *Eternal Thou*.

To step into pure relation is not to disregard everything but to see everything in the *Thou*, not to renounce the world but to establish it on its true basis.

To look away from the world, or to stare at it, does not help a man to reach God; but he who sees the world in Him stands in His presence. "Here world, there God" is the language of *It*; "God in the world" is another language of *It*; but to eliminate or leave behind nothing at all, to include the whole world in the *Thou*, to give the world its due and its truth, to include nothing beside God but everything in Him—this is full and complete relation . . . If you explore the life of things and of conditioned being, you come to the unfathomable, if you deny the life of things and of conditioned being, you stand before nothingness, if you hallow this life you meet the living God.[44]

Buber's teaching about God has been described as a major contribution to that modern movement of thought which is known as religious empiricism and which is concerned with the analysis of the facts of religious experience. Professor Herbert W. Schneider, who so regards it, has written:

What makes Buber's contribution to religious empiricism so striking and unambiguous is his definite turning from introspective psychology with its search for the sense of the Divine Presence to a social psychology of inter-personal experience. This "dialogic" empiricism is from the start inter-personal: subject meeting subject, not subject facing object. Into this context of meetings among persons Buber places man's meeting with God, and he does so not by postulation, not by phenomenology, nor by personalism, but by telling accurately the facts of religious experience. A religious man meets, encounters, addresses, trusts, lays hold on an absolute person. All the attempts of philosophers to describe this empirical "object" in impersonal terms as an "It" (whether "wholly other" or "the Holy") Buber repudiates on empirical grounds as misrepresentations. The term "God," or the personal name of a God, is a necessary term; no other type of "being" can be introduced into religious experience as an adequate substitute, for the "primitive" objects of fear, tabu, magic, rite, and reverence are no adequate analogue to what modern man meets in his religious actions and thoughts. Buber's defense of this contention seems to me an excellent piece of philosophical empiricism.[45]

Buber repeatedly insisted that the living God, the God of Biblical faith and of religious experience, with whom he was concerned, cannot—as many of the theologians seem to think—be described or defined. He can only be encountered.

God cannot be inferred in anything—in nature, say, as its author, or in history as its master, or in the subject as the self that is thought in it. Something else is not "given" and God then elicited from it; but God is the Being that is directly, most nearly, and lastingly, over against us, that may properly only be addressed, not expressed.[46]

This God, the eternally present One, does not permit Himself to be held by anyone as an object to be used or controlled. "Woe to the man so possessed that he thinks he possesses God!"[47] One who believes that he can encase God in a logical system or enclose Him in a dialectical formula is thinking of an idol constructed by his own ingenuity and not of the real God.

One of the great merits of Judaism, according to Buber, was that it always relegated dogma to a secondary place and gave primary importance "to the remembrance and the expectation of a concrete situation: the encounter of God and men."[48] Israel's great achievement, he once said, lay not so much in that "it has told mankind of the one, real God, the origin and goal of all that exists, but rather that it has taught men that they can address this God in very reality, that men can say *Thou* to Him, that we human beings can stand face to face with Him, that there is communion between God and man."[49] Or, as he put it elsewhere, "again and again God addresses man and is addressed by him . . . To God's sovereign address, man gives his autonomous answer; if he remains silent, his silence, too, is an answer . . . The basic doctrine which fills the Hebrew Bible is that our life is a dialogue between the above and the below."[50] The dogmatics of the theologians, whether Jewish or Christian, who seek to conceptualize and define the God of the divine-human dialogue reported by the Bible, are a product of the

I-It attitude, of objectification and detachment, of a condition in which God is no longer present in a living, immediate relationship. "Whatever is enunciated *in abstracto* in the third person about the divine, on the thither side of the confrontation of *I and Thou*, is only a projection onto the conceptual construct plane . . ."[51]

The real God, the God who is met only in the dialogical relation, is known, Buber followed the Bible in proclaiming, as One who is to be loved but also feared, for He is, "to begin with, dreadful and incomprehensible." The fear of Him is the dark gateway to the love of Him.

> He who wishes to avoid passing through this gate, he who begins to provide himself with a comprehensible God, constructed thus and not otherwise, runs the risk of having to despair of God in view of the actualities of history and life, or of falling into inner falsehood. Only through the fear of God does man enter so deeply into the love of God that he cannot again be cast out of it.[52]

In the revelatory experience of God as Presence or *Eternal Thou*, man achieves "salvation" and finds the meaning of his life. But revelation yields no cognitive aspect of God, no knowledge that would take away His essential mysteriousness. Of God, Buber wrote, "in absolute contrast to all other existing beings, no objective aspect can be attained. Even a vision yields no objective viewing, and he who strains to hold fast an afterimage after the cessation of the full *I-Thou* relation has already lost the vision."[53] The man who has encountered the *Eternal Thou* realizes that he has known and received something, but not, as we have already noted, something that can be communicated or transmitted to others in propositional language or in terms of a set of universal commandments. Revelation does not tell us *what* God is in His essence but only *that* He is, for in the revelatory moment He is encountered as a living being and grasped as the One who gives to each man his life as a gift, a gift which is also a summons and a sending, and charges him with the responsibility of fulfilling these through his own unique response.

Is the God of whom Buber spoke as the *Eternal Thou* a person? That, he declared, we cannot know. "The absolute character of His personality, that paradox of paradoxes, prohibits any such statement."[54] When God is referred to as the *Eternal Thou*, the term is intended to be descriptive not of God Himself but only of our experienced relation with Him. "It is indeed legitimate," Buber wrote,

> to speak of the person of God within the religious relation and in its language; but in so doing we are making no essential statement about the Absolute which reduces it to the personal. We are rather saying that it enters into the relationship as the Absolute Person whom we call God. One may understand the personality of God as His act. It is, indeed, even permissible for the believer to believe that God became a person for love of him, because in our human mode of existence the only reciprocal relation with us that exists is a personal one.[55]

Buber was well aware that for many persons today the personal God of whom he spoke has become unreal, as has all transcendence and absoluteness. He was aware that this God has been eclipsed and, in fact, for not a few in our time has died. What has brought about the present-day eclipse or death of God? Buber suggested that both philosophy and religion have been, in large measure, responsible. Philosophy is capable of rendering a positive service to the life of faith by destroying false or inadequate images of God. But when, following its presupposition "that one sees the absolute in universals," it turns away "from the covenant of the absolute with the particular, with the concrete" and comes to regard God as the object from which all other objects are derived or as "Speech" (*Logos*), "the Unlimited," or simply "Being," it erects a barrier between man and the living, personal God Who acts and feels.[56] As for religion, it all too often lapses from the posture of Biblical faith, i.e., the direct encounter with the God Who reveals Himself only in an *I-Thou* meeting, to the three pseudo-religious substitutes of subjectivization which regards religion as essentially inward, psychic "religious experience," or magic which seeks to manipulate the divine, or gnosis which pretends to unveil its essential mystery. The latter, Buber maintained, is not restricted in modern times to occult theosophies or to systems like that of Carl Jung and other psychologists of the unconscious who have religious interests. Many theologies include such unveiling gestures behind their interpreting ones and are thus really forms of gnostic speculation. "Gnosis is not to be understood as only a historical category, but as a universal one. It—and not atheism, which annihilates God because it must reject the hitherto existing images of God—is the real antagonist of the reality of faith."[57]

An even greater contemporary obstacle to encountering the reality of the living God than gnosis or magic, or the reduction of religion to inner religious experience, Buber concluded, is the present-day dominance of objectification and detachment and the virtual disappearance of the *I-Thou* attitude before the massive power of the *I-It*.

> In our age, the *I-It* relation, gigantically swollen, has usurped, practically uncontested, the mastery and the rule. The I of this relation, an I that possesses all, makes all, succeeds with all, this I that is unable to say Thou, unable to meet a being essentially, is the Lord of the hour. This self-hood that has become omnipotent, with all the It around it, can naturally acknowledge neither God nor any genuine absolute which manifests itself to man as of non-human origin. It steps in between and shuts off from us the light of heaven.[58]

But what more than anything else have today made faith in a living, personal God Who is concerned for man difficult, indeed, virtually impossible for many—and especially for Jews—are, of course, the unspeakable historical atrocities of our time, of which Oswiecim is but one example. Though men, for their part, have "killed" God through interposing the I of the *I-It* relationship between themselves and Him and by refusing to submit to the address of transcendence, God, on his side, has been silent and has hidden His face. Our historical epoch —as Buber sorrowfully recognized—is like that of the author of the Eighty-second Psalm, who described life "in a time of God's hiddenness" when the world seems to have been entirely given over to judges who "judge unjustly" and "lift up the face of the wicked,"[59] or like that depicted by Franz Kafka whose "unexpressed, ever-present theme," Buber once wrote, "is the remoteness of the judge, the remoteness of the lord of the castle, the hiddenness, the eclipse . . ."[60]

"How," Buber asked, echoing the tormented question of many survivors and witnesses of the Nazi death camps,

> . . . is a life with God still possible in a time in which there is an Oswiecim? The estrangement has become too cruel, the hiddenness too deep. One can still "believe" in the God who allowed those things to happen, but can one still speak to him? Can one still hear His word? Can one still . . . enter at all into a dialogic relationship with Him? . . . Dare we recommend to . . . the Job of the gas chambers: "Call to Him, for He is kind, for His mercy endureth forever"?[61]

But the Biblical Job, Buber remembered, *was* answered by God. Not that Job received any reply to his agonized charge that God was "cruel" or had "removed his right" from him. No, God did not answer his charges or even touch upon them. "The true answer that Job receives is God's appearance only, only this—that distance turns into nearness, that 'his eye sees Him,' that he knows Him again. Nothing is explained, nothing adjusted; wrong has not become right, nor cruelty kindness. Nothing has happened but that man again hears God's address."[62]

To an era which lives in a time of God's silence and which, like Job, longs for a sign of His presence and address, Buber spoke a message of hope and faith, the irresistible hope and indestructible faith that have always been at the heart of Judaism. The *I-Thou* relation, he declared, may have "gone into the catacombs" in our day but "the eclipse of the light of God is no extinction; even tomorrow that which has stepped in between may give way."[63] Until then "it would be worthier not to explain it (the eclipse) in sensational and incompetent sayings such as that of the 'death' of God, but to endure it as it is and at the same time to move existentially toward a new happening . . . in which the word between heaven and earth will again be heard."[64]

NOTES

1. Buber, *Hasidism and Modern Man*, New York, Horizon Press, 1958, p. 56.
2. *Ibid.*, p. 53.
3. *Ibid.*, p. 57.
4. *Ibid.*, p. 59.
5. Kaufmann, "Buber's Religious Significance," in P. A. Schilpp, and M. Friedman, eds., *The Philosophy of Martin Buber*, La Salle, Ill., Open Court Publishing Co., 1967, pp. 680–681.
6. Buber, "The Faith of Judaism," in *Israel and the World*, New York, Shocken Books, 1948, p. 13.
7. Buber, "On National Education," in *Israel and the World*, p. 159.
8. *Loc. cit.*
9. See below, *Dialogue*, "A Conversion."
10. Buber, "Afterword: The History of the Dialogical Principle," in *Between Man and Man*, New York, The Macmillan Company, 1965, pp. 211 ff.
11. Muilenberg, "Buber as an Interpreter of the Bible," in *The Philosophy of Martin Buber*, p. 382.
12. Buber, *I and Thou*, 2nd ed. New York, Charles Scribner's Sons, 1958, p. 11.
13. R. G. Smith, *Martin Buber*, Richmond, John Knox Press, 1967, p. 16, footnote.
14. Buber, *I and Thou*, p. 102.
15. *Ibid.*, p. 32.
16. *Loc. cit.*
17. *Ibid.*, p. 34.
18. *Ibid.*, p. 16.
19. *Ibid.*, p. 33.
20. Buber, *Between Man and Man*, p. 35.
21. *Ibid.*, p. 38.
22. Buber, *I and Thou*, p. 15.
23. Buber, *The Prophetic Faith*, New York, The Macmillan Company, 1949, p. 54.
24. Buber, "The Man of Today and the Jewish Bible," *Israel and the World*, New York, Schocken Books, 1948, p. 89.
25. *Ibid.*, p. 94.
26. *Ibid.*, p. 93.
27. *Ibid.*, p. 97.
28. *Ibid.*, p. 100.
29. *Ibid.*, pp. 98–99.
30. Buber, *I and Thou*, pp. 110–111.
31. *Ibid.*, p. 111.
32. Buber, "The Education of Character," *Between Man and Man*, p. 114.
33. *Loc. cit.*

34. Buber, "The Man of Today and the Jewish Bible," *Israel and the World*, p. 94.
35. *Ibid.*, p. 102.
36. Buber, "The Faith of Judaism," *Israel and the World*, p. 27.
37. Buber, "The Two Foci of the Jewish Soul," *Israel and the World*, p. 36.
38. *Ibid.*, p. 35.
39. *Loc. cit.*
40. Buber, *I and Thou*, p. 75.
41. Buber, *Eclipse of God*, London, Victor Gollancz, Ltd., 1953, pp. 68 f.
42. Diamond, "Dialogue and Theology," *The Philosophy of Martin Buber*, p. 241.
43. Isaiah 45:15.
44. Buber, *I and Thou*, pp. 78–79.
45. Schneider, "The Historical Significance of Buber's Philosophy," *The Philosophy of Martin Buber*, pp. 470–471.
46. Buber, *I and Thou*, pp. 80–81.
47. *Ibid.*, p. 106.
48. Buber, "The Faith of Judaism," *Israel and the World*, p. 14.
49. Buber, "Spinoza, Sabbatai Zevi, and the Baal Shem," *Hasidism*, p. 76.
50. Buber, *At the Turning*, pp. 47–48.
51. Buber, "The Faith of Judaism," *Israel and the World*, p. 14.
52. Buber, "The Two Foci of the Jewish Soul," *Israel and the World*, pp. 31–32.
53. Buber, "God and the Spirit of Man," *Eclipse of God*, p. 128.
54. Buber, "The Love of God and the Idea of Deity," *Eclipse of God*, p. 81.
55. Buber, "Religion and Ethics," *Eclipse of God*, p. 127.
56. Buber, "Religion and Philosophy," *Eclipse of God*, pp. 44 f., 53–63.
57. Buber, "Reply to C. G. Jung," *Eclipse of God*, p. 175.
58. Buber, "God and the Spirit of Man," *Eclipse of God*, pp. 166–167.
59. Buber, *At the Turning*, p. 60.
60. Buber, *Two Types of Faith*, p. 168.
61. Buber, *At the Turning*, p. 61.
62. *Ibid.*, pp. 60–61.
63. Buber, "God and the Spirit of Man," *Eclipse of God*, p. 167.
64. *Ibid.*, p. 91.

*Selections from
Buber's Writings*

I-THOU AND I-IT

To MAN THE WORLD IS TWOFOLD, in accordance with his twofold attitude.

The attitude of man is twofold, in accordance with the twofold nature of the primary words which he speaks.

The primary words are not isolated words, but combined words.

The one primary word is the combination *I-Thou*.

The other primary word is the combination *I-It*; wherein, without a change in the primary word, one of the words *He* and *She* can replace *It*.

Hence the *I* of man is also twofold.

For the *I* of the primary word *I-Thou* is a different *I* from that of the primary word *I-It*.

PRIMARY WORDS DO NOT SIGNIFY THINGS, but they intimate relations.

Primary words do not describe something that might exist independently of them, but being spoken they bring about existence.

Primary words are spoken from the being.

If *Thou* is said, the *I* of the combination *I-Thou* is said along with it.

If *It* is said, the *I* of the combination *I-It* is said along with it.

The primary word *I-Thou* can only be spoken with the whole being.

The primary word *I-It* can never be spoken with the whole being.

THERE IS NO *I* TAKEN IN ITSELF, but only the *I* of the primary word *I-Thou* and the *I* of the primary word *I-It*.

When a man says *I* he refers to one or other of these. The *I* to which he refers is present when he says *I*. Further, when he says *Thou* or *It*, the *I* of one of the two primary words is present.

The existence of *I* and the speaking of *I* are one and the same thing.

When a primary word is spoken the speaker enters the word and takes his stand in it.

THE LIFE OF HUMAN BEINGS is not passed in the sphere of transitive verbs alone. It does not exist in virtue of activities alone which have some *thing* for their object.

I perceive something, I am sensible of something. I imagine something. I will something. I feel something. I think something. The life of human beings does not consist of all this and the like alone.

This and the like together establish the realm of *It*.

But the realm of *Thou* has a different basis.

When *Thou* is spoken, the speaker has no thing for his object. For where there is a thing there is another thing. Every *It* is bounded by others; *It* exists only through being bounded by others. But when *Thou* is spoken, there is no thing. *Thou* has no bounds.

When *Thou* is spoken, the speaker has no *thing*; he has indeed nothing. But he takes his stand in relation.

IT IS SAID THAT MAN EXPERIENCES HIS WORLD. What does that mean?

Man travels over the surface of things and experiences them. He extracts knowledge about their constitution from them: he wins an experience from them. He experiences what belongs to the things.

But the world is not presented to man by experiences alone. These present him only with a world composed of *It* and *He* and *She* and *It* again.

I experience something—if we add "inner" to "outer" experiences, nothing in the situation is changed. We are merely following the uneternal division that springs from the lust of the human race to whittle away the secret of death. Inner things or outer things, what are they but things and things!

I experience something—if we add "secret" to "open" experiences, nothing in the situation is changed. How self-confident is that wisdom which perceives a closed compartment in things, reserved for the initiate and manipulated only with the key. O secrecy without a secret! O accumulation of information! It, always It!

THE MAN WHO EXPERIENCES has not part in the world. For it is "in him" and not between him and the world that the experience arises.

The world has no part in the experience. It permits itself to be experienced, but has no concern in the matter. For it does nothing to the experience, and the experience does nothing to it.

AS EXPERIENCE, the world belongs to the primary word *I-It*.

The primary word *I-Thou* establishes the world of relation.

THE SPHERES IN WHICH THE WORLD OF RELATION ARISES are three.

First, our life with nature. There the relation sways in gloom, beneath the level of speech. Creatures live and move over against us, but cannot come to us, and when we address them as *Thou*, our words cling to the threshold of speech.

Second, our life with men. There the relation is open and in the form of speech. We can give and accept the *Thou*.

Third, our life with spiritual beings. There the relation is clouded, yet it discloses itself; it does not use speech, yet begets it. We perceive no *Thou*, but none the less we feel we are addressed and we answer—forming, thinking, acting. We speak the primary word with our being, though we cannot utter *Thou* with our lips.

But with what right do we draw what lies outside speech into relation with the world of the primary word?

In every sphere in its own way, through each process of becoming that is present to us we look out toward the fringe of the eternal *Thou*; in each we are aware of a breath from the eternal *Thou*; in each *Thou* we address the eternal *Thou*.

IF I FACE A HUMAN BEING AS MY *Thou*, and say the primary word *I-Thou* to him, he is not a thing among things, and does not consist of things.

Thus a human being is not *He* or *She*, bounded from any other *He* and *She*, a specific point in space and time within the net of the world; nor is he a nature able to be experienced and described, a loose bundle of named qualities. But with no neighbor, and whole in himself, he is *Thou* and fills the heavens. This does not mean that nothing exists except himself. But all else lives in *his* light.

Just as the melody is not made up of notes nor the verse of words nor the statue of lines, but they must be tugged and dragged till their unity has been scattered into these many pieces, so with the man to whom I say *Thou*. I can take out from him the colour of his hair or of his speech, or of his goodness. I must continually do this. But each time I do it he ceases to be *Thou*.

And just as prayer is not in time but time in prayer, sacrifice not in space but space in sacrifice, and to reverse the relation is to abolish the reality, so with the man to whom I say *Thou*. I do not meet with him at some time and place or other. I can set him in a particular time and place; I must continually do it: but I set only a *He* or a *She*, that is an *It*, no longer my *Thou*.

So long as the heaven of *Thou* is spread out over me the winds of causality cower at my heels, and the whirlpool of fate stays its course.

I do not experience the man to whom I say *Thou*. But I take my stand in relation to him, in the sanctity of the primary word. Only when I step out of it do I experience him once more. In the act of experience *Thou* is far away.

Even if the man to whom I say *Thou* is not aware of it in the midst of his experience, yet relation may exist. For *Thou* is more that *It* realizes. No deception penetrates here; here is the cradle of the Real Life.

THE *Thou* MEETS ME THROUGH GRACE—It is not found by seeking. But my speaking of the primary word to it is an act of my being, is indeed *the* act of my being.

The *Thou* meets me. But I step into direct relation with it. Hence the relation means being chosen and choosing, suffering and action in one; just as any action of the whole being, which means the suspension of all partial actions and consequently of all sensations of actions grounded only in their particular limitation, is bound to resemble suffering.

The primary word *I-Thou* can be spoken only with the whole being. Concentration and fusion into the whole being can never take place through my agency, nor can it ever take place without me. I become through my relation to the *Thou*; as I become *I*, I say *Thou*.

All real living is meeting.

THE RELATION TO THE *Thou* IS DIRECT. No system of ideas, no foreknowledge, and no fancy intervene between *I* and *Thou*. The memory itself is transformed, as it plunges out of its isolation into the unity of the whole. No aim, no lust, and no anticipation intervene between *I* and *Thou*. Desire itself is transformed as it plunges out of its dream into the appearance. Every means is an obstacle. Only when every means has collapsed does the meeting come about.

IN FACE OF THE DIRECTNESS of the relation everything indirect becomes irrelevant. It is also irrelevant if my *Thou* is already the *It* for other *I's* ("an object of general experience"), or can become so through the very accomplishment of this act of my being. For the real, though certainly swaying and swinging, boundary runs neither between experience and non-experience, nor between what is given and what is not given, nor yet between the world of being and the world of value; but cutting indifferently across all these provinces it lies between *Thou* and *It*, between the present and the object.

THE PRESENT, and by that is meant not the point which indicates from time to time in our thought merely the conclusion of "finished" time, the mere appearance of a termination which is fixed and held, but the real, filled present, exists only in so far as actual presentness, meeting, and relation exist. The present arises only in virtue of the fact that the *Thou* becomes present.

The *I* of the primary word *I-It*, that is, the *I* faced by no *Thou*, but surrounded by a multitude of "contents," has no present, only the past. Put in another way, in so far as man rests satisfied with the things that he experiences and uses, he lives in the past, and his moment has no present content. He has nothing but objects. But objects subsist in time that has been.

The present is not fugitive and transient, but continually present and enduring. The object is not duration, but cessation, suspension, a breaking off and cutting clear and hardening, absence of relation and of present being.

True beings are lived in the present, the life of objects is in the past.

APPEAL TO A "WORLD OF IDEAS" as a third factor above this opposition will not do away with its essential twofold nature. For I speak of nothing else but the real man, of you and of me, of our life and of our world—not of an *I*, or a state of being, in itself alone. The real boundary for the actual man cuts right across the world of ideas as well.

To be sure, many a man who is satisfied with the experience and use of the world of things has raised over or about himself a structure of ideas, in which he finds refuge and repose from the oncome of nothingness. On the threshold he lays aside his inauspicious everyday dress, wraps himself in pure linen, and regales himself with the spectacle of primal being, or of necessary being; but his life has no part in it. To proclaim his ways may even fill him with well-being.

But the mankind of mere *It* that is imagined, postulated, and propagated by such a man has nothing in common with a living mankind where *Thou* may truly be spoken. The noblest fiction is a fetish, the loftiest fictitious sentiment is depraved. Ideas are no more enthroned above our heads than resident in them; they wander amongst us and accost us. The man who leaves the primary word unspoken is to be pitied; but the man who addresses instead these ideas with an abstraction or a password, as if it were their name, is contemptible.

IN ONE OF THE THREE EXAMPLES it is obvious that the direct relation includes an effect on what confronts me. In art the act of the being determines the situation in which the form becomes the work. Through the meeting that which confronts me is fulfilled, and enters the world of things, there to be endlessly active, endlessly to become *It*, but also endlessly to become *Thou* again, inspiring and blessing. It is "embodied"; its body emerges from the flow of the spaceless, timeless present on the shore of existence.

The significance of the effect is not so obvious in the relation with the *Thou* spoken to men. The act of the being which provides directness in this case is usually understood wrongly as being one of feeling. Feelings accompany the metaphysical and metapsychical fact of love, but they do not constitute it. The accompanying feelings can be of greatly differing kinds. The feeling of Jesus for the demoniac differs from his feeling for the beloved disciple; but the love is the one love. Feelings are "entertained"; love comes to pass. Feelings dwell in man; but man dwells in his love. That is no metaphor, but the actual truth. Love does not cling to the *I* in such a way as to have the *Thou* only for its "content," its object; but love is between *I* and *Thou*. The man who does not know this, with his very being know this, does not know love; even though he ascribes to it the feelings he lives through, experiences, enjoys, and expresses. Love ranges in its effect through the whole world. In the eyes of him who takes his stand in love, and gazes out of it, men are cut free from their entanglement in bustling activity. Good people and evil, wise and foolish, beautiful and ugly, become successively real to him; that is, set free they step forth in their singleness, and confront him as *Thou*. In a wonderful way, from time to time, exclusiveness arises—and so he can be effective, helping, healing, educating, raising up, saving. Love is responsibility of an *I* for a *Thou*. In this lies the likeness—impossible in any feeling whatsoever—of all who love, from the smallest to the greatest and from the blessedly protected man, whose life is rounded in that of a loved being to him who is all his life nailed to the cross of the world, and who ventures to bring himself to the dreadful point—to love *all men*.

Let the significance of the effect in the third example, that of the creature and our contemplation of it, remain sunk in mystery. Believe in the simple magic of life, in service in the universe, and the meaning of that waiting, that alertness, that "craning of the neck" in creatures will dawn upon you. Every word would falsify; but look! round about you beings live their life, and to whatever point you turn you come upon being.

RELATION IS MUTUAL. My *Thou* affects me, as I affect it. We are moulded by our pupils and built up by our works. The "bad" man, lightly touched by the holy primary word, becomes one who reveals. How we are educated by children and by animals! We live our lives inscrutably included within the streaming mutual life of the universe.

—YOU SPEAK OF LOVE as though it were the only relation between men. But properly speaking, can you take it even only as an example, since there is such a thing as hate?

—So long as love is "blind," that is, so long as it does not see a *whole* being, it is not truly under the sway of the primary word of relation. Hate is by nature blind. Only a part of a being can be hated. He who sees a whole being and is compelled to reject it is no longer in the kingdom of hate, but is in that of human restriction of the power to say *Thou*. He finds himself unable to say the primary word to the other human being confronting him. This word consistently involves an affirmation of the being addressed. He is therefore compelled to reject either the other or himself. At this barrier the entering on a relation recognizes its relativity, and only simultaneously with this will the barrier be raised.

Yet the man who straightforwardly hates is nearer to relation than the man without hate and love.

BUT THIS IS THE EXALTED MELANCHOLY OF OUR FATE, that every *Thou* in our world must become an *It*. It does not matter how exclusively present the *Thou* was in the direct relation. As soon as the relation has been worked out or has been permeated with a means, the *Thou* becomes an object among objects—perhaps the chief, but still one of them, fixed in its size and its limits. In the work of art realization in one sense means loss of reality in another. Genuine contemplation is over in a short time; now the life in nature, that first unlocked itself to me in the mystery of mutual action, can again be described, taken to pieces, and classified—the meeting-point of manifold systems of laws. And love itself cannot persist in direct relation. It endures, but in interchange of actual and potential being. The human being who was even now single and unconditioned, not something lying to hand, only present, not able to be experienced, only able to be fulfilled, has now become again a *He* or a *She*, a sum of qualities, a given quantity with a certain shape. Now I may take out from him again the color of his hair or of his speech or of his goodness. But so long as I can do this he is no more my *Thou* and cannot yet be my *Thou* again.

Every *Thou* in the world is by its nature fated to become a thing, or continually to re-enter into the condition of things. In objective speech it would be said that every thing in the world, either before or after becoming a thing, is able to appear to an *I* as its *Thou*. But objective speech snatches only at a fringe of real life.

The *It* is the eternal chrysalis, the *Thou* the eternal butterfly—except that situations do not always follow one another in clear succession, but often there is a happening profoundly twofold, confusedly entangled.

(From *I and Thou*, Second Edition, pp. 3–6, 8–9, 11–18.)

THE ETERNAL THOU

THE EXTENDED LINES OF RELATIONS meet in the eternal *Thou*.

Every particular *Thou* is a glimpse through to the eternal *Thou*; by means of every particular *Thou* the primary word addresses the eternal *Thou*. Through this mediation of the *Thou* of all beings fulfillment, and non-fulfillment, of relations comes to them: the inborn *Thou* is realized in each relation and consummated in none. It is consummated only in the direct relation with the *Thou* that by its nature cannot become *It*.

MEN HAVE ADDRESSED THEIR ETERNAL *Thou* with many names. In singing of Him who was thus named they always had the *Thou* in mind: the first myths were hymns of praise. Then the names took refuge in the language of *It*; men were more and more strongly moved to think of and to address their eternal *Thou* as an *It*. But all God's names are hallowed, for in them He is not merely spoken about, but also spoken to.

Many men wish to reject the word God as a legitimate usage, because it is so misused. It is indeed the most heavily laden of all the words used by men. For that very reason it is the most imperishable and most indispensable. What does all mistaken talk about God's being and works (though there has been, and can be, no other talk about these) matter in comparison with the one truth that all men who have addressed God had God Himself in mind? For he who speaks the word God and really has *Thou* in mind (whatever the illusion by which he is held), addresses the true *Thou* of his life, which cannot be limited by another *Thou*, and to which he stands in a relation that gathers up and includes all others.

But when he, too, who abhors the name, and believes himself to be godless, gives his whole being to addressing the *Thou* of his life, as a *Thou* that cannot be limited by another, he addresses God.

IF WE GO ON OUR WAY and meet a man who has advanced towards us and has also gone on *his* way, we know only our part of the way, not his—his we experience only in the meeting.

Of the complete relational event we know, with the knowledge of life lived, our going out to the relation, our part of the way. The other part only comes upon us, we do not know it; it comes upon us in the meeting. But we strain ourselves on it if we speak of it as though it were some thing beyond the meeting.

We have to be concerned, to be troubled, not about the other side but about our own side, not about grace but about will. Grace concerns us in so far as we go out to it and persist in its presence; but it is not our object.

The *Thou* confronts me. But I step into direct relation with it. Hence the relation means being chosen and choosing, suffering and action in one; just as any action of the whole being which means the suspension of all partial actions, and consequently of all sensations of actions grounded only in their particular limitation, is bound to resemble suffering.

This is the activity of the man who has become a whole being, an activity that has been termed doing nothing: nothing separate or partial stirs in the man any more, thus he makes no intervention in the world; it is the whole man, enclosed and at rest in his wholeness, that is effective—he has become an effective whole. To have won stability in this state is to be able to go out to the supreme meeting.

To this end the world of sense does not need to be laid aside as though it were illusory. There is no illusory world, there is only the world—which appears to us as twofold in accordance with our twofold attitude. Only the barrier of separation has to be destroyed. Further, no "going beyond sense-experience" is necessary; for every experience, even the most spiritual, could yield us only an *It*. Nor is any recourse necessary to a world of ideas and values; for they cannot become presentness for us. None of these things is necessary. Can it be said what really is necessary?—Not in the sense of a precept. For everything that has ever been devised and contrived in the time of the human spirit as precept, alleged preparation, practice, or meditation, has nothing to do with the primal, simple fact of the meeting. Whatever the advantages in knowledge or the wielding of power for which we have to thank this or that practice, none of this affects the meeting of which we are speaking; it all has its place in the world of *It* and does not lead one step, does not take *the* step, out of it. Going out to the relation cannot be taught in the sense of precepts being given. It can only be indicated by the draw-

ing of a circle which excludes everything that is not this
going out. Then the one thing that matters is visible,
full acceptance of the present.

To be sure, this acceptance presupposes that the further a man has wandered in separated being the more
difficult is the venture and the more elemental the turning. This does not mean a giving up of, say the *I*, as
mystical writings usually suppose: the *I* is as indispensable to this, the supreme, as to every relation, since relation is only possible between *I* and *Thou*. It is not the *I*,
then, that is given up, but that false self-asserting instinct that makes a man flee to the possessing of things
before the unreliable, perilous world of relation which
has neither density nor duration and cannot be surveyed.

EVERY REAL RELATION with a being or life in the world
is exclusive. Its *Thou* is freed, steps forth, is single, and
confronts you. It fills the heavens. This does not mean
that nothing else exists; but all else lives in *its* light.
As long as the presence of the relation continues, this
its cosmic range is inviolable. But as soon as a *Thou* becomes *It*, the cosmic range of the relation appears as an
offence to the world, its exclusiveness as an exclusion of
the universe.

In the relation with God unconditional exclusiveness
and unconditional inclusiveness are one. He who enters
on the absolute relation is concerned with nothing isolated any more, neither things nor beings, neither earth
nor heaven; but everything is gathered up in the relation. For to step into pure relation is not to disregard
everything but to see everything in the *Thou*, not to renounce the world but to establish it on its true basis. To
look away from the world, or to stare at it, does not
help a man to reach God; but he who sees the world in
Him stands in His presence. "Here world, there God" is
the language of *It*; "God in the world" is another language of *It*; but to eliminate or leave behind nothing at
all, to include the whole world in the *Thou*, to give
the world its due and its truth, to include nothing beside
God but everything in him—this is full and complete
relation.

Men do not find God if they stay in the world. They

do not find Him if they leave the world. He who goes out with his whole being to meet his *Thou* and carries to it all being that is in the world, finds him who cannot be sought.

Of course God is the "wholly Other"; but He is also the wholly Same, the wholly Present. Of course He is the *Mysterium Tremendum* that appears and overthrows; but He is also the mystery of the self-evident, nearer to me than my *I*.

If you explore the life of things and of conditioned being you come to the unfathomable, if you deny the life of things and of conditioned being you stand before nothingness, if you hallow this life you meet the living God.

(From *I and Thou*, Second Edition, pp. 75–79.)

DIALOGUE

SECTION ONE: DESCRIPTION

ORIGINAL REMEMBRANCE

Through all sorts of changes the same dream, sometimes after an interval of several years, recurs to me. I name it the dream of the double cry. Its context is always much the same, a "primitive" world meagrely equipped. I find myself in a vast cave, like the Latomias of Syracuse, or in a mud building that reminds me when I awake of the villages of the *fellahin*, or on the fringe of a gigantic forest whose like I cannot remember having seen.

The dream begins in very different ways, but always with something extraordinary happening to me, for instance, with a small animal resembling a lion-cub (whose name I know in the dream but not when I awake) tearing the flesh from my arm and being forced only with an effort to loose its hold. The strange thing is that this first part of the dream story, which in the duration as well as the outer meaning of the incidents is easily the most important, always unrolls at a

furious pace as though it did not matter. Then suddenly
the pace abates: I stand there and cry out. In the view
of the events which my waking consciousness has I
should have to suppose that the cry I utter varies in accordance with what preceded it, and is sometimes joy-
ous, sometimes fearful, sometimes even filled both with
pain and with triumph. But in my morning recollection
it is neither so expressive nor so various. Each time it is
the same cry, inarticulate but in strict rhythm, rising
and falling, swelling to a fulness which my throat
could not endure were I awake, long and slow, quiet,
quite slow and very long, a cry that is a song. When it
ends my heart stops beating. But then, somewhere, far
away, another cry moves towards me, another which is
the same, the same cry uttered or sung by another
voice. Yet it is not the same cry, certainly no "echo" of
my cry but rather its true rejoinder, tone for tone not
repeating mine, not even in a weakened form, but corresponding to mine, answering its tones—so much so,
that mine, which at first had to my own ear no sound of
questioning at all, now appear as questions, as a long
series of questions, which now all receive a response.
The response is no more capable of interpretation than
the question. And yet the cries that meet the one cry
that is the same do not seem to be the same as one another. Each time the voice is new. But now, as the
reply ends, in the first moment after its dying fall, a
certitude, true dream certitude comes to me that *now
it has happened*. Nothing more. Just this, and in this
way—*now it has happened*. If I should try to explain it,
it means that that happening which gave rise to my
cry has only now, with the rejoinder, really and undoubtedly happened.

After this manner the dream has recurred each time—
till once, the last time, now two years ago. At first it was
as usual (it was the dream with the animal), my cry
died away, again my heart stood still. But then there
was quiet. There came no answering call. I listened, I
heard no sound. For I *awaited* the response for the first
time; hitherto it had always surprised me, as though I
had never heard it before. Awaited, it failed to come.
But now something happened with me. As though I had

till now had no other access from the world to sensation save that of the ear and now discovered myself as a being simply equipped with senses, both those clothed in the bodily organs and the naked senses, so I exposed myself to the distance, open to all sensation and perception. And then, not from a distance but from the air round about me, noiselessly, came the answer. Really it did not come; it was there. It had been there—so I may explain it—even before my cry: there it was, and now, when I laid myself open to it, it let itself be received by me. I received it as completely into my perception as ever I received the rejoinder in one of the earlier dreams. If I were to report with what I heard it I should have to say "with every pore of my body." As ever the rejoinder came in one of the earlier dreams this corresponded to and answered my cry. It exceeded the earlier rejoinder in an unknown perfection which is hard to define, for it resides in the fact that it was already there.

When I had reached an end of receiving it, I felt again that certainty, pealing out more than ever, that *now it has happened.*

SILENCE WHICH IS COMMUNICATION

Just as the most eager speaking at one another does not make a conversation (this is most clearly shown in that curious sport, aptly termed discussion, that is, "breaking apart," which is indulged in by men who are to some extent gifted with the ability to think), so for a conversation no sound is necessary, not even a gesture. Speech can renounce all the media of sense, and it is still speech.

Of course I am not thinking of lovers' tender silence, resting in one another, the expression and discernment of which can be satisfied by a glance, indeed by the mere sharing of a gaze which is rich in inward relations. Nor am I thinking of the mystical shared silence, such as is reported of the Franciscan Aegidius and Louis of

France (or, almost identically, of two rabbis of the Hasidim) who, meeting once, did not utter a word, but "taking their stand in the reflection of the divine Face" experienced one another. For here too there is still the expression of a gesture, of the physical attitude of the one to the other.

What I am thinking of I will make clear by an example.

Imagine two men sitting beside one another in any kind of solitude of the world. They do not speak with one another, they do not look at one another, not once have they turned to one another. They are not in one another's confidence, the one knows nothing of the other's career, early that morning they got to know one another in the course of their travels. In this moment neither is thinking of the other; we do not need to know what their thoughts are. The one is sitting on the common seat obviously after his usual manner, calm, hospitably disposed to everything that may come. His being seems to say it is too little to be ready, one must also be really *there*. The other, whose attitude does not betray him, is a man who holds himself in reserve, withholds himself. But if we know about him we know that a childhood's spell is laid on him, that his withholding of himself is something other than an attitude, behind all attitude is entrenched the impenetrable inability to communicate himself. And now—let us imagine that this is one of the hours which succeed in bursting asunder the seven iron bands about our heart—imperceptibly the spell is lifted. But even now the man does not speak a word, does not stir a finger. Yet he does something. The lifting of the spell has happened to him—no matter from where—without his doing. But this is what he does now: he released in himself a reserve over which only he himself has power. Unreservedly communication streams from him, and the silence bears it to his neighbour. Indeed it was intended for him, and he receives it unreservedly as he receives all genuine destiny that meets him. He will be able to tell no one, not even himself, what he has experienced. What does he now "know" of the other? No more knowing is needed. For where unreserve has ruled, even wordlessly, between men, the word of dialogue has happened sacramentally.

OPINIONS AND THE FACTUAL

Human dialogue, therefore, although it has its distinctive life in the sign, that is in sound and gesture (the letters of language have their place in this only in special instances, as when, between friends in a meeting, notes describing the atmosphere skim back and forth across the table), can exist without the sign, but admittedly not in an objectively comprehensible form. On the other hand an element of communication, however inward, seems to belong to its essence. But in its highest moments dialogue reaches out even beyond these boundaries. It is completed outside contents, even the most personal, which are or can be communicated. Moreover it is completed not in some "mystical" event, but in one that is in the precise sense factual, thoroughly dovetailed into the common human world and the concrete time-sequence.

One might indeed be inclined to concede this as valid for the special realm of the erotic. But I do not intend to bring even this in here as an explanation. For Eros is in reality much more strangely composed than in Plato's genealogical myth, and the erotic is in no way, as might be supposed, purely a compressing and unfolding of dialogue. Rather do I know no other realm where, as in this one (to be spoken of later), dialogue and monologue are so mingled and opposed. Many celebrated ecstasies of love are nothing but the lover's delight in the possibilities of his own person which are actualized in unexpected fulness.

I would rather think of something unpretentious yet significant—of the glances which strangers exchange in a busy street as they pass one another with unchanging pace. Some of these glances, though not charged with destiny, nevertheless reveal to one another two dialogical natures.

But I can really show what I have in mind only by events which open into a genuine change from communication to communion, that is, in an embodiment of the word of dialogue.

What I am here concerned with cannot be conveyed

in ideas to a reader. But we may represent it by examples—provided that, where the matter is important, we do not eschew taking examples from the inmost recesses of the personal life. For where else should the like be found?

My friendship with one now dead arose in an incident that may be described, if you will, as a broken-off conversation. The date is Easter 1914. Some men from different European peoples had met in an undefined presentiment of the catastrophe, in order to make preparations for an attempt to establish a supra-national authority. The conversations were marked by that unreserve, whose substance and fruitfulness I have scarcely ever experienced so strongly. It had such an effect on all who took part that the fictitious fell away and every word was an actuality. Then as we discussed the composition of the larger circle from which public initiative should proceed (it was decided that it should meet in August of the same year) one of us, a man of passionate concentration and judicial power of love, raised the consideration that too many Jews had been nominated, so that several countries would be represented in unseemly proportion by their Jews. Though similar reflections were not foreign to my own mind, since I hold that Jewry can gain an effective and more than merely stimulating share in the building of a steadfast world of peace only in its own community and not in scattered members, they seemed to me, expressed in this way, to be tainted in their justice. Obstinate Jew that I am, I protested against the protest. I no longer know how from that I came to speak of Jesus and to say that we Jews knew him from within, in the impulses and stirrings of his Jewish being, in a way that remains inaccessible to the peoples submissive to him. "In a way that remains inaccessible to you"—so I directly addressed the former clergyman. He stood up, I too stood, we looked into the heart of one another's eyes. "It is gone," he said, and before everyone we gave one another the kiss of brotherhood.

The discussion of the situation between Jews and Christians had been transformed into a bond between the Christian and the Jew. In this transformation dialogue was fulfilled. Opinions were gone, in a bodily way the factual took place.

DISPUTATIONS IN RELIGION

Here I expect two objections, one weighty and one powerful.

One argument against me takes this form. When it is a question of essential views, of views concerning *Weltanschauung*, the conversation *must* not be broken off in such a way. Each must expose himself wholly, in a real way, in his humanly unavoidable partiality, and thereby experience himself in a real way as limited by the other, so that the two suffer together the destiny of our conditioned nature and meet one another in it.

To this I answer that the experience of being limited is included in what I refer to; but so too is the experience of overcoming it together. This cannot be completed on the level of *Weltanschauung*, but on that of reality. Neither needs to give up his point of view; only, in that unexpectedly they do something and unexpectedly something happens to them which is called a covenant, they enter a realm where the law of the point of view no longer holds. They too suffer the destiny of our conditioned nature, but they honour it most highly when, as is permitted to us, they let themselves run free of it for an immortal moment. They had already met one another when each in his soul so turned to the other that from then on, making him present, he spoke really to and towards him.

The other objection, which comes from a quite different, in fact from the opposite, side is to the effect that this may be true so far as the province of the point of view reaches, but it ceases to be true for a confession of faith. Two believers in conflict about their doctrines are concerned with the execution of the divine will, not with a fleeting personal agreement. For the man who is so related to his faith that he is able to die or to slay for it there can be no realm where the law of the faith ceases to hold. It is laid on him to help truth to victory, he does not let himself be misled by sentiments. The man holding a different, that is a false, belief must be converted, or at least instructed; direct contact with him can be achieved only outside the advocacy of the faith, it cannot proceed from it. The thesis of religious disputation cannot be allowed to "go."

This objection derives its power from its indifference to the non-binding character of the relativized spirit—a character which is accepted as a matter of course. I can answer it adequately only by a confession.

I have not the possibility of judging Luther, who refused fellowship with Zwingli in Marburg, or Calvin who furthered the death of Servetus. For Luther and Calvin believe that the Word of God has so descended among men that it can be clearly known and must therefore be exclusively advocated. I do not believe that; the Word of God crosses my vision like a falling star to whose fire the meteorite will bear witness without making it light up for me, and I myself can only bear witness to the light but not produce the stone and say "This is it." But this difference of faith is by no means to be understood merely as a subjective one. It is not based on the fact that we who live to-day are weak in faith, and it will remain even if our faith is ever so much strengthened. The situation of the world itself, in the most serious sense, more precisely the relation between God and man, has changed. And this change is certainly not comprehended in its essence by our thinking only of the darkening, so familiar to us, of the supreme light, only of the night of our being, empty of revelation. It is the night of an expectation—not of a vague hope, but of an expectation. We expect a theophany of which we know nothing but the place, and the place is called community. In the public catacombs of this expectation there is no single God's Word which can be clearly known and advocated, but the words delivered are clarified for us in our human situation of being turned to one another. There is no obedience to the coming one without loyalty to his creature. To have experienced this is our way.

A time of genuine religious conversations is beginning —not those so-called but fictitious conversations where none regarded and addressed his partner in reality, but genuine dialogues, speech from certainty to certainty, but also from one open-hearted person to another open-hearted person. Only then will genuine common life appear, not that of an identical content of faith which is alleged to be found in all religions, but that of the situation, of anguish and of expectation.

SETTING OF THE QUESTION

The life of dialogue is not limited to men's traffic with one another; it is, it has shown itself to be, a relation of men to one another that is only represented in their traffic.

Accordingly, even if speech and communication may be dispensed with, the life of dialogue seems, from what we may perceive, to have inextricably joined to it as its minimum constitution one thing, the mutuality of the inner action. Two men bound together in dialogue must obviously be turned to one another, they must therefore—no matter with what measure of activity or indeed of consciousness of activity—have turned to one another.

It is good to put this forward so crudely and formally. For behind the formulating question about the limits of a category under discussion is hidden a question which bursts all formulas asunder.

OBSERVING, LOOKING ON, BECOMING AWARE

We may distinguish three ways in which we are able to perceive a man who is living before our eyes. (I am not thinking of an object of scientific knowledge, of which I do not speak here.) The object of our perception does not need to know of us, of our being there. It does not matter at this point whether he stands in a relation or has a standpoint towards the perceiver.

The *observer* is wholly intent on fixing the observed man in his mind, on "noting" him. He probes him and writes him up. That is, he is diligent to write up as many "traits" as possible. He lies in wait for them, that none may escape him. The object consists of traits, and it is known what lies behind each of them. Knowledge of the human system of expression constantly incorporates in the instant the newly appearing individual variations, and remains applicable. A face is nothing but physiognomy, movements nothing but gestures of expression.

The *onlooker* is not at all intent. He takes up the position which lets him see the object freely, and undisturbed awaits what will be presented to him. Only at the beginning may he be ruled by purpose, everything beyond that is involuntary. He does not go around taking notes indiscriminately, he lets himself go, he is not in the least afraid of forgetting something ("Forgetting is good," he says). He gives his memory no tasks, he trusts its organic work which preserves what is worth preserving. He does not lead in the grass as green fodder, as the observer does; he turns it and lets the sun shine on it. He pays no attention to traits ("Traits lead astray," he says). What stands out for him from the object is what is not "character" and not "expression" ("The interesting is not important," he says). All great artists have been onlookers.

But there is a perception of a decisively different kind.

The onlooker and the observer are similarly orientated, in that they have a position, namely, the very desire to perceive the man who is living before our eyes. Moreover, this man is for them an object separated from themselves and their personal life, who can in fact for this sole reason be "properly" perceived. Consequently what they experience in this way, whether it is, as with the observer, a sum of traits, or, as with the onlooker, an existence, neither demands action from them nor inflicts destiny on them. But rather the whole is given over to the aloof fields of aesthesis.

It is a different matter when in a receptive hour of my personal life a man meets me about whom there is something which I cannot grasp in any objective way at all, that "says something" to me. That does not mean, says to me what manner of man this is, what is going on in him, and the like. But it means, says something *to me*, addresses something to me, speaks something that enters my own life. It can be something about this man, for instance that he needs me. But it can also be something about myself. The man himself in his relation to me has nothing to do with what is said. He has no relation to me, he has indeed not noticed me at all. It is not he who says it to me, as that solitary man silently confessed his secret to his neighbour on the seat; but *it* says it.

To understand "say" as a metaphor is not to understand. The phrase "that doesn't say a thing to me" is an outworn metaphor; but the saying I am referring to is real speech. In the house of speech are many mansions, and this is one of the inner.

The effect of having this said to me is completely different from that of looking on and observing. I cannot depict or denote or describe the man in whom, through whom, something has been said to me. Were I to attempt it, that would be the end of saying. This man is not my object; I have got to do with him. Perhaps I have to accomplish something about him; but perhaps I have only to learn something, and it is only a matter of my "accepting." It may be that I have to answer at once, to this very man before me; it may be that the saying has a long and manifold transmission before it, and that I am to answer some other person at some other time and place, in who knows what kind of speech, and that it is now only a matter of taking the answering on myself. But in each instance a word demanding an answer has happened to me.

We may term this way of perception *becoming aware*.

It by no means needs to be a man of whom I become aware. It can be an animal, a plant, a stone. No kind of appearance or event is fundamentally excluded from the series of the things through which from time to time something is said to me. Nothing can refuse to be the vessel for the Word. The limits of the possibility of dialogue are the limits of awareness.

THE SIGNS

Each of us is encased in an armour whose task is to ward off signs. Signs happen to us without respite, living means being addressed, we would need only to present ourselves and to perceive. But the risk is too dangerous for us, the soundless thunderings seem to threaten us with annihilation, and from generation to generation we perfect the defence apparatus. All our knowledge assures us, "Be calm, everything happens as it must happen, but nothing is directed at you, you are not meant; it is just 'the world,' you can experience it as you like, but whatever you make of it in yourself proceeds from you alone, nothing is required of you, you are not addressed, all is quiet."

Each of us is encased in an armour which we soon, out of familiarity, no longer notice. There are only moments which penetrate it and stir the soul to sensibility. And when such a moment has imposed itself on us and we then take notice and ask ourselves, "Has anything particular taken place? Was it not of the kind I meet every day?" then we may reply to ourselves, "Nothing particular, indeed, it is like this every day, only we are not there every day."

The signs of address are not something extraordinary, something that steps out of the order of things, they are just what goes on time and again, just what goes on in any case, nothing is added by the address. The waves of the aether roar on always, but for most of the time we have turned off our receivers.

What occurs to me addresses me. In what occurs to me the world-happening addresses me. Only by sterilizing it, removing the seed of address from it, can I take what occurs to me as a part of the world-happening which does not refer to me. The interlocking sterilized system into which all this only needs to be dovetailed is man's titanic work. Mankind has pressed speech too into the service of this work.

From out of this tower of the ages the objection will be levelled against me, if some of its doorkeepers should pay any attention to such trains of thought, that it is nothing but a variety of primitive superstition to hold that cosmic and telluric happenings have for the life of the human person a direct meaning that can be grasped. For instead of understanding an event physically, biologically, sociologically (for which I, inclined as I always have been to admire genuine acts of research, think a great deal, when those who carry them out only know what they are doing and do not lose sight of the limits of the realm in which they are moving), these keepers say, an attempt is being made to get behind the event's alleged significance, and for this there is no place in a reasonable world continuum of space and time.

Thus, then, unexpectedly I seem to have fallen into

the company of the augurs, of whom, as is well-known, there are remarkable modern varieties.

But whether they haruspicate or cast a horoscope, their signs have this peculiarity, that they are in a dictionary, even if not necessarily a written one. It does not matter how esoteric the information that is handed down: he who searches out the signs is *well up in* what life's juncture this or that sign means. Nor does it matter that special difficulties of separation and combination are created by the meeting of several signs of different kinds. For you can "look it up in the dictionary." The common signature of all this business is that it is for all time: things remain the same, they are discovered once for all, rules, laws, and analogical conclusions may be employed throughout. What is commonly termed superstition, that is, perverse faith, appears to me rather as perverse knowledge. From "superstition" about the number 13 an unbroken ladder leads into the dizziest heights of gnosis. This is not even the aping of a real faith.

Real faith—if I may so term presenting ourselves and perceiving—begins when the dictionary is put down, when you are done with it. What occurs to me says something to me, but what it says to me cannot be revealed by any esoteric information; for it has never been said before nor is it composed of sounds that have ever been said. It can neither be interpreted nor translated, I can have it neither explained nor displayed; it is not a *what* at all, it is said into my very life; it is no experience that can be remembered independently of the situation, it remains the address of that moment and cannot be isolated, it remains the question of a questioner and will have its answer.

(It remains the question. For that is the other great contrast between all the business of interpreting signs and the speech of signs which I mean here: this speech never gives information or appeasement.)

Faith stands in the stream of "happening but once" which is spanned by knowledge. All the emergency structures of analogy and typology are indispensable for the work of the human spirit, but to step on them when the question of the questioner steps up to you, to me, would be running away. Lived life is tested and fulfilled in the stream alone.

With all deference to the world continuum of space and time, I know as a living truth only concrete world reality which is constantly, in every moment, reached out to me. I can separate it into its component parts, I can compare them and distribute them into groups of similar phenomena, I can derive them from earlier and reduce them to simpler phenomena; and when I have done all this I have not touched my concrete world happening once only, it gazes upon me with a horrifying look. So in Stravinsky's ballet the director of the wandering marionette show wants to point out to the people at the annual fair that a pierrot who terrified them is nothing but a wisp of straw in clothes: he tears it asunder —and collapses, gibbering, for on the roof of the booth the *living* Petrouchka sits and laughs at him.

The true name of concrete reality is the creation which is entrusted to me and to every man. In it the signs of address are given to us.

A CONVERSION

In my earlier years the "religious" was for me the exception. There were hours that were taken out of the course of things. From somewhere or other the firm crust of everyday was pierced. Then the reliable permanence of appearances broke down; the attack which took place burst its law asunder. "Religious experience" was the experience of an otherness which did not fit into the context of life. It could begin with something customary, with consideration of some familiar object, but which then became unexpectedly mysterious and uncanny, finally lighting a way into the lightning-pierced darkness of the mystery itself. But also, without any intermediate stage, time could be torn apart—first the firm world's structure, then the still firmer self-assurance flew apart and you were delivered to fulness. The "religious" lifted you out. Over there now lay the accustomed existence with its affairs, but here illumination and ecstasy and rapture held, without time or sequence. Thus your own being encompassed a life here and a life beyond, and there was no bond but the actual moment of the transition.

The illegitimacy of such a division of the temporal life, which is streaming to death and eternity and which only in fulfilling its temporality can be fulfilled in face of these, was brought home to me by an everyday event, an event of judgment, judging with that sentence from closed lips and an unmoved glance such as the ongoing course of things loves to pronounce.

What happened was no more than that one forenoon, after a morning of "religious" enthusiasm, I had a visit from an unknown young man, without being there in spirit. I certainly did not fail to let the meeting be friendly, I did not treat him any more remissly than all his contemporaries who were in the habit of seeking me out about this time of day as an oracle that is ready to listen to reason. I conversed attentively and openly with him—only I omitted to guess the questions which he did not put. Later, not long after, I learned from one of his friends—he himself was no longer alive—the essential content of these questions; I learned that he had come to me not casually, but borne by destiny, not for a chat but for a decision. He had come to me, he had come in this hour. What do we expect when we are in despair and yet go to a man? Surely a presence by means of which we are told that nevertheless there is meaning.

Since then I have given up the "religious" which is nothing but the exception, extraction, exaltation, ecstasy; or it has given me up. I possess nothing but the everyday out of which I am never taken. The mystery is no longer disclosed, it has escaped or it has made its dwelling here where everything happens as it happens. I know no fulness but each mortal hour's fulness of claim and responsibility. Though far from being equal to it, yet I know that in the claim I am claimed and may respond in responsibility, and know who speaks and demands a response.

I do not know much more. If that is religion, then it is just *everything*, simply all that is lived in its possibility of dialogue. Here is space also for religion's highest forms. As when you pray you do not thereby remove yourself from this life of yours but in your praying refer your thought to it, even though it may be in order to yield it; so too in the unprecedented and surprising, when you are called upon from above, required, chosen, empowered, sent, you with this your mortal bit of life are referred to, this moment is not extracted from it, it rests on what has been and beckons to the remainder which has still to be lived, you are not swallowed up in a fulness without obligation, you are willed for the life of communion.

Who Speaks?

In the signs of life which happens to us we are addressed. Who speaks?

It would not avail us to give for reply the word "God," if we do not give it out of that decisive hour of personal existence when we had to forget everything we imagined we knew of God, when we dared to keep nothing handed down or learned or self-contrived, no shred of knowledge, and were plunged into the night.

When we rise out of it into the new life and there begin to receive the signs, what can we know of that which—of him who gives them to us? Only what we experience from time to time from the signs themselves. If we name the speaker of this speech God, then it is always the God of a moment, a moment God.

I will now use a *gauche* comparison, since I know no right one.

When we really understand a poem, all we know of the poet is what we learn of him in the poem—no biographical wisdom is of value for the pure understanding of what is to be understood: the *I* which approaches us is the subject of this single poem. But when we read other poems by the poet in the same true way their subjects combine in all their multiplicity, completing and confirming one another, to form the one polyphony of the persons's existence.

In such a way, out of the givers of the signs, the speakers of the words in lived life, out of the moment Gods there arises for us with a single identity the Lord of the voice, the One.

ABOVE AND BELOW

Above and below are bound to one another. The word of him who wishes to speak with men without speaking with God is not fulfilled; but the word of him who wishes to speak with God without speaking with men goes astray.

There is a tale that a man inspired by God once went out from the creaturely realms into the vast waste. There he wandered till he came to the gates of the mystery. He knocked. From within came the cry: "What do you want here?" He said, "I have proclaimed your praise in the ears of mortals, but they were deaf to me. So I come to you that you yourself may hear me and reply." "Turn back," came the cry from within. "Here is no ear for you. I have sunk my hearing in the deafness of mortals."

True address from God directs man into the place of lived speech, where the voices of the creatures grope past one another, and in their very missing of one another succeed in reaching the eternal partner.

RESPONSIBILITY

The idea of responsibility is to be brought back from the province of specialized ethics, of an "ought" that swings free in the air, into that of lived life. Genuine responsibility exists only where there is real responding.

Responding to what?

To what happens to one, to what is to be seen and heard and felt. Each concrete hour allotted to the person, with its content drawn from the world and from destiny, is speech for the man who is attentive. Attentive, for no more than that is needed in order to make a beginning with the reading of the signs that are given to you. For that very reason, as I have already indicated, the whole apparatus of our civilization is necessary to preserve men from this attentiveness and its consequences. For the attentive man would no longer, as his custom is, "master" the situation the very moment after it stepped up to him: it would be laid upon him to go up to and into it. Moreover, nothing that he believed he possessed as always available would help him, no

knowledge and no technique, no system and no pro-
gramme; for now he would have to do with what cannot
be classified, with concretion itself. This speech has no
alphabet, each of its sounds is a new creation and only
to be grasped as such.

It will, then, be expected of the attentive man that he
faces creation as it happens. It happens as speech, and
not as speech rushing out over his head but as speech
directed precisely at him. And if one were to ask another if he too heard and he said he did, they would
have agreed only about an experiencing and not about
something experienced.

But the sounds of which the speech consists—I repeat
it in order to remove the misunderstanding, which is
perhaps still possible, that I referred to something extraordinary and larger than life—are the events of the
personal everyday life. In them, as they now are, "great"
or "small," we are addressed, and those which count as
great yield no greater signs than the others.

Our attitude, however, is not yet decided through our
becoming aware of the signs. We can still wrap silence
about us—a reply characteristic of a significant type of
the age—or we can step aside into the accustomed way;
although both times we carry away a wound that is not
to be forgotten in any productivity or any narcotism.
Yet it can happen that we venture to respond, stammering perhaps—the soul is but rarely able to attain
to surer articulation—but it is an honest stammering, as
when sense and throat are united about what is to be
said, but the throat is too horrified at it to utter purely
the already composed sense. The words of our response
are spoken in the speech, untranslatable like the address, of doing and letting—whereby the doing may be-
have like a letting and the letting like a doing. What
we say in this way with the being is our entering upon
the situation, into the situation, which has at this moment stepped up to us, whose appearance we did not
and could not know, for its like has not yet been.

Nor are we now finished with it, we have to give up that
expectation: a situation of which we have become aware
is never finished with, but we subdue it into the substance of lived life. Only then, true to the moment, do
we experience a life that is something other than a sum

of moments. We respond to the moment, but at the same time we respond on its behalf, we answer for it. A newly-created concrete reality has been laid in our arms; we answer for it. A dog has looked at you, you answer for its glance, a child has clutched your hand, you answer for its touch, a host of men moves about you, you answer for their need.

MORALITY AND RELIGION

Responsibility which does not respond to a word is a metaphor of morality. Factually, responsibility only exists when the court is there to which I am responsible, and "self-responsibility" has reality only when the "self" to which I am responsible becomes transparent into the absolute. But he who practises real responsibility in the life of dialogue does not need to name the speaker of the word to which he is responding—he knows him in the word's substance which presses on and in, assuming the cadence of an inwardness, and stirs him in his heart of hearts. A man can ward off with all his strength the belief that "God" is there, and he tastes him in the strict sacrament of dialogue.

Yet let it not be supposed that I make morality questionable in order to glorify religion. Religion, certainly, has this advantage over morality, that it is a phenomenon and not a postulate, and further that it is able to include composure as well as determination. The reality of morality, the demand of the demander, has a place in religion, but the reality of religion, the unconditioned being of the demander, has no place in morality. Nevertheless, when religion does itself justice and asserts itself, it is much more dubious than morality, just because it is more actual and inclusive. Religion as risk, which is ready to give itself up, is the nourishing stream of the arteries; as system, possessing, assured and assuring, religion which believes in religion is the veins' blood, which ceases to circulate. And if there is nothing that can so hide the face of our fellow-man as morality can, religion can hide from us as nothing else can the face of God. Principle there, dogma here, I appreciate the "objective" compactness of dogma, but behind both there lies in wait the—profane or holy—war against the situation's power of dialogue, there lies in wait the "once-for-all" which resists the unforeseeable moment. Dogma, even when its claim of origin remains uncontested, has become the most exalted form of invulnerability against revelation. Revelation will tolerate no perfect tense, but man with the arts of his craze for security props it up to perfectedness.

SECTION TWO: LIMITATION

The Realms

The realms of the life of dialogue and the life of mono-logue do not coincide with the realms of dialogue and monologue even when forms without sound and even without gesture are included. There are not merely great spheres of the life of dialogue which in appearance are not dialogue, there is also dialogue which is not the dialogue of life, that is, it has the appearance but not the essence of dialogue. At times, indeed, it seems as though there were only this kind of dialogue.

I know three kinds. There is genuine dialogue—no matter whether spoken or silent—where each of the participants really has in mind the other or others in their present and particular being and turns to them with the intention of establishing a living mutual rela-tion between himself and them. There is technical dia-logue, which is prompted solely by the need of objective understanding. And there is monologue disguised as dia-logue, in which two or more men, meeting in space, speak each with himself in strangely tortuous and cir-cuitous ways and yet imagine they have escaped the torment of being thrown back on their own resources. The first kind, as I have said, has become rare; where it arises, in no matter how "unspiritual" a form, witness is borne on behalf of the continuance of the organic substance of the human spirit. The second belongs to the inalienable sterling quality of "modern existence." But real dialogue is here continually hidden in all kinds of odd corners and, occasionally in an unseemly way, breaks surface surprisingly and inopportunely—certainly still oftener it is arrogantly tolerated than downright scandalizing—as in the tone of a railway guard's voice, in the glance of an old newspaper vendor, in the smile of the chimney-sweeper. And the third. . . .

A *debate* in which the thoughts are not expressed in the way in which they existed in the mind but in the speaking are so pointed that they may strike home in the sharpest way, and moreover without the men that are spoken to being regarded in any way present as persons; a *conversation* characterized by the need neither to communicate something, nor to learn something, nor to influence someone, nor to come into connexion with someone, but solely by the desire to have one's own self-reliance confirmed by marking the impression that is made, or if it has become unsteady to have it strengthened; a *friendly chat* in which each regards himself as absolute and legitimate and the other as relativized and questionable; a *lovers' talk* in which both partners alike enjoy their own glorious soul and their precious experience—what an underworld of faceless spectres of dialogue!

The life of dialogue is not one in which you have much to do with men, but one in which you really have to do with those with whom you have to do. It is not the solitary man who lives the life of monologue, but he who is incapable of making real in the context of being the community in which, in the context of his destiny, he moves. It is, in fact, solitude which is able to show the innermost nature of the contrast. He who is living the life of dialogue receives in the ordinary course of the hours something that is said and feels himself approached for an answer. But also in the vast blankness of, say, a companionless mountain wandering that which confronts him, rich in change, does not leave him. He who is living the life of monologue is never aware of the other as something that is absolutely not himself and at the same time something with which he nevertheless communicates. Solitude for him can mean mounting richness of visions and thoughts but never the deep intercourse, captured in a new depth, with the incomprehensibly real. Nature for him is either an *état d'âme*, hence a "living through" in himself, or it is a passive object of knowledge, either idealistically brought within the soul or realistically alienated. It does not become for him a word apprehended with senses of beholding and feeling.

Being, lived in dialogue, receives even in extreme der-eliction a harsh and strengthening sense of reciprocity; being, lived in monologue, will not, even in the tender-est intimacy, grope out over the outlines of the self.

This must not be confused with the contrast between "egoism" and "altruism" conceived by some moralists. I know people who are absorbed in "social activity" and have never spoken from being to being with a fellow-man. I know others who have no personal relation ex-cept to their enemies, but stand in such a relation to them that it is the enemies' fault if the relation does not flourish into one of dialogue.

Nor is dialogic to be identified with love. I know no one in any time who has succeeded in loving every man he met. Even Jesus obviously loved of "sinners" only the loose, lovable sinners, sinners against the Law; not those who were settled and loyal to their inheritance and sinned against him and his message. Yet to the latter as to the former he stood in a direct relation. Dialogic is not to be identified with love. But love without dialogic, without real outgoing to the other, reaching to the other, and companying with the other, the love remaining with itself—this is called Lucifer.

Certainly in order to be able to go out to the other you must have the starting place, you must have been, you must be, with yourself. Dialogue between mere in-dividuals is only a sketch, only in dialogue between per-sons is the sketch filled in. But by what could a man from being an individual so really become a person as by the strict and sweet experiences of dialogue which teach him the boundless contents of the boundary?

What is said here is the real contrary of the cry, heard at times in twilight ages, for universal unreserve. He who can be unreserved with each passer-by has no sub-stance to lose; but he who cannot stand in a direct rela-tion to each one who meets him has a fulness which is futile. Luther is wrong to change the Hebrew "com-panion" (out of which the Seventy had already made one who is near, a neighbour) into "nearest." If every-thing concrete is equally near, equally nearest, life with the world ceases to have articulation and structure, it ceases to have human meaning. But nothing needs to mediate between me and one of my companions in the companionship of creation, whenever we come near one another, because we are bound up in relation to the same centre.

THE BASIC MOVEMENTS

I term basic movement an essential action of man (it may be understood as an "inner" action, but it is not there unless it is there to the very tension of the eyes' muscles and the very action of the foot as it walks), round which an essential attitude is built up. I do not think of this happening in time, as though the single action preceded the lasting attitude; the latter rather has its truth in the accomplishing, over and over again, of the basic movement, without forethought but also without habit. Otherwise the attitude would have only aesthetic or perhaps also political significance, as a beautiful and as an effective lie. The familiar maxim, "An attitude must first be adopted, the rest follows of itself" ceases to be true in the circle of essential action and essential attitude— that is, where we are concerned with the wholeness of the person.

The basic movement of the life of dialogue is the turning towards the other. That, indeed, seems to happen every hour and quite trivially. If you look at someone and address him you turn to him, of course with the body, but also in the requisite measure with the soul, in that you direct your attention to him. But what of all this is an essential action, done with the essential being? In this way, that out of the incomprehensibility of what lies to hand this one person steps forth and becomes a presence. Now to our perception the world ceases to be an insignificant multiplicity of points to one of which we pay momentary attention. Rather it is a limitless tumult round a narrow breakwater, brightly outlined and able to bear heavy loads—limitless, but limited by the breakwater, so that, though not engirdled, it has become finite in itself, been given form, released from its own indifference. And yet none of the contacts of each hour is unworthy to take up from our essential being as much as it may. For no man is without strength for expression, and our turning towards him brings about a reply, however imperceptible, however quickly smothered, in a looking and sounding forth of the soul that are perhaps dissipating in mere inwardness and yet do exist. The notion of modern man that this turning to the other is sentimental and does not correspond to the compression of life today is a grotesque error, just as his affirmation that turning to the other is impractical in the bustle of this life today is only the masked confession of his weakness of initiative when confronted with the state of the time. He lets it dictate to him what is possible or permissible, instead of stipulating, as an unruffled partner, what is to be stipulated to the state of *every* time, namely, what space and what form it is bound to concede to creaturely existence.

The basic movement of the life of monologue is not turning away as opposed to turning towards; it is "reflexion."

When I was eleven years of age, spending the summer on my grandparents' estate, I used, as often as I could do it unobserved, to steal into the stable and gently stroke the neck of my darling, a broad dapple-grey horse. It was not a casual delight but a great, certainly friendly, but also deeply stirring happening. If I am to explain it now, beginning from the still very fresh memory of my hand, I must say that what I experienced in touch with the animal was the Other, the immense otherness of the Other, which, however, did not remain strange like the otherness of the ox and the ram, but rather let me draw near and touch it. When I stroked the mighty mane, sometimes marvellously smooth-combed, at other times just as astonishingly wild, and felt the life beneath my hand, it was as though the element of vitality itself bordered on my skin, something that was not I, was certainly not akin to me, palpably the other, not just another, really the Other itself; and yet it let me approach, confided itself to me, placed itself elementally in the relation of *Thou* and *Thou* with me. The horse, even when I had not begun by pouring oats for him into the manger, very gently raised his massive head, ears flicking, then snorted quietly, as a conspirator gives a signal meant to be recognizable only by his fellow-conspirator; and I was approved. But once—I do not know what came over the child, at any rate it was childlike enough—it struck me about the stroking, what fun it gave me, and suddenly I became conscious of my hand. The game went on as before, but something had changed, it was no longer the same thing. And the next day, after giving him a rich feed, when I stroked my friend's head he did not raise his head. A few years later, when I thought back to the incident, I no longer supposed that the animal had noticed my defection. But at the time I considered myself judged.

Reflexion is something different from egoism and even from "egotism." It is not that a man is concerned with himself, considers himself, fingers himself, enjoys, idolizes and bemoans himself; all that can be added, but it is not integral to reflexion. (Similarly, to the turning towards the other, completing it, there can be added the realizing of the other in his particular existence, even the encompassing of him, so that the situations common to him and oneself are experienced also from his, the other's, end.) I term it reflexion when a man withdraws from accepting with his essential being another person in his particularity—a particularity which is by no means to be circumscribed by the circle of his own self, and though it substantially touches and moves his soul is in no way immanent in it—and lets the other exist only as his own experience, only as a "part of myself." For then dialogue becomes a fiction, the mysterious intercourse between two human worlds only a game, and in the rejection of the real life confronting him the essence of all reality begins to disintegrate.

THE WORDLESS DEPTHS

Sometimes I hear it said that every *I and Thou* is only superficial; deep down word and response cease to exist, there is only the one primal being unconfronted by another. We should plunge into the silent unity, but for the rest leave its relativity to the life to be lived, instead of imposing on it this absolutized *I* and absolutized *Thou* with their dialogue.

Now from my own unforgettable experience I know well that there is a state in which the bonds of the per-

sonal nature of life seem to have fallen away from us and
we experience an undivided unity. But I do not know—
what the soul willingly imagines and indeed is bound
to imagine (mine too once did it)—that in this I had
attained to a union with the primal being or the godhead. That is an exaggeration no longer permitted to
the responsible understanding. Responsibly—that is, as a
man holding his ground before reality—I can elicit from
those experiences only that in them I reached an un-
differentiable unity of myself without form or content. I
may call this an original pre-biographical unity and suppose that it is hidden unchanged beneath all biographical change, all development and complication of the
soul. Nevertheless, in the honest and sober account of
the responsible understanding this unity is nothing but
the unity of this soul of mine, whose "ground" I have
reached, so much so, beneath all formations and contents, that my spirit has no choice but to understand it
as the groundless. But the basic unity of my own soul
is certainly beyond the reach of all the multiplicity it has
hitherto received from life, though not in the least beyond individuation, or the multiplicity of all the souls in
the world of which it is one—existing but once, single,
unique, irreducible, this creaturely one: one of the
human souls and not the "soul of the All"; a defined and
particular being and not "Being"; the creaturely basic
unity of a creature, bound to God as in the instant before
release the creature is to the *creator spiritus*, not bound
to God as the creature to the *creator spiritus* in the moment of release.

The unity of his own self is not distinguishable in the
man's feeling from unity in general. For he who in the
act or event of absorption is sunk beneath the realm of
all multiplicity that holds sway in the soul cannot experience the cessation of multiplicity except as unity itself. That is, he experiences the cessation of his own
multiplicity as the cessation of mutuality, as revealed or
fulfilled absence of otherness. The being which has become one can no longer understand itself on this side of
individuation nor indeed on this side of *I and Thou*. For
to the border experience of the soul "one" must apparently mean the same as "the One."

But in the actuality of lived life the man in such a moment is not above but beneath the creaturely situation, which is mightier and truer than all ecstasies. He is not above but beneath dialogue. He is not nearer the God who is hidden above *I and Thou*, and he is farther from the God who is turned to men and who gives himself as the *I* to a *Thou* and the *Thou* to an *I*, than that other who in prayer and service and life does not step out of the position of confrontation and awaits no wordless unity, except that which perhaps bodily death discloses.

Nevertheless, even he who lives the life of dialogue knows a lived unity: the unity of *life*, as that which once truly won is no more torn by any changes, not ripped asunder into the everyday creaturely life and the "deified" exalted hours; the unity of unbroken, raptureless perseverance in concreteness, in which the word is heard and a stammering answer dared.

Of Thinking

To all unprejudiced reflection it is clear that all *art* is from its origin essentially of the nature of dialogue. All music calls to an ear not the musician's own, all sculpture to an eye not the sculptor's, architecture in addition calls to the step as it walks in the building. They all say, to him who receives them, something (not a "feeling" but a perceived mystery) that can be said only in this one language. But there seems to cling to *thought* something of the life of monologue to which communication takes a second, secondary place. Thought seems to arise in monologue. Is it so? Is there here—where, as the philosophers say, pure subject separates itself from the concrete person in order to establish and stabilize a world for itself—a citadel which rises towering over the life of dialogue, inaccessible to it, in which man-with-himself, the single one, suffers and triumphs in glorious solitude?

Plato has repeatedly called thinking a voiceless colloquy of the soul with itself. Everyone who has really thought knows that within this remarkable process there is a stage at which an "inner" court is questioned and replies. But that is not the arising of the thought but the first trying and testing of what has arisen. The arising of the thought does not take place in colloquy with oneself.

The character of monologue does not belong to the insight into a basic relation with which cognitive thought begins; nor to the grasping, limiting and compressing of the insight; nor to its moulding into the independent conceptual form; nor to the reception of this form, with the bestowal of relations, the dovetailing and soldering, into an order of conceptual forms; nor, finally, to the expression and clarification in language (which till now had only a technical and reserved symbolic function). Rather are elements of dialogue to be discovered here. It is not himself that the thinker addresses in the stages of the thought's growth, in their answerings, but as it were the basic relation in face of which he has to answer for his insight, or the order in face of which he has to answer for the newly arrived conceptual form. And it is a misunderstanding of the dynamic of the event of thought to suppose that these apostrophizings of a being existing in nature or in ideas are "really" colloquies with the self.

But also the first trying and testing of the thought, when it is provisionally completed, before the "inner" court, in the platonic sense the stage of monologue, has besides the familiar form of its appearance another form in which dialogue plays a great part, well-known to Plato if to anyone. There he who is approached for judgment is not the empirical self but the *genius*, the spirit I am intended to become, the image-self, before which the new thought is borne for approval, that is, for taking up into its own consummating thinking.

And now from another dimension which even this lease of power does not satisfy there appears the longing for a trying and testing in the sphere of pure dialogue. Here the function of receiving is no longer given over to the *Thou-I* but to a genuine *Thou* which either remains one that is thought and yet is felt as supremely living and "other," or else is embodied in an intimate person. "Man," says Wilhelm von Humboldt in his significant treatise on *The Dual Number* (1827), "longs even for the sake of his mere thinking for a *Thou* corresponding to the *I*. The conception appears to him to reach its definiteness and certainty only when it reflects from another power of thought. It is produced by being torn away from the moving mass of representation and shaped in face of the subject into the object. But the objectivity appears in a still more complete form if this separation does not go on in the subject alone, if he really sees the thought outside himself; and this is possible only in another being, representing and thinking like himself. And between one power of thought and another there is no other mediator but speech." This reference, simplified to an aphorism, recurs with Ludwig Feuerbach in 1843: "True dialectic is not a monologue of the solitary thinker with himself, it is a dialogue between *I* and *Thou*."

But this saying points beyond that "reflecting" to the fact that even in the original stage of the proper act of thought the inner action might take place in relation to a genuine and not merely an "inward" (Novalis) *Thou*. And where modern philosophy is most earnest in the desire to ask its questions on the basis of human existence, situation and present, in some modifications an important further step is taken. Here it is certainly no longer just that the *Thou* is ready to receive and disposed to philosophize along with the *I*. Rather, and preeminently, we have the *Thou* in opposition because we truly have the other who thinks other things in another way. So, too, it is not a matter of a game of draughts in the tower of a castle in the air, but of the binding business of life on the hard earth, in which one is inexorably aware of the otherness of the other but does not at all contest it without realizing it; one takes up its nature into one's own thinking, thinks in relation to it, addresses it in thought.

This man of modern philosophy, however, who in this way no longer thinks in the untouchable province of pure ideation, but thinks in reality—does he think in reality? Not solely in a reality framed by thought? Is the other, whom he accepts and receives in this way, not solely the other framed by thought, and therefore unreal? Does the thinker of whom we are speaking hold his own with the bodily fact of otherness?

If we are serious about thinking between *I* and *Thou* then it is not enough to cast our thoughts towards the other subject of thought framed by thought. We should also, with the thinking, precisely with the thinking, live towards the other man, who is not framed by thought but bodily present before us; we should live towards his concrete life. We should live not towards another thinker of whom we wish to know nothing beyond his thinking but, even if the other is a thinker, towards his bodily life over and above his thinking—rather, towards his person, to which, to be sure, the activity of thinking also belongs.

When will the action of thinking endure, include, and refer to the presence of the living man facing us? When will the dialectic of thought become dialogic, an unsentimental, unrelaxed dialogue in the strict terms of thought with the man present at the moment?

EROS

The Greeks distinguished between a powerful, world-begetting Eros and one which was light and whose sphere was the soul; and also between a heavenly and a profane Eros. Neither seems to me to indicate an absolute distinction. For the primal god Desire from whom the world is derived, is the very one who in the form of a "tender elfin spirit" (Jacob Grimm) enters into the sphere of souls and in an arbitrary daimonic way carries out here, as mediator of the pollination of being, his cosmogonic work: he is the great pollen-bearing butterfly of psychogenesis. And the Pandemos (assuming it is a genuine Eros and not a Priapos impudently pretending to be the higher one) needs only to stir his wings to let the primal fire be revealed in the body's games.

Of course, the matter in question is whether Eros has not forfeited the power of flight and is now condemned to live among tough mortals and govern their mortality's paltry gestures of love. For the souls of lovers do to one another what they do; but lame-winged beneath the rule of the lame-winged one (for his power and powerlessness are always shown in theirs) they cower where they are, each in his den, instead of soaring out each to the beloved partner and there, in the beyond which has come near, "knowing."

Those who are loyal to the strong-winged Eros of dialogue know the beloved being. They experience his particular life in simple presence—not as a thing seen and touched, but from the innervations to his movements, from the "inner" to his "outer." But by this I mean nothing but the bipolar experience, and—more than a swinging over and away in the instant—a contemporaneity at rest. That inclination of the head over there—you feel how the soul enjoins it on the neck, you feel it not on your neck but on that one over there, on the beloved one, and yet you yourself are not as it were snatched away, you are here, in the feeling self-being, and you receive the inclination of the head, its injunction, as the answer to the word of your own silence. In contemporaneity at rest you make and you experience dialogue. The two who are loyal to the Eros of dialogue, who love one another, receive the common event from the other's side as well, that is, they receive it from the two sides, and thus for the first time understand in a bodily way what an event is.

The kingdom of the lame-winged Eros is a world of mirrors and mirrorings. But where the winged one holds sway there is no mirroring. For there I, the lover, turn to this other human being, the beloved, in his otherness, his independence, his self-reality, and turn to him with all the power of intention of my own heart. I certainly turn to him as to one who is there turning to me, but in that very reality, not comprehensible by me but rather comprehending me, in which I am there turning to him. I do not assimilate into my own soul that which lives and faces me, I vow it faithfully to myself and myself to it, I vow, I have faith.

The Eros of dialogue has the simplicity of fulness; the Eros of monologue is manifold. Many years I have wandered through the land of men, and have not yet reached an end of studying the varieties of the "erotic man" (as the vassal of the broken-winged one at times describes himself). There a lover stamps around and is in love only with his passion. There one is wearing his differentiated feelings like medal-ribbons. There one is enjoying the adventures of his own fascinating effect. There one is gazing enraptured at the spectacle of his own supposed surrender. There one is collecting excitement. There one is displaying his "power." There one is preening himself with borrowed vitality. There one is delighting to exist simultaneously as himself and as an idol very unlike himself. There one is warming himself at the blaze of what has fallen to his lot. There one is experimenting. And so on and on—all the manifold monologists with their mirrors, in the apartment of the most intimate dialogue!

I have spoken of the small fry, but I have had more in mind the leviathans. There are some who stipulate to the object they propose to devour that both the doing as a holy right and the suffering as a sacred duty are what is to be called heroic love. I know of "leaders" who with their grip not only cast into confusion the plasma of the growing human being but also disintegrate it radically, so that it can no longer be moulded. They relish this power of their influence, and at the same time deceive themselves and their herd into imagining they are moulders of youthful souls, and call on *Eros*, who is inaccessible to the *profanum vulgus*, as the tutelary god of this work.

They are all beating the air. Only he who himself turns to the other human being and opens himself to him receives the world in him. Only the being whose otherness, accepted by my being, lives and faces me in the whole compression of existence, brings the radiance of eternity to me. Only when two say to one another with all that they are, "It is *Thou*," is the indwelling of the Present Being between them.

COMMUNITY

In the view customary to-day, which is defined by politics, the only important thing in groups, in the present as in history, is what they aim at and what they accomplish. Significance is ascribed to what goes on within them only in so far as it influences the group's action with regard to its aim. Thus it is conceded to a band conspiring to conquer the state power that the comradeship which fills it is of value, just because it strengthens the band's reliable assault power. Precise obedience will do as well, if enthusiastic drill makes up for the associates remaining strangers to one another; there are indeed good grounds for preferring the rigid system. If the group is striving even to reach a higher form of society then it can seem dangerous if in the life of the group itself something of this higher form begins to be realized in embryo. For from such a premature seriousness a suppression of the "effective" impetus is feared. The opinion apparently is that the man who whiles away his time as a guest on an oasis may be accounted lost for the project of irrigating the Sahara.

By this simplified mode of valuation the real and individual worth of a group remains as uncomprehended as when we judge a person by his effect alone and not by his qualities. The perversion of thought grows when chatter is added about sacrifice of being, about renunciation of self-realization, where possible with a reference to the favourite metaphor of the dung. Happiness, possession, power, authority, life can be renounced, but sacrifice of being is a sublime absurdity. And no moment, if it has to vouch for its relation to reality, can call upon any kind of later, future moments for whose sake, in order to make them fat, it has remained so lean.

The feeling of community does not reign where the desired change of institutions is wrested in common, but without community, from a resisting world. It reigns where the fight that is fought takes place from the position of a community struggling for its own reality as a community. But the future too is decided here at the same time; all political "achievements" are at best auxiliary troops to the effect which changes the very core, and which is wrought on the unsurveyable ways of secret history by the moment of realization. No way leads to any other goal but to that which is like it.

But who in all these massed, mingled, marching collectivities still perceives what that is for which he supposes he is striving—what community is? They have all surrendered to its counterpart. Collectivity is not a binding but a bundling together: individuals packed together, armed and equipped in common, with only as much life from man to man as will inflame the marching step. But community, growing community (which is all we have known so far) is the being no longer side by side but *with* one another of a multitude of persons. And this multitude, though it also moves towards one goal, yet experiences everywhere a turning to, a dynamic facing of, the other, a flowing from *I* to *Thou*. Community is where community happens. Collectivity is based on an organized atrophy of personal existence, community on its increase and confirmation in life lived towards one other. The modern zeal for collectivity is a flight from community's testing and consecration of the person, a flight from the vital dialogic, demanding the staking of the self, which is in the heart of the world.

The men of the "collective" look down superciliously on the "sentimentality" of the generation before them, of the age of the "youth movement." Then the concern, wide-ranging and deeply-pondered, was with the problem of all life's relations, "community" was aimed at and made a problem at the same time. They went round in circles and never left the mark. But now there is commanding and marching, for now there is the "cause." The false paths of subjectivity have been left behind and the road of objectivism, going straight for its goal, has been reached. But as there existed a pseudo-subjectivity with the former, since the elementary force of being a subject was lacking, so with the latter exists a pseudo-objectivism, since one is here fitted not into a world but into a worldless faction. As in the former all songs in praise of freedom were sung into the void, because only freeing from bonds was known, but not freeing to responsibility, so in the latter even the noblest hymns on authority are a misunderstanding. For in fact they strengthen only the semblance of authority which has been won by speeches and cries; behind this authority is hidden an absence of consistency draped in the mighty folds of the attitude. But genuine authority, celebrated in those hymns, the authority of the genuine charismatic in his steady response to the lord of Charis, has remained unknown to the political sphere of the present. Superficially the two generations are different in kind to the extent of contradiction, in truth they are stuck in the same chaotic condition. The man of the youth movement, pondering his problems, was concerned (whatever the particular matter at different times) with his very own share in it, he "experienced" his *I* without pledging a self—in order not to have to pledge a self in response and responsibility. The man of the collective undertaking, striding to action, succeeded beforehand in getting rid of himself and thus radically escaping the question of pledging a self. Progress is nevertheless to be recorded. With the former monologue presented itself as dialogue. With the latter it is considerably simpler, for the life of monologue is by their desire driven out from most men, or they are broken of the habit; and the others, who give the orders, have at least no need to feign any dialogic.

Dialogue and monologue are silenced. Bundled together, men march without *Thou* and without *I*, those of the left who want to abolish memory, and those of the right who want to regulate it: hostile and separated hosts, they march into the common abyss.

SECTION THREE: CONFIRMATION

CONVERSATION WITH THE OPPONENT

I hope for two kinds of readers for these thoughts: for the *amicus* who knows about the reality to which I am pointing with a finger I should like to be able to stretch out like Grüenwald's Baptist; and for the *hostis* or *adversarius* who denies this reality and therefore contends with me, because I point to it (in his view misleadingly) as to a reality. Thus he takes what is said here just as seriously as I myself do, after long waiting writing what is to be written—just as seriously, only with the negative sign. The mere *inimicus*, as which I regard everyone who wishes to relegate me to the realm of ideology and there let my thoughts count, I would gladly dispense with.

I need say nothing at this point to the *amicus*. The hour of common mortality and the common way strikes in his and in my ears as though we stood even in the same place with one another and knew one another.

But it is not enough to tell the *adversarius* here what I am pointing at—the hiddenness of his personal life, his secret, and that, stepping over a carefully avoided threshold, he will discover what he denies. It is not enough. I dare not turn aside his gravest objection. I must accept it, as and where it is raised, and must answer.

So now the *adversarius* sits, facing me in his actual form as he appears in accordance with the spirit of the time, and speaks, more above and beyond me than towards and to me, in accents and attitude customary in the universal duel, free of personal relation.

"In all this the actuality of our present life, the conditioned nature of life as a whole, is not taken into account. All that you speak of takes place in the never-never-land, not in the social context of the world in which we spend our days, and by which if by anything our reality is defined. Your 'two men' sit on a solitary seat, obviously during a holiday journey. In a big city office you would not be able to let them sit, they would not reach the 'sacramental' there. Your 'interrupted conversation' takes place between intellectuals who have leisure a couple of months before the huge mass event to spin fantasies of its prevention through a spiritual influence. That may be quite interesting for people who are not taken up with any duty. But is the business employee to 'communicate himself without reserve' to his colleagues? Is the worker at the conveyor belt to 'feel himself addressed in what he experiences'? Is the leader of a gigantic technical undertaking to 'practise the responsibility of dialogue'? You demand that we enter into the situation which approaches us, and you neglect the enduring situation in which everyone of us, so far as we share in the life of community, is elementally placed. In spite of all references to concreteness, all that is pre-war individualism in a revised edition."

And I, out of a deep consciousness of how almost impossible it is to think in common, if only in opposition, where there is no common experience, reply.

Before all, dear opponent, if we are to converse with one another and not at and past one another, I beg you to notice that I do not demand. I have no call to that and no authority for it. I try only to say that there is something, and to indicate how it is made: I simply record. And how could the life of dialogue be demanded? There is no ordering of dialogue. It is not that you *are* to answer but that you *are able*.

You are really able. The life of dialogue is no privilege of intellectual activity like dialectic. It does not begin in the upper story of humanity. It begins no higher than where humanity begins. There are no gifted and ungifted here, only those who give themselves and those who withhold themselves. And he who gives himself tomorrow is not noted to-day, even he himself does not know that he has it in himself, that we have it in ourselves, he will just find it, "and finding be amazed."

You put before me the man taken up with duty and business. Yes, precisely him I mean, him in the factory, in the shop, in the office, in the mine, on the tractor, at the printing-press: man. I do not seek for men. I do not seek men out for myself, I accept those who are there, I have them, I have him, in mind, the yoked, the wheel-treading, the conditioned. Dialogue is not an affair of spiritual luxury and spiritual luxuriousness, it is a matter of creation, of the creature, and he is that, the man of whom I speak, he is a creature, trivial and irreplaceable.

In my thoughts about the life of dialogue I have had to choose the examples as "purely" and as much in the form of paradigm as memory presented them to me in order to make myself intelliglble about what has become so unfamiliar, in fact so sunk in oblivion. For this reason I appear to draw my tales from the province which you term the "intellectual," in reality only from the province where things succeed, are rounded off, in fact are exemplary. But I am not concerned with the pure; I am concerned with the turbid, the repressed, the pedestrian, with toil and dull contrariness—and with the break-through. With the break-through and not with a perfection, and moreover with the break-through not out of despair with its murderous and renewing powers; no, not with the great catastrophic breakthrough which happens once for all (it is fitting to be silent for a while about that, even in one's own heart), but with the breaking through from the status of the dully-tempered disagreeableness, obstinacy, and contrariness in which the man, whom I pluck at random out of the tumult, is living and out of which he can and at times does break through.

Whither? Into nothing exalted, heroic or holy, into no Either and no Or, only into this tiny strictness and grace of every day, where I have to do with just the very same "reality" with whose duty and business I am taken up in such a way, glance to glance, look to look, word to word, that I experience it as reached to me and myself to it, it as spoken to me and myself to it. And now, in all the clanking of routine that I called my reality, there appears to me, homely and glorious, the effective reality, creaturely and given to me in trust and responsibility. We do not find meaning lying in things nor do we put it into things, but between us and things it can happen.

It is not sufficient, dear opponent, first of all to ascribe to me the pathos of "all or nothing" and then to prove the impossibility of my alleged demand. I know neither what all nor what nothing is, the one appears to me to be as inhuman and contrived as the other. What I am meaning is the simple *quantum satis* of that which this man in this hour of his life is able to fulfil and to receive—if he gives himself. That is, if he does not let himself be deceived by the compact plausibility that there are places excluded from creation, that he works in such a place and is able to return to creation when his shift is over; or that creation is outstripped, that it once was but is irrevocably over, now there is business and now it is a case of stripping off all romanticism, gritting the teeth and getting through with what is recognized as necessary. I say—if he does not let himself be deceived.

No factory and no office is so abandoned by creation that a creative glance could not fly up from one working-place to another, from desk to desk, a sober and brotherly glance which guarantees the reality of creation which is happening—*quantum satis*. And nothing is so valuable a service of dialogue between God and man as such an unsentimental and unreserved exchange of glances between two men in an alien place.

But is it irrevocably an alien place? Must henceforth, through all the world's ages, the life of the being which is yoked to business be divided in two, into alien "work" and home "recovery"? More, since evenings and Sundays cannot be freed of the workday character but are unavoidably stamped with it, must such a life be divided out between the business of work and the business of recovery without a remainder of directness, of unregulated surplus—of freedom? (And the freedom I mean is established by no new order of society.)

Or does there already stir, beneath all dissatisfactions that can be satisfied, an unknown and primal and deep dissatisfaction for which there is as yet no recipe of satisfaction anywhere, but which will grow to such mightiness that it dictates to the technical leaders, the promoters, the inventors, and says, "Go on with your rationalizing, but humanize the rationalizing *ratio* in yourselves. Let it introduce the living man into its purposes and its calculations, him who longs to stand in a mutual relation with the world." Dear opponent, does the longing already stir in the depths—an impulse to great construction or a tiny spark of the last revolution—to fill business with the life of dialogue? That is, in the formulation of the *quantum satis*, the longing for an order of work in which business is so continually soaked in vital dialogic as the tasks to be fulfilled by it allow? And of the extent to which they can allow it there is scarcely an inkling to-day, in an hour when the question which I put is at the mercy of the fanatics, blind to reality, who conform to the time, and of the heralds, blind to possibility, of the impervious tragedy of the world.

Be clear what it means when a worker can experience even his relation to the machine as one of dialogue, when, for instance, a compositor tells that he has understood the machine's humming as "a merry and grateful smile at me for helping it to set aside the difficulties and obstructions which disturbed and bruised and pained it, so that now it could run free." Must even you not think then of the story of Androclus and the Lion?

But when a man draws a lifeless thing into his passionate longing for dialogue, lending it independence and as it were a soul, then there may dawn in him the presentiment of a world-wide dialogue, a dialogue with the world-happening that steps up to him even in his environment, which consists partly of things. Or do you seriously think that the giving and taking of signs halts on the threshold of that business where an honest and open spirit is found?

You ask with a laugh, can the leader of a great technical undertaking practise the responsibility of dialogue? He can. For he practises it when he makes present to himself in its concreteness, so far as he can, *quantum satis*, the business which he leads. He practises it when he experiences it, instead of as a structure of mechanical centres of force and their organic servants (among which latter there is for him no differentiation but the functional one), as an association of persons with faces and names and biographies, bound together by a work that is represented by, but does not consist of, the achievements of a complicated mechanism. He practises it when he is inwardly aware, with a latent and disciplined fantasy, of the multitude of these persons, whom naturally he cannot separately know and remember as such; so that now, when one of them for some reason or other steps really as an individual into the circle of his vision and the realm of his decision, he is aware of him without strain not as a number with a human mask but as a person. He practises it when he comprehends and handles these persons as persons—for the greatest part necessarily indirectly, by means of a system of mediation which varies according to the extent, nature and structure of the undertaking, but also directly, in the parts which concern him by way of organization. Naturally at first both camps, that of capital and that of the proletariat, will decry his masterly attitude of fantasy as fantastic nonsense and his practical attitude to persons as dilettantist. But just as naturally only until his increased figures of production accredit him in their eyes. (By this of course is not to be implied that those increases necessarily come to pass: between truth and success there is no pre-stabilized harmony.) Then, to be sure, something worse will follow. He will be pragmatically imitated, that is, people will try to use his "procedure" without his way of thinking and imagining. But this demoniac element inherent in spiritual history (think only of all the magicizing of religion) will, I think, shipwreck here on the power of discrimination in men's souls. And meanwhile it is to be hoped that a new generation will arise, learning from what is alive, and will take all this in real seriousness as he does.

Unmistakably men are more and more determined by "circumstances." Not only the absolute mass but also the relative might of social objectives is growing. As one determined partially by them the individual stands in each moment before concrete reality which wishes to reach out to him and receive an answer from him; laden with the situation he meets new situations. And yet in all the multiplicity and complexity he has remained Adam. Even now a real decision is made in him, whether he faces the speech of God articulated to him in things and events—or escapes. And a creative glance towards his fellow-creature can at times suffice for response.

Man is in a growing measure sociologically determined. But this growing is the maturing of a task not in the "ought" but in the "may" and in "need," in longing and in grace. It is a matter of renouncing the pantechnical mania or habit with its easy "mastery" of every situation; of taking everything up into the might of dialogue of the genuine life, from the trivial mysteries of everyday to the majesty of destructive destiny.

The task becomes more and more difficult, and more and more essential, the fulfilment more and more impeded and more and more rich in decision. All the regulated chaos of the age waits for the break-through, and wherever a man perceives and responds, he is working to that end.

(From *Between Man and Man*, pp. 1–39.)

THE FAITH OF JUDAISM

1. THE WAY OF FAITH

My subject is not the religion but only the faith of Judaism. I do not wish to speak to you about cult, ritual, and moral-religious standards, but about faith, and faith taken in its strictest and most serious sense. Not the so-called faith which is a strange mingling of assumptions and cognitions, but that faith which means trust and loyalty. It follows that I do not start from a Jewish theology, but from the actual attitude of faithful Jews from the earliest days down till our own time. Even though I must of necessity use theological concepts when I speak of this realm of faith, I must not for a moment lose sight of the nontheological material from which I draw those concepts: the popular literature, and my own impressions of Jewish life in Eastern Europe—but there is nothing in the East something of which may not be found in the West, as well.

When I refer to this popular material, it often happens that people say to me, "You mean, I take it, hasidism?" That is a question which is natural enough, only it is not primarily hasidism which I have in mind. In hasidism I see merely a concentrated movement, the concentration of all those elements which are to be found in a less condensed form everywhere in Judaism, even in "rabbinic" Judaism. Only, in rabbinic Judaism this movement is not visible in the structure of the community, but holds sway over the inaccessible structure of the personal life. What I am trying to formulate may be called the theologoumena of a popular religion.

It is impossible to trace any one of these theologoumena back to any one epoch; my intention is to present the unity to be found in the changing forms. Religious truths are generally of a dynamic kind; they are truths which cannot be understood on the basis of a cross-section of history, but only when they are seen in the whole line of history, in their unfolding, in the dynamic of their changing forms. The most important testimony to the truth of this conception comes from the way in which these truths clarify and fulfil themselves, and from their struggle for purity. The truth of the history of religion is the growth of the image of God, the *way* of faith. Though my subject does not impose the historical form on me, it is still of the *way* of the Jewish faith that I have to speak.

2. THE DIALOGICAL SITUATION

The question has often been raised whether a Jewish dogmatics does or does not exist. The emphasis should rather fall on the question of the relative power of dogma in Judaism. There is no need to prove that there are dogmas, in view of the incorporation of the thirteen articles of faith of Maimonides into the liturgy. But dogma remains of secondary importance. In the religious life of Judaism, primary importance is not given to dogma, but to the remembrance and the expectation of a concrete situation: the encounter of God and men. Dogma can only arise in a situation where detachment is the prevailing attitude to the concrete, lived moment—a state of detachment which easily becomes misunderstood in dogmatics as being superior to the lived moment itself.

Whatever is enunciated *in abstracto* in the third person about the divine, on the thither side of the confrontation of *I* and *Thou*, is only a projection onto the conceptual construct plane which, though indispensable, proves itself again and again to be unessential.

It is from this point of view that we must regard the problem of so-called monotheism. Israel's experience of the *Thou* in the direct relationship, the purely singular experience, is so overwhelmingly strong that any notion of a plurality of principles simply cannot arise. Over against this stands "the heathen," the man who *does not recognize* God in his manifestations. Or rather: a man is a heathen to the extent to which he does not recognize God in his manifestations.

The fundamental attitude of the Jews is characterized by the idea of the *yihud*, the "unification," a word which has been repeatedly misunderstood. *Yihud* involves the continually renewed confirmation of the unity of the Divine in the manifold nature of His manifestations, understood in a quite practical way. Again and again this recognition, acknowledgment, and reacknowledgment of the divine unity is brought about through human perception and verification [*Bewaehrung*] in the face of the monstrous contradictions of life, and especially in the face of that primal contradiction which shows itself in multitudinous ways, and which we call the duality of good and evil. But the unification is brought about not to spite these contradictions, but in spirit of love and reconciliation; not by the mere profession of the unification, but by the fulfilment of the profession. Therefore, the unification is contained in no pantheistic theorem, but in the reality of the impossible, in translating the Image into actuality, in the *imitatio Dei*. The mystery behind this fact is fulfilled in martyrdom, in the death with the cry of unity on one's lips, the "Hear, O Israel" which at this point becomes testimony in the most vital sense.

A wise man of the Middle Ages said, "My God, where can I find you, but where can I not find you?" The Eastern European Jewish beggar of today softly and unfalteringly whispers his *Gotenyu* in the trembling and dread of his harshest hour; the pet name is untranslatable, naive, but in its saying it becomes rich in meanings.

In both there is the same recognition, the same reac-knowledgement of the One.

It is the dialogical situation in which the human being stands that here finds its sublime or childlike expression.

Judaism regards speech as an event which grasps beyond the existence of mankind and the world. In contradiction to the static of the idea of Logos, the Word appears here in its complete dynamic as "that which happens." God's act of creation is speech; but the same is true of each lived moment. The world is given to the human beings who receive it, and the life of man is itself a giving and receiving. The events that occur to human beings are the great and small, untranslatable but unmistakable signs of their being addressed; what they do and fail to do can be an answer or a failure to answer. Thus the whole history of the world, the hidden, real world history, is a dialogue between God and his creature; a dialogue in which man is a true, legitimate partner, who is entitled and empowered to speak his own independent word out of his own being.

I am far from wishing to contend that the conception and experience of the dialogical situation are confined to Judaism. But I am certain that no other community of human beings has entered with such strength and fervor into this experience as have the Jews.

3. THE HUMAN ACTION

What is presupposed when one is serious about the lived dialogue, regarding the moment as word and an-swer, is, of course, that one is serious about the appoint-ment of Man to the earth.

In the strongest contrast to the Iranian conception with all its later ramifications, the Jewish conception is that the happenings of this world take place not in the sphere between two principles, light and darkness, or good and evil, but in the sphere between God and men, these mortal, brittle human beings who yet are able to face God and withstand his word.

The so-called evil is fully and as a primary element included in the power of God, who "forms the light, and creates darkness" (Isa. 45:7). The divine sway is not answered by anything which is evil in itself, but by the individual human beings, through whom alone the so-called evil, the directionless power, can become real evil. Human choice is not a psychological phenomenon but utter reality, which is taken up into the mystery of the One who is. Man is truly free to choose God or to reject him, and to do so not in a relationship of faith which is empty of the content of this world, but in one which contains the full content of the everyday. The "Fall" did not happen once and for all and become an inevitable fate, but it continually happens here and now in all its reality. In spite of all past history, in spite of all his inheritance, every man stands in the naked situation of Adam: to each, the decision is given. It is true that this does not imply that further events are deducible from that decision; it only implies that the human being's choice is that side of reality which concerns him as one called upon to act.

It is only when reality is turned into logic and A and non-A dare no longer dwell together, that we get determinism and indeterminism, a doctrine of predestination and a doctrine of freedom, each excluding the other. According to the logical conception of truth only one of two contraries can be true, but in the reality of life as one lives it they are inseparable. The person who makes a decision knows that his deciding is no self-delusion; the person who has acted knows that he was and is in the hand of God. The unity of the contraries is the mystery at the innermost core of the dialogue.

I said above that "evil" is to be taken only as a primary element; humanly speaking, as passion. Passion is only evil when it remains in the directionless state, when it refuses to be subject to direction, when it will not accept the direction that leads toward God—there is no other direction. In Judaism there recurs again and again in many forms the insight that passion, "the Evil Urge," is simply the elemental force which is the sole origin of the great human works, the holy included. The verse in the Scripture which says that at the end of the last day of creation God allowed himself to see his work "that it was very good" has been taken by tradition to refer to the so-called Evil Urge. Of all the works of creation, it is passion which is the very good, without which man cannot serve God, or truly live. The words,

"And thou shalt love the Lord thy God with all thine heart" (Deut. 6:5) are interpreted, "With both thy Urges," with the evil, undirected, elemental, urge, as well as the good, because directed, urge. It is of this so-called Evil Urge that God says to man, "You have made it evil."

Consequently, "inertia" is the root of all evil. The act of decision implies that man is not allowing himself any longer to be carried along on the undirected swirl of passion, but that his whole power is included in the move in the direction for which he has decided—and man can decide only for the direction of God. The evil, then, is only the "shell," the wrapping, the crust of the good, a shell that requires active piercing.

Some time ago a Catholic theologian saw in this conception a "Jewish activism" to which grace is unknown. But it is not so. We are not less serious about grace because we are serious about the human power of deciding, and through decision the soul finds a way which will lead it to grace. Man is here given no complete power; rather, what is stressed is the ordered perspective of human action, an action which we may not limit in advance. It must experience limitation as well as grace in the very process of acting.

The great question which is more and more deeply agitating our age is this: How can we act? Is our action valid in the sight of God, or is its very foundation broken and unwarranted? The question is answered as far as Judaism is concerned by our being serious about the conception that man has been appointed to this world as an originator of events, as a real partner in the real dialogue with God.

This answer implies a refusal to have anything to do with all separate ethics, any concept of ethics as a separate sphere of life, a form of ethics which is all too familiar in the spiritual history of the West. Ethical life has entered into religious life, and cannot be extracted from it. There is no responsibility unless there is One to whom one is responsible, for there is no reply where there is no appeal. In the last resort, "religious life" means concreteness itself, the whole concreteness of life *without reduction*, grasped dialogically, included in the dialogue.

Thus, man has a real start in the dialogue over and over again. However, mysteriously, something has been allotted to man, and that something is the beginning. Man cannot finish, and yet he must begin, in the most serious, actual way. This was once stated by a hasid in a somewhat paradoxical interpretation of the first verse of Genesis: " 'In the beginning'—that means: for the sake of the beginning; for the sake of beginning did God create heaven and earth." For the sake of man's beginning; that there might be one who would and should begin to move in the direction of God.

At the end of the tractate of the Mishnah which deals with the Day of Atonement there occurs a great saying, which must be understood in the same way as the hasid understood the words of Genesis. Here Rabbi Akiba is speaking to Israel: "Happy are ye, O Israel. Before whom do ye cleanse yourselves, and who is it who makes you clean? Your Father who is in Heaven." Here both the reality and the insufficiency of man's action are clearly expressed, the reality of man's action and his dependence upon grace. And, pregnant with meaning, the saying ends with words whose origin is a daring scriptural exegesis: "The Lord is the waters of immersion of Israel."

4. THE TURNING

This "beginning" by process of man manifests itself most strongly in the act of the turning. It is usual to call it "repentance," but to do so is a misleading attempt to psychologize; it is better to take the word in its original, literal meaning. For what it refers to is not something which happens in the secret recesses of the soul, showing itself outwardly only in its "consequences" and "effects"; it is something which happens in the immediacy of the reality between man and God. The turning is as little a "psychic" event as is a man's birth or death; it comes upon the whole person, is carried out by the whole person, and does not take place as a man's self-intercourse, but as the plain reality of primal mutuality.

The turning is a human fact, but it is also a world-embracing power. We are told that when God contemplated creating the world, and sat tracing it on a stone, in much the same way as a master-builder draws his ground plan, he saw that the world would have no stability. He then created the turning, and the world had stability. For from that time on, whenever the world was lost in the abyss of its own self, far away from God, the gates of deliverance were open to it.

The turning is the greatest form of "beginning." When God tells man: "Open me the gate of the turning as narrow as the point of a needle, and I shall open it so wide that carriages can enter it"; or when God tells Israel: "Turn to me, and I shall create you anew," the meaning of human beginning becomes clear as never before. By turning, man arises anew as God's child.

When we consider that the turning means something so mighty, we can understand the legend that Adam learned the power to turn from Cain. We can understand the saying which is reminiscent of a New Testament text, but which is quite independent of it, "In the place where those who have turned stand, the perfectly righteous cannot stand."*

Again we see that there is no separate sphere of ethics in Judaism. This, the highest "ethical" moment, is fully received into the dialogical life existing between God and man. The turning is not a return to an earlier "sinless" state; it is the revolution of the whole being—in whose process man is projected onto the way of God. This, ἡ ὁδὸς τοῦ θεοῦ however, does not merely indicate a way which God enjoins man to follow; it indicates that he, God himself, walks in the person of his *Shekhinah,* his "indwelling," through the history of the world; he takes the way, the fate of the world upon himself. The man who turns finds himself standing in the traces of the living God.

When we remember this, we understand the full, pregnant meaning of the word with which first the Baptist, then Jesus, then the disciples begin their preaching, the word which is falsely rendered by the Greek μετανοεῖτε referring to a spiritual *process,* but which in the original Hebrew or Aramaic idiom cannot have been anything else than that cry of the prophets of old: "Turn

* Talmud, Berakhot 34 b.

ye!" And when we remember this, we can also understand how the following sentence is linked to that beginning of the sermon: "For ἡ βασιλεία τῶν οὐρανῶν is at
hand," which, according to the Hebrew or Aramaic usage
of the time cannot have meant the "Kingdom of Heaven"
in the sense of "another world"; *shamayim*, Heaven, was
at that time one of the paraphrases for the name of God;
malkhut shamayim, ἡ βασιλεία τῶν οὐρανῶν, does not
mean the Kingdom of Heaven, but the Kingdom of
God, which wills to fulfil itself in the whole of creation,
and wills thus to complete creation. The Kingdom of
God is at the hand of man, it wills him to grasp and
realize it, not through any theurgical act of "violence,"
but through the turning of the whole being; and not as
if he were capable of accomplishing anything through
so doing but because the world was created for the sake
of his "beginning."

5. AGAINST GNOSIS AND MAGIC

The two spiritual powers of gnosis and magic, mas-
querading under the cloak of religion, threaten more
than any other powers the insight into the religious
reality, into man's dialogical situation. They do not attack religion from the outside; they penetrate into religion, and once inside it, pretend to be its essence. Because Judaism has always had to hold them at bay and
to keep separate from them, its struggle has been largely
internal. This struggle has often been misunderstood as
a fight against myth. But only an abstract-theological
monotheism can do without myth, and may even see it
as its enemy; living monotheism needs myth, as all religious life needs it, as the specific form in which its central events can be kept safe and lastingly remembered
and incorporated.

Israel first confronted gnosis and magic in its two great
neighboring cultures: gnosis, the perception of the knowable mystery, in the Babylonian teaching about the stars
whose power holds all earthly destinies in custody,
which was later to reach its full development in the
Iranian doctrine concerning the world-soul imprisoned
in the cosmos; and magic, the perception of the dom-

itable mystery, in the Egyptian doctrine that death can be conquered and everlasting salvation attained by the performance of prescribed formulas and gestures.

The tribes of Jacob could only become Israel by disentangling themselves from both gnosis and magic. He who imagines that he knows and holds the mystery fast can no longer face it as his "Thou"; and he who thinks that he can conjure it and utilize it, is unfit for the venture of true mutuality.

The gnostic temptation is answered by "the Instruction," the Torah, with the truly fundamental cry: "The secret things belong unto the Lord our God; but the things that are revealed belong unto us and to our children for ever, that we may do all the words of this instruction" (Deut. 29:28). Revelation does not deal with the mystery of God, but with the life of man. And it deals with the life of man as that which can and should be lived in the face of the mystery of God, and turning toward that mystery, even more, the life of man *is* so lived, when it is his true life.

The magical temptation is confronted with the word of God from out of the burning bush. Moses expected the people in their distress to ask him what was the name of the god as whose messenger he spoke (not, what was the name of the "God of their Fathers"!—[cf. Exod. 3:13]). For according to the usage common to primitive peoples, once they seized the secret of the name, they could conjure the god, and thus coerce him to manifest himself to them and save them. But when Moses voices his scruple as to what reply he should give to the people, God answers him by revealing the sense of the name, for he says explicitly in the first person that which is hidden in the name in the third. Not "I am that I am" as alleged by the metaphysicians—God does not make theological statements—but the answer which his creatures need, and which benefits them: "I shall be there as I there shall be" (Exod. 3:14). That is: you need not conjure me, for I am here, I am with you; but you cannot conjure me, for I am with you time and again in the form in which I choose to be with you time and again; I myself do not anticipate any of my manifestations; you cannot learn to meet me; you meet me, when *you* meet me: "It is not in heaven; that thou shouldst say: 'Who shall go up for us to heaven, and bring it unto us, and make us to hear it that we may do it . . .' Yea, the word is very nigh unto thee, in thy mouth, and in thy heart, that thou mayest do it" (cf. Deut. 30:14).

It is also in the light of its own inner battle against the infiltration of gnosis and magic that the dynamic of later Judaism must be understood, and especially that vexatious Talmud. We can only grasp some of its apparently abstract discussions when we keep in mind this constant double threat to the religious reality, the threat from gnosis taking the form of the late-Iranian teaching of the double principles and the intermediary substances, and the threat from magic taking the form of the Hellenistic practice of theurgy. Both of these amalgamated inside Judaism and became the Kabbalah, that uncannily powerful undertaking by the Jew to wrest himself free of the concreteness of the dialogical situation.

The Kabbalah was overcome because it was taken just as it was into the primal Jewish conception of the dialogical life. This overcoming of the Kabbalah is the significant work of hasidism. Hasidism caused all intermediary substances to fade before the relationship between God's transcendence, to be named only "the Unlimited," the suspension of all limited being, and his immanence, his "indwelling." The mystery of this relationship is, however, no longer knowable, but is applied directly to the pulsating heart of the human person as the *yihud*, the unification which man must profess and verify [*bewaehren*] in every moment of his life, and in his relationship to all the things of the world. On the other hand, hasidism drains theurgy of its poison, not by attempting to deny the influence of humanity on deity, but by proclaiming that, far above and beyond all formulas and gestures, above all exercises, penances, preparations, and premeditated actions, the hallowing of the whole of the everyday is the one true bearer of the human influence. Thus it dissolves the technique of theurgy, and leaves no "practicable," specific means behind, no means which are valid once and for all and applicable everywhere. In this way hasidism renews the insight into the mutuality where the whole of life is put unreservedly at stake; the insight into the dialogical relationship of the undivided human being to the undi-

vided God in the fulness of this earthly present, with its
unforeseeable, ever changing and ever new situations;
the insight into that differentiation between "secret" and
"revelation," and the union of both in that unknowable
but ever to be experienced "I shall be there"; the insight
into the reality of the divine-human meeting.

Gnosis misunderstands that meeting; magic offends it.
The meaning of revelation is that it is to be prepared;
hasidism interprets that revelation is to be prepared in
the whole reality of human life.

6. THE TRIAD OF WORLD TIME

The insight which Judaism has with regard to the
dialogical situation, or rather the fact that it is completely imbued with the dialogical situation, gives Judaism its indestructible knowledge of the threefold
chord in the triad of time: creation, revelation, redemption.

Within early Christianity the Gospel according to
John was the first to try to substitute a duad for the
triad by weaving revelation and redemption into one.
The light which shone in darkness and was not received
by the darkness, the light enlightening the whole man,
which comes into the world—that light is at the same
time revelation and redemption; by his coming into the
world God reveals himself, and the soul is redeemed.
The Old Testament shrinks into a prologue to the New
Testament.

Marcion went further: he tried to substitute a monad
for the duad by banishing creation from religious reality;
he tore God the Creator apart from God the Redeemer,
and declared that the former was not worthy of being
adored. The "alien" God, who reveals himself in redeeming the world, redeems the soul from the cosmos
and simultaneously from the cosmos' builder, who becomes the merely "righteous"—not "good"—God of the
Jews, the demiurge, the lawgiver, the sham god of this
aeon. The Old Testament was rejected as being anti-
God.

Marcion's work has not been accepted by the Church,
which has indeed fought a great battle against it. The
extent to which Marcion's influence has persisted in

Christian thought, however, is shown by Adolf von Harnack's Marcionizing thesis, which is only one of many evidences. In his thesis Harnack stamps the "preservation" of the Old Testament in Protestantism as a canonical document as "the consequence of religious and ecclesiastical paralysis." But more would be gained with the victory of this thesis than the separation of two books, and the profanation of one for Christendom: man would be cut off from his origin, the world would lose its history of creation, and with that its creaturely character; or creation would itself become the Fall. Existence would be divided not only cosmologically, but in the last resort it would be divided religiously beyond possibility of redress into a "world" of matter and moral law, and an overworld of spirit and love. Here the Iranian teaching of dual principles reaches its Western completion, and the duality of man, estranged from his natural, vitally trustful faith, finds its theological sanction. No longer does redemption crown the work of creation; redemption vanquishes creation. The world *as such* can no longer become the Kingdom of God. "The Unknown" who is worshipped at this point is the spirit of *reduction*.

For the Western peoples such an issue would only have meant a threat of disintegration; for Judaism it would have meant certain dissolution. What saved Judaism is not, as the Marcionites imagine, the fact that it failed to experience "the tragedy," the contradiction in the world's process, deeply enough; but rather that it experienced that "tragedy" in the dialogical situation, which means that it experienced *the contradiction as theophany*. This very world, this very contradiction, unabridged, unmitigated, unsmoothed, unsimplified, unreduced, this world shall be—not overcome—but consummated. It shall be consummated in the Kingdom, for it is that world, and no other, with all its contrariety, in which the Kingdom is a latency such that every reduction would only hinder its consummation, while every unification of contraries would prepare it. It is a redemption not from the evil, but of the evil, as the power which God created for his service and for the performance of his work.

If it is true that the whole world, all the world process, the whole time of the world, unsubtracted, stands in the dialogical situation; if it is true that the history of the world is a real dialogue between God and his creature—then the triad, as which that history is perceived, becomes not a man-made device for his own orientation, but actual reality itself. What comes to us out of the abyss of origin and into the sphere of our uncomprehending grasp and our stammering narrative, is God's cry of creation into the void. Silence still lies brooding before him, but soon things begin to rise and give answer—their very coming into existence is answer. When God blesses his creatures and gives them their appointed work, revelation has begun; for revelation is nothing else than the relation between giving and receiving, which means that it is also the relation between desiring to give and failing to receive. Revelation lasts until the turning creature answers and his answer is accepted by God's redeeming grace. Then the unity emerges, formed out of the very elements of contrariety, to establish amidst all the undiminished multiplicity and manifoldness the communion of creatures in the name of God and before his face.

Just as God's cry of creation does not call to the soul, but to the wholeness of things, as revelation does not empower and require the soul, but all of the human being—so it is not the soul, but the whole of the world, which is meant to be redeemed in the redemption. Man stands created, a whole body, ensouled by his relation to the created, enspirited by his relation to the Creator. It is to the whole man, in this unity of body, soul, and spirit, that the Lord of Revelation comes and upon whom he lays his message. So it is not only with his thought and his feelings, but with the sole of his foot and the tip of his finger as well, that he may receive the sign-language of the reality taking place. The redemption must take place in the whole corporeal life. God the Creator wills to consummate nothing less than the whole of his creation; God the Revealer wills to actualize nothing less than the whole of his revelation; God the Redeemer wills to draw into his arms nothing less than the all in need of redemption.

(From *Israel and the World*, pp. 13–27.)

Selected Bibliography

Shestov

Shestov, Lev. *All Things Are Possible*. Translated by S. S. Koteliansky, with an introduction by D. H. Lawrence. New York, Robert M. McBride, 1920.
————. *Athens and Jerusalem*. Translated, with an introduction, by Bernard Martin. Athens, Ohio University Press, 1966.
————. *Chekhov and Other Essays*. Ann Arbor, University of Michigan Press, 1966.
————. *Dostoevsky, Tolstoy and Nietzsche*. Translated by Bernard Martin and Spencer Roberts, with an introduction by Bernard Martin. Athens, Ohio University Press, 1969.
————. *In Job's Balances*. Translated by Camilla Coventry and C. A. Macartney. London, Dent and Sons, 1932.
————. *Kierkegaard and Existential Philosophy*. Translated by Elinor Hewitt. Athens, Ohio University Press, 1969.
————. *Potestas Clavium*. Translated, with an introduction, by Bernard Martin. Athens, Ohio University Press, 1968.

Rosenzweig

Rosenzweig, Franz. *On Jewish Learning*. New York, Schocken Books, 1955.
————. *The Star of Redemption*. Translated by William Hallo. New York, Holt, Rinehart and Winston, 1970.
————. *Understanding the Sick and the Healthy*. New York, Noonday Press, 1954.
Agus, Jacob B. *Modern Philosophies of Judaism*. New York, Behrman House, 1941.
Bergman, Samuel H. *Faith and Reason: An Introduction to Modern Jewish Thought*. Washington, B'nai B'rith Hillel Foundation, 1961.
Glatzer, Nahum N. *Franz Rosenzweig: His Life and Thought*. New York, Schocken Books, 1953.
Guttman, Julius. *Philosophies of Judaism*. New York, Holt, Rinehart and Winston, 1964.
Rotenstreich, Nathan. *Jewish Philosophy in Modern Times*. New York, Holt, Rinehart and Winston, 1968.

Schwarzschild, Steven S. *Franz Rosenzweig: Guide to Reversioners*. London, Education Committee of the Hillel Foundation, 1960.

Buber

Buber, Martin. *Between Man and Man*. New York, The Macmillan Co., 1965.

———. *Eclipse of God*. New York, Harper and Brothers, 1952.

———. *Hasidism*. New York, The Philosophical Library, 1948.

———. *I and Thou*. New York, Charles Scribner's Sons, Second Edition, 1958.

———. *Israel and the World*. New York, Schocken Books, 1948.

———. *Moses*. Oxford, East and West Library, 1946.

———. *The Prophetic Faith*. New York, The Macmillan Company, 1949.

———. *Two Types of Faith*. New York, The Macmillan Co., 1952.

Diamond, Malcolm. *Martin Buber: Jewish Existentialist*. New York, Oxford University Press, 1960.

Friedman, Maurice. *Martin Buber: The Life of Dialogue*. New York, Harper Torchbooks, 1960.

Schilpp, P. A. and M. Friedman, eds. *The Philosophy of Martin Buber*. Lasalle, Open Court Publishing Co., 1967.